GREAT FOOL

GREAT FOOL

Zen Master Ryōkan

*Poems, Letters, and
Other Writings*

Translated with Essays by
RYŪICHI ABÉ AND PETER HASKEL

University of Hawai'i Press
Honolulu

07 06 05 04 03 02   8 7 6 5 4 3

Library of Congress Cataloging-in-Publication Data
Ryōkan, 1758-1831.
   Great Fool : Zen master Ryōkan—poems, letters, and other writings
/ translated with essays by Ryūichi Abé and Peter Haskel.
       p.   cm.
   Includes bibliographical references and index.
   ISBN 0-8248-1741-9 (cloth : alk. paper). — ISBN 0-8248-1777-X
(paper : alk. paper)
   1. Ryōkan, 1758-1831. I. Abé, Ryūichi, 1954-   . II. Haskel,
Peter, 1945-   . III. Title.
PL797.6.Z5R8   1996
895.6'134—dc20   95-42750
                                                    CIP

University of Hawai'i Press books are printed on acid-free
paper and meet the guidelines for permanence and durability
of the Council on Library Resources

Book design by Kenneth Miyamoto

For our teacher
Yoshito Hakeda,
who led us to
Ryōkan's door

Contents

Acknowledgments

MANY PEOPLE have contributed to the completion of this book. Particular thanks are due to the following individuals for their many helpful suggestions during the manuscript's preparation: Professors Paul Anderer, Haruo Shirane, Robert A. F. Thurman and Philip Yampolsky of Columbia University, and Professors George Tanabe and H. Paul Varley of the University of Hawai'i.

Among those who graciously assisted in editing and proofreading were Maria Collora, Mary Farkas, and John Storm. We are also indebted to Alexander Brown, Kenneth Harlin, Amy Heinrich, Yasuko Makino, D. John McClure, and other librarians and staff members at Columbia's Starr East Asian Library for their support of our research. In particular, we thank the library's Rongxiang Zhang for her kind assistance.

Ryūichi Abé would like to express his gratitude to the late Professor Barbara Stoller Miller of Barnard College, whose love of poetry and the art of translation were his source of inspiration for studying Ryōkan's poems.

Finally, this volume has greatly benefited from the encouragement and advice of Patricia Crosby, our editor at the University of Hawai'i Press, and the superior editorial work of Sally Serafim, managing editor at the press, and Susan Stone.

Introduction

GENERATIONS have called this beggar-monk of the early nineteenth century "Ryōkan-san," the informal suffix *"san"* expressing affectionate respect. Only two other eminent Buddhist figures in Japanese history have received this particular honor: "Kōbō-san" or "Daishi-san," Kūkai, the ninth-century founder of Shingon Buddhism, who is remembered in popular legends as a savior–miracle worker; and "Ikkyū-san," the fifteenth-century Zen monk whose eccentric life-style has inspired numerous folk stories in which he is depicted as a marvelously quick-witted child novice. Ryōkan is a singularly attractive figure. Minakami Tsutomu, the celebrated contemporary novelist, explains why, despite countless earlier works examining the minutest details of Ryōkan's life, he could not escape the urge to write about the Zen monk-poet:

> The reason is simple. I, among others, would like to follow in the footsteps of this unthinkably kind yet strict Buddhist practitioner, who entrusted his thoughts to kanshi [poems composed in classical Chinese] and waka [poems composed in the Japanese syllabary] and strove day and night in the path of literary art. Why did Ryōkan, who, under the guidance of a famous master, had grasped the depths of Zen, refer to himself as "Great Fool" and say he "belonged to neither priesthood nor laity"? Why did he not live in a temple? He excelled in studying the scriptures, in calligraphy and in poetry . . . yet he ran away from the monastery. And it was in the residence of a lay follower that he died. He is indeed an enchantingly mysterious monk.[1]

Minakami's words provide a clue to Ryōkan's ever-increasing popularity in Japan. Ryōkan, despite his religious and artistic sophistication, refused to place himself within the cultural elite of his age and lived instead among villagers. It is this curious interplay of opposites—of dignity and familiarity—that continues to inspire books on Ryōkan by historians, literary critics, poets, novelists, and journalists.

Miya Eiji, an authority on Ryōkan's biography, has commented on the recent upsurge in Ryōkan-related books. Writing in 1985, Miya reported that the past hundred years had seen the publication of over 3,600 books on Ryōkan. In 1930 alone, for instance, sixty-four books on Ryōkan were issued by major publishing houses. Since the 1970s, the number of works published on Ryōkan has grown each year, to 271 in 1980, and in 1983 reaching 362. "In the past three years, new books on Ryōkan have appeared at the rate of one book every day, and this does not include many other forums—magazine articles, public lectures, broadcasts, and so forth—in which Ryōkan is being constantly discussed. . . . No day passes without Ryōkan being discussed somewhere in Japan."[2] In 1978, the Ryōkan Study Society (Ryōkan kai) was established in Ryōkan's native region of Niigata, and its membership has since spread swiftly to other areas of Japan. Currently, the All-Japan Ryōkan Study Society (Zenkoku Ryōkan kai), which comprises not only scholars, but literary figures, artists, and, above all, ordinary people who admire Ryōkan, publishes periodicals, supports research, hosts conferences, and organizes exhibitions.

Despite his current popularity and despite the massive literature of Ryōkan studies, it is not an easy task to understand who Ryōkan was. Recently in the West there has been a growth of serious academic interest in Ryōkan. However, the pioneering studies in Western languages have thus far limited the scope of their investigation mainly to Ryōkan's role as a literary figure. Yet, such an approach by itself does not help in understanding Ryōkan's phenomenal popularity in contemporary Japan. Nor does it explain Ryōkan's importance as a cultural and religious figure.

Likewise, Ryōkan cannot be discussed merely as a Zen master. True, Ryōkan was ordained in the Sōtō school of Zen, a school that was established by the celebrated Kamakura Zen master Dōgen Kigen (1200–1253) and by Ryōkan's day had grown to become one of the largest religious institutions in Japan. Ryōkan also completed rigorous Zen training under the guidance of his master Tainin Kokusen (1722–1791), abbot of Entsūji, a large Sōtō training center in western Japan, and received Kokusen's *inka,* the certificate marking the completion of his Zen study. However, identifying Ryōkan as a Sōtō Zen master is as grave an error as labeling him simply a poet or a calligrapher. In contrast to the Zen masters of his time who presided over large monaste-

Ryōkan detested poems composed by professional poets and described his own literary creations as "poems that are not poems at all."[3] But if Ryōkan's goal was not to win recognition as a poet, what was his purpose in composing poetry? How is Ryōkan's favorite activity, the writing of poems, related to his life of begging? In what way do the images of Ryōkan projected in his poems help us understand him better? Ryōkan's poems are often characterized by their simplicity and directness of expression. Many of his poems, particularly those that have been previously translated into English, seem to be straightforward descriptions of his simple rustic life or of the natural beauty of his surroundings. Ryōkan, however, also left a large number of poems that can be understood as philosophical reflections. In these, Ryōkan manifests his ideas not only in the poems' literal meanings (i.e., *what* they say) but in their figurative movements (i.e., *how* they say it) as well. Even the poems that at first glance appear to be simple descriptions of Ryōkan's solitary life are often richly troped with metaphorical and rhetorical devices. Hayden White has asserted that "troping is the soul of discourse" because it "is both a movement *from* one notion of the way things are related *to* another notion, and a connection between things so that they can be expressed in a language." Tropics—that is, the figurative strategies that White identifies as the "deep level" of the text—"is the process by which all discourse constitutes the objects which it pretends only to describe realistically."[4] It is particularly important for poetic discourse, whose referents do not always have to exist outside the text. "A Poetics of Mendicancy," our second essay, attempts to study the figurative strategies particular to Ryōkan's poems and strives to illustrate not only in their literal meanings but in the poems' tropical movements the intimate relationship between Ryōkan's writing of poetry and his daily practice of Buddhism.

Because of the proliferation of popular literature on Ryōkan, writers have not infrequently presented an overly idealized picture of the Master, relying on the legendary literature of later periods. We have made a deliberate attempt, whenever possible, to base our observations on the biographical sources recorded by Ryōkan's contemporaries. "Commemorating Ryōkan," the last introductory essay, is a bibliographical study that identifies the major primary sources for Ryōkan's life. It demonstrates that the effort to commemorate Ryōkan and to preserve his writings had already begun during his lifetime and shows that these writings about Ryōkan's life and Ryōkan's own writing of poetry were mutually related, not isolated processes.

No historical record, not even the accounts of those who were personally acquainted with Ryōkan, can claim to present *the* historical reality of Ryōkan's life, but only *an* interpretation of Ryōkan's daily existence. It is, however, possible to reconstruct the manner in which Ryōkan was *represented* in various contemporaneous biographical materials as well as in his own poems. We have striven through the web of intertwining interpretations projected by these prosaic and poetic texts to illustrate Ryōkan's multifarious qualities. We hope that our study of Ryōkan will highlight aspects of the Master that have yet to be explored fully by modern scholarship and will come close to presenting the beggar-monk known to his neighbors and friends.

R. A.

Essays

Ryōkan of Mount Kugami

Peter Haskel

SPEND TIME at one of Japan's busy commuter train stations and you will probably notice a bookstore crowded with silent rows of well-dressed "salarymen" and "salarywomen" browsing through an array of paperbacks and magazines. There, among the ubiquitous tabloids, the sex-and-violence comics, and the very latest Japanese and American bestsellers, you are likely to find several books devoted to the Zen master Taigu Ryōkan (1758–1831), a penniless monk whose life was spent in obscurity in Japan's snow country, meditating, playing with children, and writing poems that vividly describe his world. He lived by begging in the villages and towns of his native area, beloved by all, celebrated for his warmth and wisdom, and legendary for his naïveté, which made him the butt of countless practical jokes.

> Worldly people call him different things: fool, wise man, idiot, man of the Way. He never flatters the rich and important, nor disdains the poor and humble. He isn't happy when he gets things or sad when he loses them. He just goes along, natural, relaxed, a man who has transcended the dust of the world. He is always accompanied by children and, when he is out begging, can be found playing with them in the shade of trees and in the fields, tugging at blades of grass, sumo wrestling, and bouncing balls.[1]

A book on a figure like Ryōkan may seem an unusual choice for a corporate soldier confronting the frenzy of the early morning rush. But Japan is an unusual place and Ryōkan an unusual monk. Today, over one hundred fifty years after his death, Ryōkan has been elevated from a local to a national hero, and Japan remains in the grip of a *Ryōkan būmu* (boom). Ryōkan is the subject of hundreds of books, with new titles constantly swelling the shelves; tour buses ferry legions of eager pilgrims to the site of Ryōkan's rustic retreat on Mount Kugami, and people of all ages and backgrounds pack exhibits of Ryōkan's calligraphy at museums and department store galleries. Ryōkan societies dot Japan, and at Ryōkan conventions, speakers exhort their audiences to "manifest Ryōkan's mind in your own daily life." Always popular among the very young, Ryōkan is the subject of humorous stories familiar to nearly every schoolchild. All in all, "Ryōkan san" ("Mr. Ryōkan"), as he is familiarly known, is perhaps the Zen monk closest to the hearts of ordinary Japanese, revered not as an object of antiquarian interest, but as a reminder of what is unique in both Zen and Japan itself.

While there survive an abundance of tales and legends about Ryōkan, the facts of his biography remain largely unclear. The original sources for Ryōkan's life are scant, consisting for the most part of a handful of brief biographies by colleagues and contemporaries. But these, too, are vague and incomplete, providing few dates or details. No doubt deeming it unimportant, Ryōkan seems to have rarely discussed his past, even with his closest friends. Possibly he shared the feelings of another nineteenth-century poet, Walt Whitman, who wrote in "The Biography":

> I suppose men's lives, as in books, must be
>   written
> But never by me—I could not write the life of
>   a drop of rain, or a beach pebble
> Or the least insect humming in the air.[2]

Nevertheless, relying on those original, contemporary sources that we possess, it remains possible to reconstruct, or at least suggest, something of the distinct form and character of Ryōkan's life.

Ryōkan was born in 1758 in the coastal town of Izumozaki, in what is now Niigata prefecture. Facing the island of Sado across the Japan Sea, Izumozaki lies in the old northwestern province of Echigo, an area famous for its deep snows and hardy inhabitants. A scenic spot, with panoramic ocean views, Izumozaki was known in Ryōkan's day as a haunt of artists and writers. As such, it was provincial but not isolated, and in the town and its environs, literary culture was actively promoted by a prosperous middle class of brewers, doctors, and merchants. Izumozaki's wealth depended largely on its role as a strategically located port. Sado's gold mines were a valuable source of revenue for the Tokugawa Shogunate (1600–1856), and for a time, Izumozaki served as the principal transshipment point, the gold being unloaded from ships and packed onto horses for the journey to the capital at Edo (present-day Tokyo). Rice, for which Echigo was famous, was another important item of commerce, as was fish. By the mid–eighteenth century, however, Izumozaki's fortunes had begun to wane in the face of competition from the neighboring port town of Amaze, which gradually came to dominate the local economy.

Ryōkan was the eldest son and heir of the headman of Izumozaki, Yamamoto Shinzaemon (1736–1795), best known by his pen name Tachibana I'nan.[3] The second son of the Araki, a farming family from the nearby village of Yoita, I'nan had been adopted into the Yamamoto merchant clan, Izumozaki's leading family, operating under the shop name Tachibana. Ryōkan's mother, Hideko (also known as Onobu, d. 1783), was from a Sado branch of the Yamamoto, and her marriage with I'nan produced a large family of four sons and three daughters.

A locally famous haiku poet and a student of Japanese literature, Ryōkan's father was a champion of the Echigo movement to revive the style of the seventeenth-century haiku master Matsuo Bashō. I'nan seems to have been more gifted as a poet than as an administrator, and as the port of Izumozaki continued to decline, the Tachibana found their own authority and prestige successfully challenged by a rival merchant family, the Noguchi of neighboring Amaze. Tensions between the two clans reached a crisis in 1763, when I'nan failed to prevent the Noguchi from erecting their own official notice board in Amaze—an important symbolic defeat for Izumozaki and the Tachibana. I'nan seems to have consoled himself with poetry, drink, and travel, and after retiring in 1786, he took to the road and lost contact with his family. In 1795, word arrived that he had drowned himself in Kyoto's Katsura River, leaving behind only a poem preceded by the cryptic statement "At the urging of the Dharmakāya Buddha, I, I'nan, threw myself into the Katsura River."

Virtually nothing is known of Ryōkan's early years. His childhood name is given as both Eizō and Bunkō, and between 1771 and 1777, he studied Chinese literature under an important local Confucian scholar and poet, Ōmori Shiyō (d. 1791). Trained in Edo, Ōmori had opened an academy, the Kyōsenjuku, in his native village of Jizōdō, several miles northeast of Izumozaki. Here, Ryōkan received a grounding in classical Chinese culture and particularly Chinese poetry. He remained devoted to Ōmori throughout his life and must have been sorely disappointed when the scholar left for Tsuruoka (Yamagata prefecture) in 1777.

Following his *genpuku,* or coming of age ceremony, at sixteen,

Ryōkan would have assumed his duties as heir to the Tachibana clan, assisting I'nan in his work as village head. It was during this period, according to certain accounts, that Ryōkan began his study of Zen, practicing as a layman under the Sōtō school teacher Genjō Haryō (d. 1814) at Genjō's temple, Kōshōji, in Amaze. At age seventeen, after what must have been only a year as apprentice village head, Ryōkan seems to have abandoned Izumozaki and his position as I'nan's successor and entered Kōshōji as a novice. It is not known what led Ryōkan to Zen as a young man or precisely why he left his family and joined the Buddhist priesthood, shaving his head and receiving the religious name Ryōkan ("Virtuous and Tolerant"). We have only Ryōkan's statement, recorded by his biographer Ōzeki Bunchū, "People all say: 'Become a monk and then study Zen'; but I studied Zen and then became a monk."[4] All that can be known with certainty is that while at Kōshōji, Ryōkan met Genjō's teacher, the Zen master Tainin (or Dainin) Kokusen (1723–1791), and in 1779, at age twenty-one, Ryōkan left Echigo to accompany Kokusen to his temple, Entsūji, in Bitchū (present-day Okayama prefecture).[5]

Like the Rinzai school, the other major sect of Japanese Zen, the Sōtō school, to which Kokusen belonged, had experienced a period of intense ferment and self-examination between the mid-seventeenth and mid-eighteenth centuries. Developed in T'ang dynasty China, Zen is a distinctive school of Buddhism that stresses the practice of meditation and the experience of enlightenment, transmitted intuitively "mind-to-mind" from teacher to disciple. The principal lines of Japanese Zen were imported in the thirteenth century by Japanese monks who had studied on the continent and received their Chinese teachers' sanctions. During the late Middle Ages, however, both Japanese Sōtō and Rinzai teachings and lineages had become corrupt, and under Tokugawa rule, reformers in both sects were actively debating how to revive the Zen of their early medieval founders. In the Sōtō school, the reform movement centered on a return to the teachings of the school's patriarch, Dōgen Kigen (1200–1253), emphasizing the monastic regulations Dōgen instituted at his temple, Eiheiji, and the study of Dōgen's seminal work, the *Shōbōgenzō*. The Sōtō revival, led by Gesshū Sōko (1618–1696) and his noted disciple Manzan Dōhaku (1635–1714), was essentially formalistic, aiming to restore Dōgen's Zen by reasserting conventions such as those governing the transmission of the teaching from master to disciple. Others, such as Dokuan Genkō (1630–1698) and Tenkei Denson (1648–1735), objected that the way to restore the original, authentic Zen of the early masters was to stress not the form but the substance of their teachings, the primacy of the individual enlightenment experience. This, they asserted, was the true, timeless link to the mind of Dōgen and to the minds of all the enlightened masters of the past. Ultimately, the faction identified with Gesshū and Manzan prevailed, but the tension between inner authenticity and institutional orthodoxy remained unresolved.

While most Tokugawa period Zen monks pursued their vocations within the temples and monasteries, others rejected any connection with the Zen establishment and lived as independents. Sometimes traveling as impoverished vagabonds, their styles often highly eccentric, such teachers tended to view their lives as a protest against what they considered the falseness and pretense of the temple priests. The Zen master Unkei Tōsui (d. 1683), for example, abandoned his position as abbot of a Sōtō temple in Echigo, working at times as a palanquin carrier, a sweeper, and a maker of straw horseshoes. Known as "Beggar Tōsui," he is said to have worn only a paper robe and a rope belt. After a day of begging, he would take whatever he had received and make rice balls to distribute to children and beggars. Tōsui avoided residence in the temples and ended his life in a hut in Kyoto, selling vinegar at a roadside stand. It is uncertain whether Ryōkan was aware of the details of Tōsui's career, but, though they are separated by nearly a century, the parallels between the two are certainly striking. Other celebrated "independents" of the seventeenth and eighteenth centuries include the Sōtō teacher Fūgai Ekun (1568–1654), who is said to have lived in a mountain cave and who was renowned for his brushwork, and Maisaō (or Baisaō, d. 1765), "Old Tea Seller," a Zen master who composed poetry and managed a tea stall.

Ryōkan's master Kokusen was a successor in the Sōtō line of Gesshū and had studied under Manzan. Tradition has it that when Ryōkan questioned him about his style of Zen, Kokusen replied: "First make a row of stones, then put soil on top"—presumably referring to the traditional manner in which foundations are laid for Japanese buildings. But, in fact, little is known of Kokusen's Zen or of the actual character of Ryōkan's studies at his temple. Entsūji was primarily a training temple for Zen monks in Kokusen's line, with a regular population of some forty practitioners. Judging from the rules for Entsūji's daily practice[6] and the various poems in which Ryōkan recalls his years as a novice, we can presume that Ryōkan observed the usual Zen monastic routine, combining regular periods of zazen (seated meditation) and chanting of the Buddhist scriptures with begging and various manual chores. His schedule doubtless also included the intensive ninety-day meditation retreats, or *ango,* held in summer and winter, as well as private instruction from Kokusen and lectures on the writings of Dōgen.

In 1790, Ryōkan received Kokusen's *inka,* or "seal of approval," his formal acknowledgment of Ryōkan's realization of Zen. Kokusen's sanction took the form of a Chinese poem, together with a staff of wild wisteria, symbolizing the Zen teaching.[7] The opening line of the poem begins, "Ryōkan! How nice to be like a fool," and Ryōkan's other religious name, Taigu ("Great Fool"), may have been bestowed on this occasion.[8] Kokusen addresses Ryōkan in the poem by the title *anju,* "Hermitage Master," leading to speculation that Ryōkan had been given charge of a particular *an,* or subtemple, on the grounds of Entsūji. The official title by which Ryōkan was known in Kokusen's line, that of *shuso,* or "head monk," also suggests that he had advanced to a position of importance at the temple, serving as leader of Entsūji's meditation hall.

Ryōkan and the nun Gitei (1761–1837) were the last of thirty disciples who received Kokusen's *inka,* both being awarded poems and a staff. The following year, Kokusen died at age sixty-eight. Ryōkan does not seem to have been attracted to Kokusen's successors at Entsūji, and he gradually drifted away from the temple, though he remained friendly with individual priests with whom he had trained under Kokusen and kept the master's *inka* verse with him throughout his life. Clearly disillusioned with much of what passed for Zen study in the temples, Ryōkan inveighs in his poems against the ignorance and hypocrisy of the Sōtō priesthood and its betrayal of Dōgen's original teaching. However elevated the status accorded him, Ryōkan never seems to have been comfortable within an organization or a hierarchy, whether religious or secular. Ultimately, he abandoned his place in the Sōtō Zen establishment, just as earlier he had renounced his connections with the house of Tachibana and relinquished his position as successor to the headman of Izumozaki.

Ryōkan's training as a young monk apparently included years of wandering on pilgrimage, or *angya,* the traditional period of travel and study in which the Zen monk leaves his original temple to search out and examine various teachers, testing and maturing his understanding. Ryōkan's poems describe the harshness and exhilaration of his journeys, drifting across the country, meditating and camping under the stars. At the same time, Ryōkan ridicules his own youthful passion and inexperience during these years of wandering and compares his misguided attempts to discover the truth to trying to satisfy one's hunger with a picture of a rice cake. Once again, however, details are lacking. There remain only two accounts of Ryōkan's activities during this period. The first, a letter by Ryōkan's friend the nun Teishin, describes how the young Ryōkan secretly enters the compound of a reclusive Echigo Zen master, Taiji Sōryū (d. 1789), and leaves a note begging Sōryū to receive him. The master instantly agrees, to the astonishment of the other monks.[9] The second account of Ryōkan's *angya* is a memoir by Kondō Banjō (d. 1848), an Edo literatus who states that he stayed several nights in Ryōkan's hut while traveling in Tosa.[10] Contained in his work *Nezame no tomo* (A Bedside Companion), the memoir was written by Banjō in old age, long after the events he describes, and employs an identical-sounding but incorrect Chinese character for the "Ryō" in Ryōkan's name. Some Japanese scholars have consequently questioned whether the monk Banjō encounters in Tosa is the Ryōkan with whom we are familiar or another monk with a similar name. However, in the *Ryōkan zenji kiwa* (Curious Accounts of the Zen Master Ryōkan), Kera Yoshishige, who, as a child, knew Ryōkan, mentions both Banjō's stay with the Master and his record of the visit; and this together with the fact that the *Nezame no tomo* has been preserved as a treasure of the Kera family, Ryōkan's longtime supporters, tends to confirm its importance as a source for Ryōkan's biography. The full account reads:

> My name is Banjō. Long ago, when I was very young, I traveled through the province of Tosa. I was still some three *ri*[11] from the castle town,[12] when I was caught in a terrible downpour, and to make matters worse, the sun had set. Seeing a tumbledown hut at the foot of a mountain about two *chō*[13] from the road, I went to ask if I could stay the night. I found a monk with a pale, thin face, seated alone beside the hearth.
>
> "I have no food," he told me. "I haven't even a screen to keep out the wind."
>
> "So long as I have shelter from the rain," I replied, "what more do I need?"
>
> In this way, I finally prevailed upon him to let me stay the night.
>
> Till late that evening, I sat facing him across the hearth, but after our initial conversation, he did not speak at all. He did not even practice meditation, sleep, or recite the *nenbutsu*.[14] Whatever I said to him, he would simply smile. "He must be crazy!" I thought to myself.

That evening I slept beside the hearth, and when I awoke at dawn, the priest, too, was fast asleep, his head resting on his arm. The new day arrived, but the rain was coming down even more violently than on the previous night. Seeing it was impossible to continue my journey, I asked if I could stay, at least until the rain let up a bit.

"Stay as long as you wish," he replied, which made me even happier than having been allowed to stay the day before.

Around midmorning, he fed me some wheat flour mixed in hot water. Glancing about the hut, I noticed only a wooden Buddha and a small desk by the window, on which were placed two books. Apart from these, he literally hadn't a thing. Opening the books to see what they were, I found them to be a Chinese edition of *Chuang-tzu.*[15] Tucked between the leaves were some old-style Chinese poems written in cursive script, which appeared to be the monk's own compositions. Being unschooled in Chinese poetry, I was unable to judge the quality of the verses but could not help being struck by the writer's calligraphy, and taking from my carrying box two fans, I asked him to inscribe them for me. He instantly seized his brush, dipped it in ink, and began to draw—on the first, a warbler on the branch of a plum tree, on the second, Mount Fuji. Sadly, I have forgotten what he wrote, but I recall that beneath the inscription on the picture of Mount Fuji were the words "Who is it saying this? Ryōkan from Echigo."

That night, with the rain still falling and showing no sign of letting up, I stayed again with the monk beside the hearth. By the following morning, however, the rain had completely disappeared and the sun was shining. After a breakfast of the usual wheat flour, I offered my host some money in appreciation for my two-night stay. But he refused, saying simply, "What am I going to do with that?" Feeling I would have been remiss not to return his kindness, I offered him instead some calligraphy paper and poem cards, which he accepted with delight.

All this happened over thirty years ago. Recently, however, I came across a work titled *Hokuetsu kidan* (Curious Tales of Echigo) by one Tachibana Mochiyo. It tells of a certain Ryōkan from Echigo—I can't recall the exact place— the eldest son of a Mr. Tachibana, head of a prominent family. From an early age, he delighted in literature and par-

ticularly excelled in calligraphy. But he was determined to
be just like the ancient masters, even refusing to succeed to
the headship of his eminent family, and in the end he aban-
doned the world and disappeared. Having read the details of
how he lived in his hut, I realized this was none other than
the monk I had met in Tosa, and vividly recalling that time
long past, tears wet my sleeve all night. . . .

I wrote all this over twenty years ago, recording every-
thing I observed and compiling a collection titled *A Bedside
Companion,* which has remained in my possession. Recent-
ly, however, the abbot of Denchū-an[16] saw my account and
said: "I, too, am a native of Echigo and sorely miss Ryōkan.
Won't you make a copy of what you've written for me?" And
I could not refuse.

> Recorded by the seventy-year-old Banjō, Master of the
> Camellia Garden, in early summer of the second year
> of Kōka (1845)[17]

Ryōkan returned to his native Echigo probably not later than
1795, the year of I'nan's suicide. Ryōkan's mother had died some
twelve years before, and following I'nan's retirement, Ryōkan's younger
brother Yoshiyuki (or Yūshi, 1762–1834) had inherited the office of
headman of Izumozaki and control of the Tachibana family's affairs.
Yoshiyuki was to prove even less adequate as an administrator than his
father, and he soon found himself embroiled in disputes with Izumo-
zaki's townspeople. In 1810, the Tachibana were defeated in a lawsuit
accusing them of embezzling public funds, and the family property
was confiscated and Yoshiyuki banished to the ancestral village of Yoita.

Ryōkan's precise movements after his homecoming are uncer-
tain. He seems to have lived by begging, staying for a time in a lean-to
near Gōmoto, a coastal town not far from Izumozaki, and later in
vacant huts on the grounds of several local Buddhist temples. By 1800,
Ryōkan had moved to Mount Kugami, a peak some twelve miles north
of Izumozaki that was to remain closely associated with Ryōkan's life
and writings. Picturesque and remote, with commanding views of the
surrounding area, roamed by monkeys and wild deer, Mount Kugami
seems to have provided an ideal setting for both poetry and medita-
tion. By 1804, Ryōkan had established himself in a thatched hut in the
precincts of Kokujōji, a Shingon[18] temple on the mountain's western
slope. Known as Gogō-an, the hut had been named for its late tenant,
a Buddhist hermit who subsisted on a ration of five measures *(gogō)* of

rice. That Ryōkan had already achieved a certain celebrity among his neighbors is clear from the contemporary account by Tachibana Mochiyo in his *Hokuetsu kidan*[19]—the work cited in Banjō's *Nezame no tomo,* quoted earlier. Published in 1811 in Edo, it is our earliest reliable source for Ryōkan, and it presents a colorful description of the Master's life from the time of his return to Izumozaki until his move to Gogō-an. Tachibana writes:

> In this Gogō-an, there has recently lived a strange priest. His desirelessness, purity, and unworldliness have been praised by all. He is the eldest son of the Tachibana clan of Izumo-zaki, a large and wealthy family. He spent six years studying under the [Confucian] teacher Shiyō, then studied under a Zen monk and traveled extensively on pilgrimage. When he abandoned his home [to become a monk], he left behind a note assigning all responsibility for the family to his brother, and for several years afterward nothing was heard from him.
>
> Much later, in a place known as Gōmoto, which was by the seashore, there was a vacant hut, and one evening a traveling monk came and inquired at a neighboring house if he might stay in it. The following day, he went out begging in the neighborhood, and when he had received enough food to satisfy his needs for the day, he returned to the hut. If he received more than he needed, he would share it with the birds and animals. In this manner, half a year passed. People praised his virtue and some would give him clothes. Any extra clothing he would share with the poor.
>
> Because his dwelling was only a short distance from Izu-mozaki, people there heard about him, and someone told my brother: "He must be Tachibana." My brother searched the shore at Gōmoto and found the hut, but its occupant was out. The brushwood door was unfastened, and ivy covered everything. Inside, he found a desk on which lay a brush and inkstone, and a hearth containing a single clay pot. The walls of the hut were covered with poems. Reading them, he experienced an unworldly feeling, as if serene moonlight had spontaneously purified his mind. "The calligraphy is without doubt [Tachibana's]," he reported to the neighbor, who proceeded to spread the word around Izumozaki. Ryōkan's relatives then came and attempted to bring him home with them, but he refused. They then offered him food and clothing, but he insisted he had no need for it and returned it to them. His whereabouts after

this are uncertain, but years later he settled at Gogō-an. His daily life is just as I have described it. He is truly an enlightened monk for our time.[20]

Mount Kugami was to be Ryōkan's home for some twenty-six years, shaping both his poetry and the distinct character of his daily life. Though virtually all of Ryōkan's poems are undated, many refer by name to Mount Kugami, and Ryōkan's mature literary work probably has its inception in the period when he settled on the mountain and took up residence at Gogō-an. But, again, facts are few, and even the sites of Ryōkan's huts on Mount Kugami are approximate, the present huts being modern reconstructions.

Ryōkan prized the beauty and solitude of Gogō-an, but he was not bound to his hut. Even in old age, he made excursions throughout the area around Mount Kugami, staying with friends or putting up at local Buddhist temples, and on occasion he may have traveled farther afield, even setting off once more on pilgrimage. Around 1814, Ryōkan began to move between Gogō-an and a second hut, located on the grounds of Otogo jinja, a deserted Shinto shrine set in a cryptomeria forest at the foot of Kugami's southern slope. The Otogo hut, which became Ryōkan's permanent residence after 1816, stood in a grove of bamboo, within earshot of the bell that announced rare visitors to the shrine.

Ryōkan's routine varied with the weather. During rainy spells or when his hut was buried under snow, he would stay indoors, sometimes for days, meditating, reading Buddhist texts and the Chinese and Japanese classics, practicing calligraphy, and composing poetry. This pattern probably helps to explain why many of Ryōkan's poems depict inclement weather, particularly the frequent snowfall and rains typical of Echigo. On clear spring or autumn days, Ryōkan would invariably go out to beg in the nearby villages and towns. Because he was an impoverished monk without a temple or disciples, begging was Ryōkan's sole means of support. But, as his poems make clear, begging for Ryōkan was a special source of pride, as much a joy as a necessity, an expression of the Buddha's enlightenment and an opportunity to share that enlightenment with his neighbors. Taking his staff and his lacquer begging bowl, Ryōkan would leave his hut at daybreak, making his way down the steep slopes of the mountain and exulting in the early morning air. At times, he would spend the day tramping with his bowl from village to village, not returning to Mount Kugami till nightfall. Ryōkan's begging was unlike the ritualized begging of the great Zen monasteries, whose precision lines of impassive monks can still be seen proceeding grimly with their bowls through Japanese villages and towns. By contrast, Ryōkan would freely interrupt his rounds to play with children, drink raw sake with an old farmer, or visit a friend. At other times, he would stop to pick flowers and gather the wild vegetables that are a popular spring delicacy in the mountains, frequently joined by boys and girls and even other adults.

Ryōkan's relations with his neighbors were not limited to begging. Ryōkan had a genuine affection for the common people of his native area, and they seem to have reciprocated, welcoming him wherever he went. An integral part of the life of the district, Ryōkan could be found dancing through the night at village festivals or exchanging rounds of drinks with the farmers at local wineshops.

According to the accounts of his contemporaries, Ryōkan's good-natured simplicity and ingenuousness made him everyone's friend, but endeared him particularly to children, who would flock to the Master in droves. Ryōkan tells us he would always carry with him two or three balls, and when he went begging in the villages, children would swarm around him, clinging to his sleeves, shouting and clapping in delight. Ryōkan's thin, lanky frame was instantly recognizable, and his friend the poet Yamada Tokō noted how, seeing him, all the children would yell:

> Here he comes, Master Ryōkan
> Skinny as the season's first sardine![21]

Unable to refuse the children's demands that he join their games, Ryōkan would end by abandoning his rounds. At times, he would spend the entire day playing with the village girls and boys, to the astonishment and disapproval of adult passersby. "Wherever the Master went, a crowd of children would gather around him," Ryōkan's young friend Suzuki Bundai recalled. "When people asked, 'Why do you act like this?' the Master would reply: 'I love their truthfulness, their lack of pretense.' "[22]

The particular games in which Ryōkan joined are still popular with Japanese children: *onigokko,* a sort of combination tag and blindman's bluff; hide-and-seek; "grass fights," in which opponents pull apart looped blades of grass to see whose loop will break first; sumo wrestling; *ohajiki,* a game, using flat stones or seashells, played by snapping one's piece against one's opponents' to drive them out of a circle; and *temari,* Japanese handball, a game of skill involving counting and bouncing accompanied by special songs.

Children also seem to have enjoyed teasing Ryōkan, who even in old age was apparently willing to "play along." In the early part of the twentieth century, Suzuki Bundai's grandson Hōken, a professor of literature at Kyoto University, recalled his grandmother telling him that as a child she had often played with Ryōkan: "'Ryōkan was afraid of mice,' she told me, 'and when we'd play ball or blind-man's bluff, we'd say: "Ryōkan, a mouse! a mouse!" And he'd shout: "Oh my! Oh my!" and look anxiously all around. No matter how many times we'd say this, he would do the same thing over and over.'"[23]

Ryōkan's forbearance in the face of the children's constant teasing was also noted by Bundai's adopted son Tekiken:

> When the Zen Master went out, children would follow him. Sometimes they would shout at him loudly, and the Master would shout back in surprise, throwing up his hands, reeling backward and almost losing his balance. Whenever the children found the Master, they were always ready to do this. Ordinary people frowned on this behavior. My late father once questioned the Master about it. The Master laughed and told him: "When the children surprise me this way, it makes them happy. When the children are happy, it makes *me* happy. The children are happy, and I'm happy, too; everyone is happy together, and so I do it all the time. There's no truer happiness than this!" This happiness of the Master's was itself a manifestation of the ultimate truth.[24]

Nevertheless, at times Ryōkan did become exhausted and would have to make his escape. "The children like to circle around him," Ōzeki Bunchū wrote in 1818, "clapping their hands and laughing with delight. When the Teacher tires of this, he lies down and pretends to be dead. Then, when the children are no longer hemming him in, he slowly gets up and walks away."[25]

It is hardly surprising that Japanese children are raised on humorous tales about Ryōkan, many centering on Ryōkan's own child-like innocence and credulity. The following, recorded in Ryōkan's native Echigo, is typical of the stories known to nearly every Japanese child:

> Ryōkan was playing hide-and-seek, and when it came his turn to hide, he looked around for a spot where the children

wouldn't find him. Noticing a tall haystack, he crawled inside, concealing himself completely in the hay. No matter how hard they searched, the children couldn't find him. Soon they grew tired of playing, the sun began to set, and when they saw the smoke rising from the dinner fires, they deserted Ryōkan and returned to their homes. Unaware of this, Ryōkan imagined the children were still searching for him. Thinking, "Here they come to look for me!" "Now they're going to find me!" he waited and waited. He waited all night and was still waiting when dawn arrived. In farmhouses, in the morning, the kitchen hearth is lit with bundles of hay, and when the farmer's daughter came to fetch some of these, she was startled to find Ryōkan hiding in the haystack. "Ryōkan! What in the world are you doing here?" she cried. "Shhh!" Ryōkan warned her, "the children will find me!"[26]

Other tales typically play on Ryōkan's chronic forgetfulness, his tendency to misplace even his most personal and valued belongings. Ryōkan's own poems and letters make it clear that he was perennially absentminded, forgetting his walking stick, his precious begging bowl, his books, and, on one occasion, even his underwear. He attempted to keep one cherished volume from straying by inscribing on it the notice "This is mine"; and on the advice of friends, he compiled a long checklist of personal items he carried with him, such as balls, playing stones, and cash, but promptly forgot the list itself, still preserved at Suzuki Bundai's house.

Ryōkan's unconventional way of life evoked at least as much admiration as bewilderment, and he maintained a wide circle of friends, most with homes in the vicinity of Mount Kugami. Many seem to have been local rustics, unlettered farmers who were Ryōkan's neighbors; but others were amateur literati, scholars of Chinese like Suzuki Bundai and his brother Ryūzō, or poets like Harada Jakusai, Ryōkan's younger brother Yoshiyuki, and the sake brewers Abe Sadayoshi and Yamada Tokō, together with various merchants, doctors, and village headmen. Ryōkan would frequently stay at his friends' homes, and he looked forward to their visits to his hut, where, together, they would drink, talk, and compose poetry. Although, technically, liquor is forbidden to Buddhist monks, Ryōkan loved sake. But his drinking seems to have been largely social, an activity shared with friends, and he never appears to have drunk to excess. "When people give the Teacher sake," Ōzeki's biography observes, "he can imbibe and remain completely relaxed. If people urge him to get up and dance, he doesn't hesitate. When he's had enough, he simply leaves without saying anything."[27] Like pipe smoking, another favorite pastime, drinking sake with friends and neighbors seems to have been regarded by Ryōkan as a natural and perfectly harmless activity.

Despite its compensations, Ryōkan's life on Mount Kugami was a difficult one, fraught with physical hardship. Besides being obliged to haul his own water and firewood along Kugami's rugged slopes, Ryōkan remained throughout his years on the mountain an impoverished beggar, depending on the alms of neighbors who were often themselves in dire straits. Starvation seems to have been a constant threat, particularly in winter when Ryōkan was snowed in and unable to make his rounds of the towns and villages. He was frequently forced to rely on his friends to supply him with food and other necessities, and most of his roughly two hundred surviving letters are simple notes soliciting or acknowledging various forms of assistance and sometimes accompanied by brief poems. While never impolite, Ryōkan's language in these letters tends to be amusingly direct, even blunt, with no trace of pleading or unctuousness. His friends, in turn, the letters suggest, responded to his requests with unfailing generosity and warmth.

The multitude of items mentioned in the letters offer an intimate glimpse into Ryōkan's day-to-day existence on Mount Kugami. Along with staples such as rice, miso, and salt that must have sustained him through the harsh winter months, conspicuous among the goods Ryōkan mentions in his letters are "luxuries," especially tobacco and sake—clearly Ryōkan's favorite gifts—and sweets, like edible lily bulbs. Other offerings noted in Ryōkan's correspondence include an assortment of foodstuffs, among them seasonal fruits (pears and pomegranates), vegetables (eggplant, yams, daikon, or Japanese radish, burdock, ginger, parsley, red peppers), prepared foods (preserved plums, rice cakes, boiled beans, fried tofu, *yōkan,* or sweet bean jelly, sugar candy, preserved chrysanthemums), flour, tea, *konbu* (dried kelp), brandy, and even a carp. The letters also show that Ryōkan turned to his friends for clothes (a hat, *geta*—wooden Japanese platform sandals—a wadded cotton coat, underwear), household furnishings (futon, straw mats, towels, incense, candles, lamp oil, oiled paper umbrellas), paper, ink, and brushes for calligraphy, even cash. Some of these may have been one-time items, but others, like calligraphy supplies, were apparently regular gifts. An avid calligrapher whose work was much sought after,

Ryōkan seems to have been perpetually short of writing materials. His friend and biographer Bundai recalls visiting Ryōkan's hut and seeing on his desk an inkstone, several worn-out brushes, and fifty or sixty sheets of paper, each so densely covered with calligraphy that it appeared to be solid black.[28]

Along with poverty and hunger, Ryōkan suffered from a number of chronic ailments, which worsened with age and were no doubt exacerbated by the austere conditions of his life on Mount Kugami. In winter, he was afflicted by colds and lumbago, while the sticky summer months brought on vomiting, diarrhea, and skin disease. Ryōkan was fortunate in numbering among his friends many doctors, who kept him supplied with medicine; but his health during the years on Mount Kugami seems to have been poor at best, a reality reflected in the numerous poems that depict periods of illness and convalescence.

Although too humble to act as a teacher or to accept formal disciples, Ryōkan was joined at his hut in 1815 by a fourteen-year-old Shingon monk named Henchō (1801–1876), who had visited Ryōkan on Mount Kugami and begged to be allowed to remain and serve as his attendant. As Ryōkan grew older, Henchō's assistance with the tasks of carrying water and gathering firewood must have been welcome, and Henchō may also have acted as caretaker during the periods when Ryōkan was traveling or staying with friends.

By 1826, however, Ryōkan's increasing age and infirmity forced him at last to leave his beloved mountain and accept the hospitality of his friend and supporter the merchant Kimura Motouemon (1778–1848). While Henchō settled at a Shingon temple in Jizōdō, Ryōkan moved to a detached house on the grounds of the Kimura family mansion in Shimazaki, a village some seven miles south of Mount Kugami. But although warmly received by Kimura, Ryōkan seems to have been unhappy living in the town, lonely for the familiar sights and sounds of his mountain home.

It was at this low ebb in Ryōkan's fortunes that he first met the nun Teishin (1798–1872), probably in the fall of 1827. Teishin was the beautiful daughter of a samurai from Nagaoka, a castle town some fourteen miles southeast of Shimazaki. She had married a doctor but, finding herself widowed after only five years, shaved her head and became a Buddhist nun, entering a Pure Land temple near her native Nagaoka. Teishin was an accomplished writer of *tanka,* the traditional thirty-one-syllable (5-7-5-7-7) Japanese verse form, and learning of Ryōkan's fame as a poet, she determined to travel to Shimazaki and seek his instruction. At the time of their first meeting, Ryōkan was sixty-nine, Teishin only twenty-nine. The visit left them both exhilarated, and led to a close relationship that brightened Ryōkan's final years. Teishin was often at Ryōkan's side, even nursing him when he was ill, and the deep affection they shared is revealed in the many poems they exchanged, collected by Teishin under the title *Dew on the Lotus (Hachisu no tsuyu).*[29]

Ryōkan's health continued to deteriorate, and by the winter of 1830, he was confined to his bed by violent diarrhea, unable to eat, his suffering compounded by the insomnia that had plagued him over the years. Sometimes delirious, tended by Teishin and Henchō, Ryōkan continued to write throughout his final illness. The end came in late afternoon on the sixth day of the New Year, 1831. Teishin records that Ryōkan, seated in meditation posture, died "just as if he were falling asleep."[30]

Ryōkan's funeral was held at the Kimura mansion and attended by nearly three hundred mourners, including representatives from seventeen Buddhist temples and many ordinary farmers and villagers from the surrounding area. Some of Ryōkan's friends sent poems to the service, expressing their grief. Tomitori Masanari of Jizōdō[31] offered a *tanka* titled "Mourning the Passing of Zen Master Ryōkan" that suggests the intimate place Ryōkan occupied in the lives of those who knew him:

> Year after year
> We frolicked together in the spring fields
> But this year
> With whom shall I pluck
>   the young spring greens?[32]

And Ryōkan's brother Yoshiyuki wrote:

> Picking spring greens
> This, too, has become my keepsake of you
> The sky at twilight
> On a day long ago[33]

Ryōkan's poetry was much appreciated by his friends, but he seems to have written purely for his own and their enjoyment and never to have sought a wider audience for his work. Although none of Ryōkan's poems were published in his lifetime, manuscript collections circulated widely in Echigo after his death, and by the end of the nineteenth century, some of Ryōkan's kanshi and waka had begun to appear in print. In the early years of the twentieth century, Ryōkan's writings and biography were seriously studied for the first time, with new materials uncovered and published through the efforts of two Echigo schoolteachers, Nishigori Kyūgo (1866–1932) and Tamaki Reikichi (d. 1922). Ryōkan was finally catapulted to national attention by the writer Sōma Gyofū, who from 1918 till his death in 1950 produced a series of widely read works devoted to Ryōkan's life and poetry.

Postwar Japan has, meanwhile, experienced an explosion of popular interest in Ryōkan, whose appeal now extends beyond aesthetes and intellectuals to the general public. Through the works of Sōma and others who collected local tales and legends, Ryōkan has now become a part of Japanese folklore. Stories about the whimsical monk of Mount Kugami are a staple of modern Japanese children's literature, and a survey conducted in 1970 showed 99 percent of elementary school students to be familiar with Ryōkan.

At first glance, Ryōkan may seem an unlikely culture hero for modern Japan, a land often regarded as oppressively conformist, status-obsessed, and materialistic, a place where, as the Japanese themselves observe, "The nail that sticks up gets hit." By contemporary or even eighteenth-century standards, the Ryōkan we encounter in the poems and in the records of his biographers would appear to be a failure, a dropout, a loner in a society where group identity and affiliation can be all-important. Yet precisely this aspect of Ryōkan has made him popular with today's Japanese. Those qualities epitomized by Ryōkan in the popular imagination—simplicity, trust, goodness—are still regarded by many in Japan as the essence of the Japanese spirit, the basis of all Japanese social groups, from the clan to the corporation. Such qualities may be as rare in Japan as elsewhere, but in Japan they are particularly valued, even if only as an ideal. This is a fact that often eludes foreign observers, distracted by the aggressive modernity, wealth, and sophistication of bustling cities like Tokyo or Osaka; but it remains an important element of the Japanese psyche, critical to the way in which the Japanese view themselves.

Ryōkan, moreover, is revered not only as quintessentially Japanese, but as quintessentially "Zen." It is true that, unlike other famous monks, Ryōkan never founded temples, composed religious tracts, trained disciples, or delivered sermons. In fact, he seems to have studiously avoided talking about Zen at all. Instead, Ryōkan appears to have taught through his own life. If Ryōkan is admired in Japan as a paradigm of the fully liberated person, it is because he was free from both secular and religious conventions, not only playing hide-and-seek with the children and living as a beggar on the mountainside, but also joining in the village festivals and drinking sake with the local farmers. There remains uncertainty about Ryōkan's title of *zenji,* or "Zen Master," a title indicating that a Zen monk has been officially acknowledged as his teacher's heir and a teacher in his own right, qualified to transmit the Dharma to heirs of his own. Existing Sōtō sect lineage charts designate Ryōkan as Kokusen's heir, but this status could well have been conferred in retrospect to acknowledge Ryōkan's later celebrity. "Zen Master," in Ryōkan's case, may have been more a sobriquet than a formal rank, a deferential title spontaneously accorded Ryōkan by his friends and neighbors in Echigo in recognition of his spiritual attainment. Certainly Ryōkan never referred to himself as a teacher or a Zen master, but others regularly referred to him as such, including his friends Suzuki Bundai and Teishin and his brother Yoshiyuki. The village children called him simply "Ryōkan *sa!*"—*sa* being an informal local variation of the Japanese *san,* or "mister."

Ryōkan's freewheeling way of life was itself a rebuke to what he regarded as the sham and rigidity of the Japanese Zen monasteries. But although he distanced himself from the Sōtō temple establishment after his return to Echigo, Ryōkan's writings show that he remained passionately committed to Buddhism and to his role as a monk. In this sense, Ryōkan was a traditionalist. He lamented that Dōgen's teachings were no longer understood in the Sōtō temples and contended that the monk's practice of begging was the means to revive the original Buddhism of Shākyamuni. Judging by his poems and his biographers' accounts, Ryōkan was also devoted to Zen meditation. He would practice outdoors among the hills and streams around Mount Kugami or in his hut, sitting in zazen all night or sometimes for days on end when he was snowed in; he even maintained his practice when traveling and staying in the homes of his patrons and friends.

Ryōkan's approach to Buddhism was forthrightly nonsectarian. The *Lotus Sūtra,* though not specifically identified with Zen, was among Ryōkan's favorite scriptures, and he composed a series of poems based on its text and copied out the *Sūtra* in its entirety. Although a Sōtō Zen monk by training, Ryōkan never criticized other schools and readily embraced the popular forms of Buddhism traditionally practiced by the masses in rural Japan, worshiping Kannon,[34] repeating the *nenbutsu,* even serving as caretaker of a Shinto shrine. Ryōkan's hermitage

Gogō-an belonged to the Shingon, or Esoteric, sect, as did many of the temples around Mount Kugami where Ryōkan would stay on his travels in the area; and Ryōkan was buried at the Shimazaki Ryūsenji, an Ikkō sect[35] temple that served as the mortuary chapel of the Kimura family.

Ryōkan's disregard for sectarian differences would seem to reflect his identification with the fundamental concerns common to Buddhism as a whole. Much of the development of Mahāyāna Buddhism, and of the Zen school in particular, has crystallized around a single pivotal question: What is the relationship between the world of enlightenment, of original, unconditioned mind, and the transient world of ordinary human existence? The most noted teachers of Buddhism have generally been those who offered arresting responses to this problem. Most, however, agree that reality itself is a whole, that the dichotomy between enlightenment and ignorance is more apparent than real; when seen with the eye of wisdom, they maintain, the world of buddhas and the world of human beings are constantly and perfectly interfused. This is a tenet of the teachings of nearly all important Mahāyāna texts, from the *Heart* and *Lotus* sūtras to the writings of Kūkai and the records of the T'ang Zen masters.[36]

In the attempt to resolve the "great matter of birth and death," Zen, in particular, has stressed the practice of meditation and the experience of enlightenment, the realization of one's original nature. But Zen, it is said, demands one thing more. To be truly enlightened, the old masters insist, it is not enough simply to *realize* original nature; it must somehow be actualized, manifested. And to many Japanese, Ryōkan's own daily life, the qualities he reveals in his poems, his brushwork, and his at times almost comical innocence, constitute his direct and personal demonstration of the mind of enlightenment at work in the world of ordinary humanity.

A Poetics of Mendicancy
Nondualist Philosophy and Ryōkan's Figurative Strategies

Ryūichi Abé

> Who says that my poems are poems?
> My poems aren't poems at all
> When you understand
> That my poems really aren't poems
> Then we can talk poetry together
> Ryōkan

"*Text* means *Tissue*," writes Roland Barthes, "but whereas hitherto we have always taken this tissue as a product, a ready-made veil, behind which lies, more or less hidden, meaning (truth), we are now emphasizing, in the tissue, the generative idea that the text is made, is worked out in a perpetual interweaving."[1] Barthes' proposal to understand text as the topos of incessant semantic production—rather than as the representation of fixed meanings outside of it—speaks eloquently of the seminal shift of emphasis in contemporary philosophical and literary theories in their approach to studying text. Such a reminder, however, seems unnecessary for Ryōkan, who, more than a century earlier than Barthes, articulated as follows the essentials of waka, the traditional Japanese poetry composed in the native *kana* syllabary, consisting of forty-eight characters.

> Weaving the countless
> Varying tinges of texture
> Are the forty-eight phonetic letters
> Weaving them with their voices
> And echoes, the warp and woof[2]

The ever-changing shades of color in his poetry have captivated its readers, who return to it time and again, discovering something new with each rereading. It is probably because of the poet's emphasis on such dynamic, generative aspects of poetic composition over conventional rhetorical regulations that his poems have been eagerly studied and eulogized by many of the twentieth-century poets who have radically transformed the Japanese poetic tradition: Masaoka Shiki (1867–1902), Itō Sachio (1864–1913), Saitō Mokichi (1882–1953), Hagiwara Sakutarō (1886–1942), and Aizu Yaichi (1881–1956), to name only a few.

In one of his collected essays, the prominent Japanese critic Karaki Junzō relates that, following the death of his famed mentor, the Kyoto school philosopher Tanabe Hajime (1885–1962), he discovered in a drawer of his late teacher's desk sheets of paper on which Tanabe had copied out thirty times a poem composed by Ryōkan.[3] Each character of the poem, each stroke of the characters, Karaki recalls, was inscribed by Tanabe with the utmost care as if to emulate Ryōkan's original style of calligraphy. As Karaki's experience shows, Ryōkan is also highly acclaimed for his mastery of calligraphy. Already during his lifetime Ryōkan's brushwork, as much as his poetry, was widely admired. Even ordinary villagers pursued Ryōkan to obtain his calligraphy;[4] among the literati, Ryōkan's repute spread beyond his own locale to the capital of Edo;[5] and counterfeits of his works even began to circulate among connoisseurs.[6] It appears, however, that Ryōkan himself did not enjoy his fame either as a calligrapher or as a poet. Kera Yoshishige (1810–1859), the village chief of Makigahana, who in his childhood had been one of Ryōkan's regular playing companions on his daily begging rounds, reports: "When anyone asked the Master for a sample of his calligraphy, the Master would say: 'After I practice and become good at it, I'll write something for you.' At other times, in the grip of inspiration, he would toss off one sheet of calligraphy after another. He never complained about the quality of his materials. The Master would write his poems from memory, and that's why there were sometimes missing characters and some small variations in wording, so that there is no definitive version of his poems."[7] In a poem comically titled "Inspiration," Ryōkan complains:

> Shaving my head, becoming a monk
> I spent years on the road
>   pushing aside wild grasses
>   peering hard into the wind
> Now, everywhere I go
>   people just hand me paper and brush:
>   "Do some calligraphy!" "Write me a poem!"[8]

Suzuki Bundai, a Confucian teacher who was a friend of Ryōkan's and himself a poet, recalled in 1849: "He [Ryōkan] once said, 'There are three things I detest: professional calligraphers' calligraphy; professional poets' poems; and professional cooks' food.' "[9] Bundai's statement suggests that Ryōkan did not wish to be recognized merely as a calligrapher or a poet. Just as Ryōkan is unique among eminent poets, his poems are renowned for their transgression of conventional rules. This is true for both of the literary formats in which he composed his poems: *kanshi,* poetry composed in classical Chinese characters, recited not in the original Chinese pronunciation, but in the pronunciation and grammatical order of Japanese transliteration; and *waka,* native Japanese poetry composed in *kana,* the Japanese phonetic alphabet, with rhythmically alternating five- and seven-syllable phrases. In his waka, Ryōkan intentionally avoids the ornate style upheld by Dōjōha —the mainstream school claiming to be the inheritor of *kokin denju,* the esoteric technical tradition originating from the medieval poet Tō Tsuneyori (1401–1494)—and takes as his source of inspiration the *Man'yōshū,* an eighth-century compendium of ancient poems, known for its archaic vocabulary and crude but direct style.[10] As for Ryōkan's kanshi, modern Japanese scholars have repeatedly pointed out a particular stylistic affinity between his poems and those of the *Han-shan shih-chi* (Cold Mountain Poems), the collected poems of Han-shan, Shih-te, and Feng-kang, legendary T'ang dynasty Zen recluses on Mount T'ien-t'ai.[11] Ryōkan mentions in several of his own poems that reading the *Han-shan shih-chi* was one of his favorite activities in his mountain hut.[12] However, a discussion on the relationship between Ryōkan and Han-shan based strictly on their styles can be misleading. One of Han-shan's poems reads:

> There's a certain scholar called Wang
> He laughs at my poems
>   for their many errors
> He says: "You don't know about 'bee's waist'
> "You don't understand 'crane's knee'
> "You don't even know how to place *p'ing-tse!*
> "Careless, you string together
>   trite words"
> But I laugh at him: "The way you make poems:
> The blind striving in vain
>   to compose poems about the sun!"[13]

"Bee's waist" *(heng-yao)* and "crane's knee" *(ho-hsi)* are two violations of the rules governing the balanced distribution of characters with identical sound and pitch.[14] *P'ing-tse* is a rule regulating the allocation of accentuated and unaccentuated characters in classical Chinese poetry.[15] As with Han-shan's poems, Ryōkan's kanshi are often criticized for violating the traditional rules of Chinese poetry. Ryōkan defends his own attitude toward poetry as follows: "Who says that my poems are poems? / My poems aren't poems at all / When you understand that my poems really aren't poems / Then we can talk poetry together."[16] Ryōkan appears not to care if his poems fail to be recognized as such. What is it, then, he aims to accomplish through his poetry? Ōzeki Bunchū (d. 1834), one of Ryōkan's literary friends and a local physician, provides a clue: "Once, someone remarked that the Master's kanshi contained many technical errors. The Master replied: 'I just say whatever is in my mind. What do I know about technical matters? If there are people schooled in such matters, they can make the corrections themselves.' Abashed, the fellow slunk off."[17] Ryōkan underscores this point in the following poem:

> How pitiful, those virtuous fellows!
> Moving into the recesses, they immerse
>   themselves in composing poetry
> For Ancient Style, their models
>   are the poems of Han and Wei
> For Recent Form,
>   the T'ang poets are their guide
> With gaudy words their lines are formed
> And further adorned by
>   novel and curious phrases
> Yet if they fail to express
>   what's in their own minds
> What's the use, no matter
>   how many poems they compose![18]

This poem makes explicit that the affinity between Ryōkan and the *Han-shan shih-chi* cannot be revealed fully merely in terms of style. Ryōkan's poetry shares with that of the recluses on Cold Mountain its bold intent to break free from stylistic limitations, its direct, earnest voice unadulterated even by poetic conventions, ready to "say whatever is in my mind."

The celebrated Meiji novelist Natsume Sōseki (1867–1916) is among those who appreciate the particular freedom manifested in Ryōkan's creation. On 17 January 1914, Sōseki wrote a thank you letter to a friend in Niigata who had sent him a copy of Ryōkan's collected poems. "I deeply appreciate your kindness," Sōseki writes. "I find the Reverend's [Ryōkan's] poetry so lofty that only a handful of poets from the ancient past would compare with him fairly. It also seems to me that he pays almost no attention to *p'ing-tse* and other regulations. What is your own opinion? Although I am no expert in this matter [of poetry], I find myself perfectly satisfied when I, as a Japanese, just recite his verses. As I read his poems, I always enjoy their subtlety manifesting itself right before me in their lines, phrases, and characters."[19] The letter goes on to convey Sōseki's request for original pieces of Ryōkan's calligraphy. On 16 March 1916, in a letter to his physician and friend Morinari Rinzō, Sōseki describes his ecstasy at finally acquiring, with Morinari's help, a treasure he had been pursuing for years: handwritten kanshi by Ryōkan. "Everyone in the world wishes to have Ryōkan's calligraphy. But I insisted on Ryōkan not because he is an excellent calligrapher, but because he is Ryōkan. I even get upset when I see collectors displaying Ryōkan's work on their walls, evaluating it in the same way as [the works of other renowned calligraphers and poets such as] Shōō, San'yō, and so forth.[20] They do not deserve to be the owners of a piece by Ryōkan."[21]

Sōseki's letters point to an interesting yet serious problem: on the one hand, Ryōkan's phenomenal popularity is in large part attributable to his unusual talent at poetry and calligraphy; on the other hand, it is impossible to understand Ryōkan's person by reducing him merely to a poet or a calligrapher. While this contradiction may well be the key to explaining Ryōkan's unique attraction, it also presents a difficulty for Ryōkan scholars who attempt to understand Ryōkan and his artistic creations.

Characterizing Ryōkan: Poet or Zen Master?

In the introduction to his 1977 translation of Ryōkan's poems, Burton Watson states that his book was intended to fulfill the prophecy of Saitō Mokichi, an eminent modern Japanese poet, who predicted that the time would come when Ryōkan's poems would be appreciated in China as well as in the West.[22] For the most part, the study of Ryōkan in Western languages has followed Watson's lead in characterizing Ryōkan as a literary figure. Although Watson and other earlier translators are responsible for introducing Ryōkan's name to students in the West, their approach falls short of illustrating Ryōkan's multifarious characteristics. Nor does it help in understanding the exceptional popularity Ryōkan's poems enjoy in contemporary Japan, where interpretation of Ryōkan is divided between two opposing camps.

The first camp consists of a group of scholars whose core is made up of local historians and ethnographers of the Echigo (present Niigata) region, who understand Ryōkan above all as a religious-cultural hero. Probably the best-known figure in this group is Sōma Gyofū (1883–1950), a native of the city of Itoigawa, Niigata, and a nationally renowned poet and literary critic, whose widely read 1919 biography *Taigu Ryō-kan* (Ryōkan the Great Fool)[23] was singularly instrumental in expanding Ryōkan's popularity among the general public throughout Japan. In the same year, Tamaki Reikichi, a local historian and grammar school teacher and a native of the village of Kugami (formerly one of Ryōkan's regular begging sites), published the first edition of Ryōkan's collected writings, *Ryōkan zenshū* (Complete Collection of Ryōkan's Works),[24] which triggered the rapid growth of new bibliographical and historiographical research during the 1920s and 1930s. The work of these scholars—preserving Ryōkan's calligraphy, discovering new historical documents, collecting local oral traditions, establishing the Ryōkan Study Society (Ryōkan kai), and publishing academic and nonacademic periodicals dedicated to Ryōkan—provided the foundation for the formation of the voluminous literature of modern Ryōkan studies. Among other prominent figures in this group of scholars are Miya Eiji, renowned for his study of Ryōkan's calligraphy; Satō Kichitarō, who prepared a detailed local history of Ryōkan's home province; and Tanigawa Toshirō, who produced the most comprehensive bibliographical catalog of Ryōkan studies to date.[25]

In his article "Ryōkan's Religiosity,"[26] Hasegawa Yōzō, another Niigata native, a professor at Waseda University and an active member of the Ryōkan Study Society, characterizes Ryōkan as follows:

> I address Ryōkan, as many others do, as Zen master *(zenji)*. I would like to make it clear that I am using the term *zenji* in its literal sense, as a "master who excelled in meditative training and who is qualified to serve people as a teacher," and not as the honorific title that the emperors of the past granted to high priests. The "zen" in my usage of *zenji* refers to the practice of meditation and not to a particular school of Zen. . . . Ryōkan did not have any sectarian affiliation. He simply lived his life as a Buddhist through the practice of meditation. Because of this freedom, Ryōkan enjoyed from

time to time even reciting *nenbutsu* [of the Pure Land school]. (pp. 341–342)

Ryōkan is characterized as *zenji* because, Hasegawa argues, the term illustrates Ryōkan's unique quality as an ideal teacher for ordinary people. That is, Ryōkan communicates his wisdom wrought by meditative practice to people without the authoritative arrogance of a high priest, without the biased obstinacy of a sectarian propagandist. Hasegawa continues:

> It seems apparent to me that Ryōkan did actually attain enlightenment. People often overlook this because, contrary to the cases of many high Zen monks, Ryōkan's enlightenment was not dramatized. However, one locates his religiosity directly in the same stream of True Dharma that runs through Shākyamuni, Bodhidharma, Hui-neng and Dōgen. . . . Precisely because he realized his original nature through and through and succeeded in dropping off the duality of body and mind *(shinjin datsuraku)* . . . and because of his genuine attainment of the *samadhi* of blissfulness *(jijuyō sanmai)*—despite the fact that he neither resided in a temple nor produced disciples—he was able to transmit his Buddhist teaching to countless beings through his poetry and calligraphy. (p. 345)

For Hasegawa, Ryōkan is not merely an enlightened Zen master. He is a superior teacher whose enlightenment is so thorough that he rejected such conventional means as formal lectures or doctrinal writings. Instead, Ryōkan's poetry and calligraphy became his vehicle for expressing Buddhist teaching. Ryōkan's distance from the ecclesiastic establishment, his freedom from sectarianism, and his exposition of religiosity through literature and art make him a superior Buddhist teacher. "In some respects, Ryōkan even went further than Dōgen. This does not mean that Ryōkan was superior to Dōgen. It means that Ryōkan was an extraordinary talent who demonstrated greater flexibility than Dōgen in accepting and absorbing various Buddhist and non-Buddhist teachings. Ryōkan is larger than the framework provided by the institutional lineage of Dōgen's school" (p. 343).

In his detailed study *Ryōkan's Life and Anecdotes*,[27] Tanigawa Toshirō describes Ryōkan's nonsectarianism:

> Ryōkan's family had been the village chiefs *(nanushi)* and, for generations, had served as head priests of the Shintō

shrine at Ishii. His family was also affiliated with Enmyōji, a
Buddhist temple of the Shingon school at Izumozaki. Ryō-
kan became a monk at Kōshōji, a temple of the Sōtō school
at Amaze, and was trained at Entsūji, a Sōtō monastery at
Tamashima. After his return home, he first found temporary
quarters in Shōmyōji, a Shingon temple at Teradomari, and
thereafter settled at Gogō-an, a hut located on the grounds
of Kokujōji, another temple of the same school. Later, Ryō-
kan lived in a hut at the Shintō shrine of Otogo, and in his
last years he stayed in quarters in the house of the Kimura
family, followers of the True Pure Land school. His grave is
located at Ryūsenji, another True Pure Land temple. (p. 384)

Based on these events in Ryōkan's life, Tanigawa lends support to Hase-
gawa's characterization of Ryōkan's tolerant attitude toward different
religions:

The *Lotus Sūtra* was his favorite reading in his hut. . . .
Besides the *Lotus,* he was well-versed in the Pure Land
sūtras as well as in the *Analects* and the *Chuang-tzu.* . . .
One may say he transcended the differences between Shintō,
Buddhism, Confucianism, and Taoism. . . . Precisely because
Ryōkan was brimming with boundless compassion and gen-
erosity, the very fountainhead of Buddhism, Ryōkan's reli-
gion appeared to ordinary people to be the religion of no
religion. People kept coming to him to seek this something
of Ryōkan's that transcended all doctrinal teachings. (pp.
384–385)

Ryōkan's "religion of no religion," for both Hasegawa and Tanigawa,
makes him superior to typical Zen masters of his day, who, having been
assigned to their resident temples with a number of disciples to serve
them, sustained the sectarian lineage of Dharma transmission largely
on paper.

At the opposite pole from Hasegawa and Tanigawa are scholars
who characterize Ryōkan as a nonreligious poet. According to their
view, Ryōkan turned away from the feudalistic religion of Tokugawa
Buddhism and composed his poems as a tribute to the oppressed
masses. Such a reading of Ryōkan has rather a short history that does
not go back farther than the beginning of the postwar era in 1945.
However, it quickly gained support and thrived, particularly in the
dominantly Marxist atmosphere of the Japanese intelligentsia of the
1960s and 1970s.

Imoto Nōichi, a leading scholar of classical Japanese literature, argues in his voluminous study *Ryōkan* that, if Ryōkan was enlightened, it is "contradictory that he left a large number of poems expressing the depression and alienation of old age. . . . One must consider Ryōkan as a figure of agony, sorrow, and suffering."[28] For Imoto, Ryōkan is a quitter of Zen training who found comfort in a reclusive life of poetry and art:

> If one strives hard in religious training to reach the realm of nirvāṇa, he will certainly have a positive attitude toward life. [Ryōkan] once led such a life. Particularly when he was studying with the Abbot Kokusen, he singlemindedly devoted himself to sitting in meditation. However, having left Entsūji, he traveled here and there, wandering across the land, and hid himself in the mountains of Echigo, losing his positive attitude toward attaining the ultimate state of nirvāṇa. . . . Instead, he found pleasure in appreciating flowers, getting drunk, writing calligraphy, and playing *go*. (p. 94)

Imoto goes on to say that it is precisely Ryōkan's withdrawal from religion to art that lends "modernity" to his poetry: "For Ryōkan, art is the escape from affliction and despair. . . . He barely succeeded in dispersing them from his mind by composing poetry and producing calligraphy" (p. 88). In agreement with Imoto, the renowned critic Kurita Isamu, in his *Introduction to Ryōkan,* identifies the darkness of night, the sound of rainfall, and the deep snow concealing mountains and forests as major motifs of Ryōkan's poetry and asserts that they all aim at expressing Ryōkan's tormenting isolation.

> Can such a heart-devouring loneliness be called a state of enlightenment? . . . Here one does not find the enlightenment of pureness, thoroughness, and steadfastness that characterizes Dōgen. Nor is there the peace of mind to be found in entrusting oneself completely to the Buddha of the Pure Land. What Ryōkan expresses in his poems are the ultimate states of the same agonizing solitude that we experience in our own everyday life.[29]

Iriya Yoshitaka, an expert on Zen Buddhist literature, shares this view. By pointing to the empty begging bowl as the principal icon in Ryōkan's poems of his solitude, Iriya, in his *Collected Poems of Ryōkan,*[30] discusses the following poem as a testimony to Ryōkan's depressed state of mind:

Will my stupidity and stubbornness ever end?
Poor and alone—that's my life
Twilight on the streets of a ramshackle town
Going home again with an empty bowl[31]

Iriya says: "What dominate here are dark, downcast thoughts that res-
onate with one another in self-scorn. . . . Precisely because Ryōkan in
his old age had many days filled with such depressive thoughts, he
sought in composing poems and playing with children emancipation
from a self dull with stupidity and heavy with stubbornness" (p. 40).
For Iriya, Ryōkan is certainly not an exemplar of Zen enlightenment:
"It is absolutely unnecessary to regard Ryōkan's Zen as having reached
the highest realm of enlightenment, comparable to that of the Sixth
Patriarch or Bodhidharma. Nor is it necessary to describe it as actualiz-
ing Dōgen's ideal of 'transcending buddhas, transcending patriarchs,'
and penetrating the mysterious depths" (p. 39).

The arguments put forth in the interpretations representing the
second group of Japanese Ryōkan scholars can be summarized with
two points. First, Ryōkan is a Zen monk who failed to attain enlighten-
ment. This does not diminish the value of studying Ryōkan because,
they assert, Ryōkan's historical importance rests not on his religiosity
but on his talent as a poet. Second, for a poet, Ryōkan's nonenlighten-
ment is not a liability but an asset. It is Ryōkan's escape from religion
to art and his discovery there of a refuge from the torment of existen-
tial solitude that makes his poetry most appealing to the modern mind
of a secularized, alienated society.

These contradictory characterizations of Ryōkan—the enlight-
ened Zen master versus the secularized poet—proposed by the two
opposing camps of Japanese Ryōkan scholarship suggest that neither
has succeeded in providing interpretations comprehensive enough to
illustrate Ryōkan's multifaceted character. Furthermore, their failure
has created a new problem: their unbridgeable difference has posthu-
mously split Ryōkan's person between the religious and the literary.
This seems to explain why there has not been a thorough study cap-
able of illustrating exactly in what sense Ryōkan's poems are related to
his religion. Interestingly, and ironically, such an intellectualized prob-
lematic separating Ryōkan's poetry from his religious life belies a gen-
eral consensus among Ryōkan scholars, both Japanese and American
(see, for example, Nobuyuki Yuasa, *The* Zen Poems *of Ryōkan* [Prince-
ton, 1981]; Burton Watson, *Ryōkan,* Zen Monk-Poet *of Japan* [New

York, 1977]; John Stevens, *One Robe, One Bowl: The* Zen Poetry *of Ryōkan* [New York, 1977]), that Ryōkan's poems are "Zen poems." A careful review of the way in which primary materials were used by the two camps of scholars reveals that conclusions regarding Ryōkan's enlightenment or nonenlightenment are not the outcome of their analysis but are ideological premises on which their argumentations are constructed. The question of enlightenment, just like the proof or disproof of the presence of God in theological literature, lies beyond the scope of an academic inquiry that attempts to understand Ryōkan's life and his poems.

The first group of scholars draw their strength from the massive historical data, both written and oral, collected in Ryōkan's homeland of Echigo. Although many of these written texts and oral traditions are later legendary accounts, they also include earlier biographical records left by Ryōkan's contemporaries, primary sources that many historians claim to be the most reliable accounts of Ryōkan's everyday life.

One of the earliest biographical accounts of Ryōkan can be found in an anthology of classical Chinese poems composed in 1814 by the young Confucian scholar Suzuki Bundai (1796–1870).[32] Ryōkan was then living at his hut Gogō-an on Mount Kugami, and Bundai became acquainted with Ryōkan through his Confucian teacher Yamada Shizan, a frequent visitor to Ryōkan's mountain hut. Through Shizan, Bundai was introduced to Ryōkan's kanshi and became a devoted student of his poetry. Bundai speaks of Ryōkan in his anthology: "Worldly people call him different things—fool, wise-man, idiot, man of the Way. He neither flatters the rich and important, nor disdains the poor and humble. He isn't happy when he gets things, or sad when he loses them. He just goes along, natural, relaxed, a man who has transcended the dust of the world."[33] The Ryōkan portrayed by Bundai shows no trace of the bitterness, agony, and affliction suggested by the second camp of scholars. Bundai continues: "He is always accompanied by children and, when he is out begging, can be found playing with them in the shade of trees and in the fields, tugging at blades of grass, sumo wrestling and bouncing balls. His mind is like a mirror, looking neither forward nor backward."[34]

Two years later, in 1816, Bundai edited Ryōkan's kanshi and prepared them for publication in a volume called *Sōdōshū* (Grass Hut Collection). In his new preface to this volume, composed in 1849, Bundai recalls the affinity between Ryōkan's mirrorlike mind, focused on the here-and-now, and the minds of children: "Whenever the Master would appear in the village, he would follow the boys and girls and play. . . . Wherever the Master went, a crowd of children would gather around him. When people asked, 'Why do you act like this?' the Master would reply: 'I love their truthfulness, their lack of pretense.' "[35]

Four years after Bundai's poetic anthology, in 1818, his friend Ōzeki Bunchū (d. 1834), a student of Chinese classics and medicine, composed *Ryōkan zenji den* (Record of Zen Master Ryōkan), the first independent bibliographical work on Ryōkan. Bunchū observes: "The Master chants sūtras or sits in meditation; sometimes he composes poems or practices calligraphy, just taking up each as the spirit moves him. . . . He is pure, without desire, with no trace of defilement. Concealing his virtue, hiding his wisdom, calling himself a fool, he goes along, enjoying himself, doing just as he pleases."[36] In conclusion, Bunchū declares: "Isn't this truly someone who has realized the mind transmitted by Bodhidharma?"

Other contemporaneous records include those by Sugae Masumi (1754-1829), a nationally renowned ethnographer, Ryōkan's disciple the nun Teishin (1798-1872), and Kera Yoshishige (1810-1859), the chief of Makigahana, whose house had long been among the regular stopovers of Ryōkan's daily rounds of begging.[37] Similar to the accounts of Bundai and Bunchū, these accounts also describe Ryōkan as a Zen master with an exceptional talent in poetry and calligraphy. The Ryōkan delineated in these contemporaneous accounts seems to lend support to the view held by the first group of scholars that Ryōkan was a religious-cultural hero, a Zen master endowed with superior enlightenment. One does not find in these records any hint of a secularized monk-poet who, depressed by poverty, old age, and estrangement, led a tragic existence at the margins of society.

However, precisely because these scholars take these contemporaneous accounts for granted, they fail to explain *why* Ryōkan's early biographers understood Ryōkan as an enlightened Zen master. As Bundai's statement quoted above—"worldly people call him different things—fool, wise-man, idiot, man of the Way"—shows, and in contrast to the idealized image depicted in many later accounts, not everyone who knew Ryōkan loved him and approved his unconventional life as a beggar-monk. There were those who labeled Ryōkan an idiot, a failure, a pariah. What these earlier records demonstrate as historical fact is, therefore, not Ryōkan's enlightenment but *an* interpretive perspective shared by the contemporaneous biographers through which they viewed Ryōkan, despite his appearance as a fool and his eccentricity, as a superior Zen master. That is to say, this happened to be the particular perspective that prevailed and preserved Ryōkan's name in history.

At this juncture, one recognizes the merit of the second group of Japanese scholars, who argue that it is Ryōkan's own poems, rather than the traditional historical and legendary accounts, that must first be considered as the most dependable source for understanding who Ryōkan was and how he actually lived his life. The logic behind their assertion is that because the poems are Ryōkan's own words, it is they, not the biographies, that have the final say about the nature of Ryōkan's life. True, many of Ryōkan's poetic self-portraits of solitude provide a picture that supports these scholars' projection that Ryōkan was not an extraordinary teacher but an ordinary being who lived, like others, a life of suffering. For instance, in one of his poems Ryōkan portrays a picture of misery in his lonely abode.

> Who is there to pity this life of mine?
> A pepper tree props up the brushwood gate
> Mugwort obliterates the narrow garden path
> On my bamboo fence dangles a solitary gourd
> Across the valley
>   I hear the sounds of trees being felled
> And spend the clear morning
>   with my head on the pillow
> A mountain bird trills a few notes as it passes
> As if trying to console me in my solitude[38]

For the second group of scholars, such a poem is Ryōkan's own testimonial to the failure of his life, to his defeat in the struggle to attain enlightenment. Ryōkan is important not because of his pitiable life but because of his unusual talent for expressing this life in poetry. Thus, when Ryōkan says, "Will my stupidity and stubbornness ever end? / Poor and alone—that's my life," Iriya interprets it *literally* as evidence of Ryōkan's failure in attaining enlightenment and, accordingly, regards the latter half of Ryōkan's life as characterized by dejection and alienation.

One must not overlook, however, that not all of Ryōkan's self-portrait poems reveal him as downcast. In fact, Ryōkan composed as many poems of spiritual uplift as of depression.

> Finished begging my food in a ramshackle town
> I return to my home among the green hills

The evening sun drops behind the western peaks
A pale moon lights the stream that runs by my door
I wash my feet, climb onto a rock
Burn incense and sit in meditation
I am, after all, a Buddhist monk
How can I let the years just drift uselessly by?[39]

A Buddhist monk of the old Indians' school
I hid myself on Mount Kugami
   I don't recall how many springtimes ago
I've worn out countless pairs of robes
But my staff has never left my side
Following the mountain streams
   I wander singing along distant paths
Or sit and watch the white clouds
   billowing from jagged peaks
Pity the traveler in the floating world
   of fame and fortune
His life spent chasing after specks of
   swirling dust![40]

    If Ryōkan's poems are the one truly reliable witness to his daily life, as asserted by the second group of scholars, these poems suggest that Ryōkan, whether or not he was enlightened, remained faithful to his commitment as a Buddhist practitioner. He does not look like a "Zen quitter," as Imoto infers, who found refuge by escaping into the art of poetry. Ryōkan composed poems in diverse lyrical moods. In some poems Ryōkan suffers an unbearable burden of solitude; in others he confidently describes his mind purified by the practice of meditation; in yet others he joyfully plays with the village children. If one insists on interpreting Ryōkan's poems literally, they only provide conflicting pictures of his daily life. It is problematic to assess the state of Ryōkan's enlightenment or lack of enlightenment, as the second group of scholars have done, based only on one particular category of the poems, those describing moments of sadness and gloom.

    There is another, perhaps more serious, problem in the way the second group of scholars treat Ryōkan's poetry. One of their central assertions is that because Ryōkan's poems are his own words, they are the most reliable records for understanding his life. However, poems are not the same as historical documents in their signifying practices. Poems do not have to, and indeed in many cases do not, account for actual happenings. When, for instance, T. S. Eliot says in the *Waste Land:*

"Footsteps shuffled on the stair / Under the firelight, under the brush, her hair / Spread out in fiery points / Glowed into word, then would be savagely still," he is certainly not talking about a woman who was aflame. Instead, he is describing the metaphorical overlapping between the glowing sheen of the woman's hair lit by fire *and* her fiery words, which burn themselves into the silence of ashes. The heart of poetry lies not in its literal description but in its figurative strategies that constantly transform its signification from the denotative to the connotative.[41] One cannot accuse a poet of distorting facts. A poet, in short, does not have to be an accurate witness either to actual events or to particular inner emotions.

Many of Ryōkan's poems look descriptive. However, a careful reading of even those poems reveals that they are often only deceptively so. To take just one example, Ryōkan's long poem on Dōgen's magnum opus *Eiheiroku* describes his reading of the text throughout a spring night, an experience that caused him to shed tears.[42] In the morning, his neighbor, an old man, visits him and asks: "Why are these volumes all wet?" Ryōkan says: "I try to tell him, but I can't, and it tears at my heart. . . . Finally I say: 'Last night the rain came in and soaked all my books.'" The poem does not tell us at what stage in Ryōkan's life this event occurred, nor does it hint at the old man's identity. We cannot tell what indeed wet the volumes. Was it Ryōkan's tears or the passing evening shower? Did it really rain that night? Is it actually possible that Ryōkan cried so hard and so long that all the volumes became soaked? There is no way to tell. Indeed, everything could have happened in Ryōkan's poetic imagination. Yet the poem's rhetoric unfailingly manifests its major motif: Ryōkan's deep attachment to this text that conveys Dōgen's own words.

Therefore, even poems that are descriptive in outlook cannot be divorced from elements of the metaphorical. As Paul Ricoeur notes on the role of metaphor in poetic representation, "Metaphor is the rhetorical process by which discourse unleashes the power that certain fictions have to redescribe reality."[43] The creativity of poetic language, *poiēsis,* emerges from metaphor's integration of the fictive, *mythos,* and the imitative, *mimēsis,* for *re*description. Poetry, accordingly, "is an imitation of human actions; but this *mimēsis* passes through creation of a plot [i.e., *mythos*], a tale, which shows signs of composition and order lacked by the dramas of everyday life" (p. 244). Poetic reference arises out of the suspension by the metaphorical of the literal reference, a suspension that generates a condition to unleash poetry's power to redescribe what is conventionally accepted as reality. What poetry represents is, to use Ricoeur's expression, "metaphorical truth," not because the representation is less than real, but because it arises through the semiogenetic passages of *mythos* and *mimēsis* to redeem language's primordial power of revealing things as reality.[44]

This is certainly not to say that poetry is devoid of historicity. Just as historical writings cannot be complete without their literary qualities, poems reflect within their own textuality the historical situations in which poets engage in their literary craft. However, one must not forget that poems do not aim at representing historical facts in all their details as would historical records. Aristotle's classic definition discloses the distinction between the poetic and historical discourses —the distinction not of their essences but in their workings—which seems to have escaped the attention of the second camp of Ryōkan scholars:

> The historian and the poet do not differ according to whether they write in verse or without verse. . . . But the difference is that the former relates things that have happened, the latter things that may happen. For this reason poetry is more philosophical than history; poetry tends to speak of universals, history of particulars. A universal is the sort of thing that a certain kind of person may well say or do in accordance with probability or necessity—this is what poetry aims at.[45]

One may say that historians produce their discourse in a dominantly indicative mood, while poets compose their texts by means of subjunctivity.

This uniquenesss of poetic representation—both in its metaphoricity and in its subjunctivity—suggests that Ryōkan's poems can depict his daily life and disclose his inner experience. However, they do so not necessarily through their literal meanings but through the figurative movements. When studied as a whole, Ryōkan's poems evince that, throughout his career as a poet, he kept composing poems on his religious practices of begging, meditation, and textual study *and* that he continued to produce many poems expressing his sorrow, dejection, and agony. The most essential dilemma for students of Ryōkan lies, therefore, not in contradictory characterizations in terms of "enlightenment" versus "nonenlightenment," but in the seeming disjunction between the positive, optimistic depiction of Ryōkan in the contemporaneous biographies and Ryōkan's own poems of suffering.

Neither camp of modern Ryōkan studies has succeeded in bridging this gulf separating Ryōkan's life from his poetry. By contrast, many of Ryōkan's contemporaneous biographers, such as Bundai, Bunchū, and Teishin, were themselves poets and directly responsible for preserving Ryōkan's poems, collecting, compiling, and editing Ryōkan's kanshi and waka. While in their biographies they all respectfully portray Ryōkan as a Zen master, they did not exclude from their poetic anthologies those of Ryōkan's poems that the second group of modern scholars regard as evidence of "nonenlightenment." This suggests that the contemporaneous biographers' understanding of Ryōkan's life was radically different both from that of the scholars of the second camp who attempt to efface any trace of religious qualities from their picture of Ryōkan's life as a poet *and* from that of the first camp of modern scholars who posit Ryōkan's significance as grounded in an "enlightenment" free of worldly suffering. The contemporaneous accounts of Ryōkan point to the lack in the current Ryōkan scholarship of a theory, or theories, that allows one to read Ryōkan's poems—whether or not they are "Zen" poems—*in relation to* his life of religious practice, a practice of Buddhism that was marked by his nonsectarianism.

Discussions in the following sections strive to locate two areas of Ryōkan's poetry that demonstrate the intertwining aspects of his literary production and his life as Buddhist practitioner. First, there is a group of poems expressing the Mahāyāna Buddhist philosophy of nonduality, which helps explain Ryōkan's insistence on sustaining his life through the practice of begging. Reading these poems along with Ryōkan's various essays on Buddhism suggests that it was this philosophy of nonduality, and its deconstructive stance in particular, that served as the guiding principle for Ryōkan's chosen life style of mendicancy. Second, Ryōkan composed a large number of poems in which he relates important events in his own life, such as becoming a monk, leaving his monastery, and returning home. Many of these "autobiographical" poems were constructed with aphorisms, parables, and metaphors drawn from scriptural texts. They provide a unique intertextual space where Ryōkan's act of reading Buddhist texts, as a part of his religious training, and his act of composing poems meet.

Ryōkan's Poems of Philosophical Reflection

Ōzeki Bunchū writes in 1818 that once Ryōkan was at Kokujōji, a large local temple complex on Mount Kugami to which his hermitage of Gogō-an belonged, and he delivered a series of lectures on Abhidhar-

makosha, a complex system of Buddhist analytic philosophy attributed
to the fifth-century Indian theoretician Vasubandhu. "So exhaustive
was his exposition of the meaning of the text that the assembly of
monks was filled with awe. But after only ten days, the Master left. Pur-
sued by the monks, who pleaded with him to return, the Master said:
'Enough is enough!' "[46] In the following poem, Ryōkan warns against
an overly intellectualized approach to Buddhism.

> Buddha is a conception of your mind
> The Way isn't anything that is made
> Now that I've told you this
>   take it to heart
> Don't let yourself be misled
> If to reach [the southern land of] Yüeh
>   you point your cart north
> When can you ever hope to arrive?[47]

Elsewhere Ryōkan succinctly describes the relationship between
religious studies and enlightenment.

> Because of the finger
>   you can point to the moon
> Because of the moon
>   you can understand the finger
> The moon and the finger
> Are neither different nor the same
> This parable is used only
> To lead students to enlightenment
> Once you've really seen things as they are
> There's no more moon, no more finger[48]

The moon and the pointing finger are common metaphors in
Buddhist literature. The moon is symbolic of enlightenment, which
can be revealed by the pointing finger of Buddhist teaching. While the
moon and the finger must be distinguished to prevent practicing Bud-
dhists from becoming entangled only in bookish learning, it is also
wrong, Ryōkan emphasizes, to regard the two as completely distinct.
Ryōkan's poems are often characterized by their crystallization of the
serenity of nature, as seen in his description of valley streams in deep
recesses, his solitary abode buried in the snow, and his tireless play
with the village children. It must not be forgotten, however, that Ryō-
kan also composed many poems that evince the rigor of his theoretical
training in Buddhist philosophy. Together with Ryōkan's other poems

on his meditative experience, these poems are the expressions of Ryō-kan's religious insight. (See the poems translated in this volume under the headings "Meditations" and "Butterfly Dreams.")

> What was right yesterday
> Is wrong today
> How do you know what's right today
> Wasn't wrong the day before?
> Right and wrong aren't something fixed
> You can't tell in advance the pros and cons
> The foolish are stuck on a single note
> So wherever they go, they're out of tune
> The wise penetrate to the source of things
> And pass their time roaming free and at ease
> Forget about knowledge and ignorance both
> And you can call yourself one who has the Way[49]

As epitomized in this poem, underlying these poems of philosophical reflection is Ryōkan's emphasis on the theory of nonduality (Skt. *advaita, advaya;* J. *funi*), which sees reality in one's freedom from the dichotomous opposites of extremes. This nondualist thinking forms the central thread not only of Buddhism, but of major Asian philosophical traditions, including Advaita Vedanta and Sāṃkhya Yoga of Hinduism, the Lu-Wang school of Neo-Confucianism, and Taoism. David Loy, for example, states in his ambitious study of comparative philosophy: "No concept is more important in Asian philosophical and religious thought than *nonduality.*"[50] Loy is also quick to point out that nondualist perspective—especially its decentering of the subject and deconstructing of the subject-object duality—can be observed in the writings of seminal Western thinkers, such as Spinoza, Schopenhauer, Bergson, Nietzsche, Heidegger, and Wittgenstein.[51]

> Where did my life come from?
> Where will it go? . . .
> Even the present moment
>   can't be pinned down
> Everything changes, everything is empty
> And in that emptiness, this "I" exists
>   only for a little while
> How can one say anything is or is not?
> Best just to hold to these little thoughts
> Let things simply take their way
>   and so be natural and at your ease[52]

Ryōkan's emphasis on nonduality in his poetic reflections sheds a new light on the next poem, which is often interpreted negatively as an expression of his lethargy and withdrawal from the world.

> I've never bothered about getting ahead
> But just gone leisurely along
>   letting things take their way
> In my bag are three measures of rice
> A bundle of firewood sits by the hearth
> Who cares about delusion and enlightenment?
> What use is there in fame and fortune?
> In my hut, I listen to the evening rain
> And stretch my legs without a care in the world[53]

It is interesting to note in this poem—of which the philosopher Tanabe Hajime is said to be so fond—that for Ryōkan nonduality can be realized by transcending all forms of opposition. As if mocking the polemic of modern Ryōkan scholarship, Ryōkan asserts that, to be genuinely enlightened, practitioners must free themselves from the dualities of "enlightenment" and "nonenlightenment."

One must take care, however, not to treat the above poems as evidence of Ryōkan's own enlightenment. To repeat the point raised in the previous section, as a system of poetic representation, these writings neither ascertain nor disprove Ryōkan's personal enlightenment. They demonstrate that Ryōkan was deeply concerned with religious and ethical problems, that Ryōkan did discuss the issue of enlightenment in his own words, and that he delineated his strategy for attaining a nondualist perspective, whether for his own heuristic purposes or for the sake of instructing others.

> Delusion and enlightenment
>   two sides of a coin
> Universal and particular
>   just parts of one whole
> All day long I read the wordless scriptures
> All night I practice no-practice meditation
> On the riverbank, a bush warbler
>   sings in the weeping willow
> In the sleeping village
>   a dog bays at the moon
> Nothing troubles the free flow of my feelings
> But how can this mind be passed on?[54]

Ryōkan's nondualist strategy of transcending both enlightenment and nonenlightenment can be seen as a direct expression of the central theme of Mahāyāna Buddhist literature: the practice of the bodhisattva path. Bodhisattvas, the buddhas-to-be, out of compassion for others, defer their own salvation and dedicate themselves to saving sentient beings from the world of suffering, saṃsāra, the realm of endless transmigratory rebirths perpetuated by greed, rage, and delusion. These bodhisattvas, advanced practitioners who champion Mahāyāna, locate their deliverance—or nirvāṇa, the state of release from saṃsāra—not outside saṃsāra but in their own activity of saving others within saṃsāra. It is the deliverance defined in Mahāyāna literature as *apratiṣṭha nirvāṇa* (J. *mujūsho nehan*), the nirvāṇa of nonabiding, or the "nirvāṇa of no particular address." That is to say, for the bodhisattvas, anywhere in saṃsāra is a potential topos for the realization of nirvāṇa.

The *Awakening of Faith,*[55] perhaps the single most important Mahāyāna treatise in East Asia, describes the ideals of bodhisattva practice: "[A bodhisattva] is to meditate on the fact that all things are the products of the union of the primary and coordinating causes, and that the effect of karma will never be lost." That is to say, all things in this world are ephemeral and there is no end to sentient beings' saṃsāric sufferings. Therefore, the bodhisattva is "to cultivate great compassion, practice meritorious deeds, and accept and transform sentient beings equally, without abiding in nirvāṇa . . . because he is to follow the nonabiding of the essential nature of Reality *(dharmatā)*."[56] Yoshito Hakeda comments on his translation of this passage: "The term 'nonabinding' *(a-partiṣṭha)* suggests freedom, spontaneity, nonattachment, nondogmatism, etc. It is a way of life, a practical application of 'emptiness' *(shunyatā)* in a life situation encompassing both intellectual and affectional aspects."[57] In Ryōkan's poems, too, the idea of nonabiding seems to be an important motif of his religious cultivation.

> Ever since becoming a monk
> I've been drawn to the country's clouds and mists
> I spend my time with fishermen and woodcutters
> Or join the children in their games
> What is the glory of kings to me?
> Even the immortality of gods holds no appeal
> Wherever I happen to be is home
> It's no different from Bodhidharma's Mount Sung
> Riding the changes each new day brings
> I live out the years soaring calm and free[58]

The conceptual underpinning of the bodhisattvas' "nonabiding nirvāṇa" is Mahāyāna philosophy's exposure of the illusory nature of the seemingly obvious division between saṁsāra and nirvāṇa. The *Awakening of Faith* illustrates this with a celebrated simile, which places enlightenment and nonenlightenment in a nondual relationship: "Ignorance does not exist apart from enlightenment. . . . This is like the relationship that exists between the water of the ocean [i.e., enlightenment] and its waves [i.e., modes of mind] stirred by the wind [i.e., ignorance]." Based on this reasoning, redolent with poetic imagery, the text then explicates its major doctrine, that of an original enlightenment: "Water and wind are inseparable; but water is not mobile by nature, and if the wind stops the movement ceases. But the wet nature remains undestroyed. Likewise, man's Mind, pure in its own nature, is stirred by the wind of ignorance." That is to say, while enlightenment and nonenlightenment are inseparably intertwined, the latter, like the waves, is secondary, transient, and has no innate essence. True, the water may become muddy because of the turbulent waves; but turbulence cannot destroy the intrinsic quality of water, or of Mind, which is clear, purifying, and, when calm and undisturbed, naturally functions as a mirror, reflecting all things as they are. To attain enlightenment is not to attempt physically to smooth the surface of water, which only gives rise to more waves, but rather to realize thoroughly the indestructible quality of the originally enlightened mind amid the ever-changing waves of ignorance. Thus, the text concludes: "Both Mind and ignorance have no particular forms of their own and they are inseparable. . . . But the essential nature of wisdom remains undestroyed."[59] In the following poem Ryōkan plays with the ambivalence of water imagery—the ever-changing flow reminiscent of the transiency of saṁsāric existence and the always pristine fountainhead evoking original enlightenment—to depict the nonabiding nirvāṇa of nondualism.

> Walking along
> I followed the drifting stream to its source
> But reaching the headwaters left me stunned
> That's when I realized that the true source
> isn't a particular place you can reach
> So now, wherever my staff sets down
> I just play in the current's eddies and swirls[60]

As pointed out in the pioneering studies of Robert Magliola, David Loy, Harold Coward, and other scholars of comparative philosophy, the Mahāyāna theory of nonduality demonstrates a striking paral-lel to contemporary deconstructionist theories.[61] The same case can be made for Ryōkan. A comparison with the Derridian theory, for exam-ple, helps illustrate Ryōkan's deconstructive perspective disclosing various discriminatory conventions hidden in everyday language. Bar-bara Johnson, in her introduction to one of Jacques Derrida's texts, explains Derridian deconstruction as aimed at "not only the Western philosophical tradition but 'everyday' thought and language as well." Derrida's criticism is directed at the failure of Western metaphysics to see that everyday thought and language, as well as the metaphysical system based on them, "has always been structured in terms of dichot-omies, of polarities: good vs. evil, being vs. nothingness, presence vs. absence, truth vs. error, identity vs. difference, mind vs. matter, man vs. woman, soul vs. body, life vs. death." A careful reading, however, of these oppositions reveals that such binary opposites are neither equal nor autonomous. "The second term in each pair is considered the neg-ative, corrupt, undesirable version of the first, a fall away from it. . . . The two terms are not simply opposed in their meaning, but are arranged in a hierarchical order which gives the first term *priority,* in both the temporal and the qualitative sense of the word."[62] As if to con-firm Johnson's exposition Ryōkan writes:

> Where you have beauty
>   you have ugliness, too
> Where you have right
>   you will also have wrong
> Knowledge and ignorance are each other's cause
> Delusion and enlightenment produce one another
> It's always been so
> It didn't start now
> You get rid of this, then grab hold of that
> Don't you see how stupid it is!
> If you're determined to find the innermost truth
> Why trouble about the changing face of things?[63]

Beauty-ugliness, right-wrong, knowledge-ignorance—such binary, hierarchical oppositions provide the values and meanings of daily life and the foundation of the social order, and are, therefore, neither deter-minate nor self-evident. For Ryōkan, systems of values are not based on things that are intrinsically good or bad, but, instead, are constructed by means of linguistic articulation, simultaneously giving rise to both good and bad, articulated as the differences that distinguish each from the other. Johnson explains: "Instead of 'A is opposed to B' we have 'B is both added to A and replaces A.' A and B are no longer opposed, nor are they equivalent. Indeed, they are no longer even equivalent to themselves. They are their own difference from themselves" (p. xiii). That is to say, knowledge becomes knowledge only because of its difference from ignorance; ignorance always resides in knowledge as its difference, as its other; and the identity of knowledge to itself is always preceded by its difference. This also exposes as illusory the apparent immediacy of perception of that which is referred to by the sign, the thing itself. As Derrida states: "The sign is usually said to be put in the place of the thing itself, the present thing, 'thing' here standing equally for meaning or referent. The sign represents the present in its absence. It takes the place of the present. . . . The sign, in this sense, is deferred presence."[64] Language, in other words, is a system of difference, what Derrida calls *différance*,[65] which is neither presence nor absence but a relation that is at once differential and deferral. In everyday thinking built on the concepts of hierarchical oppositions, one cannot see this deep level of différance, the "mystic writing-pad"[66] of language—the level that corresponds to the water/mind of the *Awakening of Faith* that gives rise as its own difference-deferral to all forms of waves/conceptions—because, as Johnson notes, "what these hierarchical oppositions do is to privilege unity, identity, immediacy, and temporal and spatial presentness over distance, difference, dissimulation and deferment" (p. viii).

For Ryōkan, too, the deconstructive approach strives to capture this concealed movement of difference and expose the fact that "the very possibility of opposing the two terms on the basis of presence vs. absence or immediacy vs. representation is an illusion." Besides difference, there is nothing substantial or fixed at the root of the hierarchical opposites that gives structure to everyday language and its value system. In the light of difference, these oppositions are as arbitrary, transient, and whimsical as dancing waves or fleeting reflections. Johnson concludes: "The illusion of the self-presence of meaning or of consciousness is thus produced by the repression of the differential structures from which they spring" (p. ix).

> Who was it said, "Names are the guests of reality"?
> These words have come down to us from ancient times
> But even if people know that names aren't real
> They don't see that reality itself has no root
> Name, reality—both are beside the point
> Just naturally find joy in the ever-changing flow[67]

Ryōkan's basing himself, or, perhaps more precisely, non/basing himself, on the "ever-changing flow" of difference epitomizes his non-dualist deconstructive perspective directed at the repressive, discriminatory forces inherent in ordinary social conventions. This, in turn, makes it possible to understand Ryōkan's life as a beggar-monk as a conscious strategy to maintain his critical distance from the authoritarian structure of Tokugawa society and to neutralize the oppressive institutionalizing processes that had integrated Zen and other Buddhist schools within the Tokugawa political establishment.

Ryōkan's Mendicancy and Its Deconstructive Stance

> Ryōkan! How nice to be like a fool
>   for then one's Way is grand beyond measure
> Free and easy, letting things take their course—
>   who can fathom it?
> I therefore entrust to you this staff of wild wisteria
> Whenever you lean it against the wall
> Let it bring the peace of a noonday nap[68]

In 1790 at age thirty-two, Ryōkan received this poem from his master Tainin Kokusen (1723–1791), abbot of Entsūji, a large Sōtō Zen monastic center at Tamashima in the province of Bitchū in western Japan. Kokusen gave Ryōkan the poem as his *inka,* the testimonial of the completion of Ryōkan's decade-long training at Entsūji. Ryōkan then held the rank of *shuso,* head priest.[69] It was customary for high-ranked priests of large monasteries to become their masters' heirs or to receive appointment as resident priests at local branch temples. However, shortly after Kokusen's death, Ryōkan left Entsūji for many years of wandering on pilgrimage.

In 1795, still on pilgrimage, Ryōkan learned of his father's death. In the next few years, he returned as a nameless beggar-monk to his native town of Izumozaki in the province of Echigo in northern Japan. He had grown up there as the eldest son of the prominent house of Yamamoto, which for generations had been holding the post of village chief. Ryōkan first moved into an abandoned hut on the seashore near the town of Izumozaki. There he began his life of mendicancy, making daily trips to nearby villages for alms.[70] It appears that Ryōkan was at first an object of the villagers' ridicule: the son of the most respected family of Izumozaki returning home to live as a beggar. However, friends and supporters soon began to form around him. It was with

their help that in 1797, at age thirty-nine, Ryōkan found a home for
himself at a hermitage on Mount Kugami, where he remained for the
next two decades.[71] In 1816, at age fifty-eight, he moved to another hut
at Otogo, a Shintō shrine on the foothills of the mountain.[72] However,
until 1826, at the age of sixty-eight, when deteriorating health forced
Ryōkan to retire to the residence of his patron Kimura Motouemon in
the village of Shimazaki, his daily routine remained unchanged: beg-
ging for food in neighboring villages, playing with the children, visit-
ing his friends in the local literary circle, even occasionally drinking
with farmers and fishermen.[73] Ryōkan's routine in his mountain hut
included studying scriptures, practicing meditation, composing poems,
and producing calligraphy.

It is this extended period of Ryōkan's life of mendicancy that
was most vividly commemorated by his biographers. The great major-
ity of his poems also originate from this period. From the point of view
of the monastic establishment, however, Ryōkan's mendicant life, how-
ever celebrated, is an anomalous deviation. Ryōkan appears not to
have been particularly fastidious about observing details of the pre-
cepts for the ordained: he was fond of drinking with his friends, often
stayed for days as a guest at his patrons' lay households, and even loved
dancing with villagers at the annual festivals in the local Shintō
shrines.[74] Ryōkan never returned to a Sōtō Zen temple, nor did he
establish himself as a master for educating disciples in the school.
Should Ryōkan be criticized for his failure to produce Dharma heirs to
carry on the Sōtō school's lineage? Why did he insist instead on a life
of mendicancy, which kept him traveling back and forth between his
mountain hermitage and the nearby villages?

The eccentricity of Ryōkan's life as a beggar-monk independent
of sectarian organizations strongly contrasts with the excessive insti-
tutionalization of the Buddhist establishment in the late Tokugawa
period. Tamamuro Taijō, an expert on the social history of Japanese
religions, explains the symbiotic relationship that had been constructed
between the Tokugawa regime and the Buddhist schools. First, in the
framework of the "headquarters-branch" (honmatsu) system, all the
temples in Japan, regardless of size and location, were forced by the
government to become members of one of the major Buddhist schools.
In each school, the headquarters temple alone held the right to
appoint or discharge the head priests of member temples. These tem-
ples, in turn, were classified into stratified ranks according to size, loca-
tion, assets, history, and prestige. Second, it was mandatory for all

households to be "affiliated families" *(danka)* of a local, branch temple. Under this affiliated family system, each household had to perform funerals and commemorative ceremonies for ancestors under the supervision of the head priest of the family temple *(bodaiji)*, who alone had the government's sanction to perform these rites and collect fees. Third, the government gave the local temples the power to issue various official documents concerning the daily lives of the villagers and townsfolk. The "temple entrustment" *(terauke)* system transformed local temples into extensions of the government administrative apparatus, with the sole right to issue certificates for birth, marriage, moving, adoption, and death, and the responsibility to maintain these records. These certificates issued by the family temples constituted proof of the household's obedience to the government and to its prohibition against Christianity. In return, the government gave the headquarters temples vast domains, whose tax revenues supported their religious activities.[75]

Through this threefold system of control, the priesthood was transformed into a bureaucracy. Priests labored to acquire new affiliated families, thus promoting their temples in the school's hierarchy. This promotion, in turn, offered opportunities for appointment to higher office in the central administration at the headquarters temple. The nature of the alms provided by the laity, too, was gradually transformed: no longer an expression of religious devotion, they became taxes paid to maintain the temples' official functions. Understandably, in Buddhist temples of Ryōkan's time, begging had already become a ceremonial act practiced only on a few fixed days of each month. In an essay titled "Priesthood,"[76] Ryōkan delivers a sharp criticism of monastic life:

> I see those who have become monks thoughtlessly raising their voices night and day. Only concerned with filling their stomachs, they spend their lives pursuing externals. For a layman to lack dedication to the Way may be excused; but for a monk to be like this is obscene.
>
> When you shave your head, you sever all attachment to the three worlds [of the profane]. When you don the monk's robes, you destroy the world of appearances. Casting off all bonds of affection, you enter the realm of the unconditioned, indifferent to "right" and "wrong."
>
> Wherever one goes in the world, men and women have their allotted tasks: without weaving, how can one make

clothes? Without tilling the fields, how can one feed one-
self? Those who nowadays call themselves Shākyamuni
Buddha's disciples have neither practice nor enlightenment.
They uselessly consume the offerings of the faithful, heed-
less of the offenses they commit. Instead, they band together
and "talk big," going on like this from morning till night.[77]

Ryōkan deplores not only the bureaucratization of the Buddhist
order but the resultant formation of a "mundane" world within the
monastic community.

Outwardly they pretend to be superior, playing on the gull-
ibility of old peasant women and congratulating themselves
on their cleverness. Alas! Will they ever come to their
senses? A monk would sooner walk among a pride of
mother tigers than tread the path of fame and fortune. Let
the smallest lust for fame and fortune enter the mind, and all
the waters of the ocean will not wash it away. What have
you been doing with your time since your father sent you to
become a monk? You may burn incense or pray to the gods
and buddhas that your dedication to the Way will always be
firm; but if you remain as you are today, your path will be
blocked at every turn. . . .

A good opportunity is easily lost, the true teaching hard
to encounter. You've got to make a fresh start! Don't wait for
me to tell you again and extend a helping hand. I'm pleading
with you earnestly now, but for me it's a cheerless task.
From here on, I want you to reflect carefully and change
your ways. Strive hard, you successors of the Buddha, that
you may have no regrets![78]

As if to bear out Ryōkan's criticism, the Sōtō school of his time
was divided by an intense factional struggle for hegemony between
Eiheiji and Sōjiji, the school's two traditional headquarters founded,
respectively, by Dōgen and Keizan Jōkin (1268–1325), the "great patri-
arch" *(taiso)* of the Sōtō school.[79] A bitter struggle between these
headquarters to win the allegiance of major local temples broke out
during the Tenmei era (1781–1788)—the period coinciding with Ryō-
kan's training at Entsūji and his pilgrimage. The confrontation between
Eiheiji and Sōjiji remained unresolved long after the fall of the Toku-
gawa regime in 1868. As this perennial strife within the Sōtō school
demonstrates, the priests' very separation from secular life, intended
to free them from worldly duties, could easily become a snare entan-

gling them in their own sanctimonious pretense. In the following poems, Ryōkan warns the priests of his day against this danger:

> All these monks traveling on pilgrimage—
> what a pitiful lot!
> Unless you've studied at the great temples,
> they say,
> You can't call yourself a real Zen monk
> That's why students leave their original teachers
> Grab their staffs and take to the road
> wandering from place to place
> Summer at one temple, winter at another
> They spend their whole lives idly parroting masters
> But meet one of these monks
> surprise him with a question
> And he's just as pitiful as he was at the start![80]

In another essay, "On Begging One's Food,"[81] Ryōkan under-scores the importance of the practice of mendicancy for Buddhism as a signpost pointing to the path trod by the exemplary teachers of the past.

> The practice of begging for one's food is the very lifeblood of the tradition of monkhood. That is why there exist the particular forms for begging and for eating with the wooden bowl. . . . The practice [of begging] is common to all the buddhas. Know that all the buddhas practiced begging in realizing the Way. The successive generations of patriarchs, too, practiced begging in transmitting the torch of the teaching. Therefore it is said that a monk should receive food obtained in the proper manner and should not receive food obtained in a manner that is improper. It is further said that overeating makes one drowsy and slothful, while eating too little deprives one of energy to pursue enlightenment.

By quoting sūtra passages, Ryōkan emphasizes that begging is aimed at producing religious merit for both donors and recipients.

> The *Last Admonition Sūtra*[82] says: "O monks, receive offer-ings of food and drink just as you would medicine. Whether [the food] is good or bad, your response must not differ."[83] It is also said: "During those periods when eating is allowed, you should nourish yourself in a pure fashion and endeavor to dispel all afflictions. You must not be greedy and thereby destroy good intentions [i.e., both your own and those of

the food's donors]. Just so, one who is wise knows what
load his ox can bear and will not let it exhaust itself."[84] The
Vimalakīrti Sūtra says: "Once Mahākāshyapa, as a deliber-
ate act of kindness, went begging in a poor village. Vimala-
kīrti upbraided him, saying: 'You should beg from all alike.
For one who is impartial, receiving food of any sort, has real-
ized the impartiality of Dharma.' "[85]

Ryōkan's quote from the *Vimalakīrti Sūtra,* a celebrated Mahā-
yāna scripture, concerns an episode in which Mahākāshyapa, the Bud-
dha's leading disciple, renowned for his mastery of meditation and the
legendary progenitor of the Zen lineage, was rebuked by the protago-
nist Vimalakīrti, a lay practitioner who had thoroughly fathomed the
wisdom of nonduality. In the sūtra's story, Vimalakīrti is ill, and Shākya-
muni Buddha urges his disciples to visit him. However, recalling how
Vimalakīrti reproved them in the past for their poor understanding of
Dharma, the disciples are too embarrassed to bring themselves to go.
Even Mahākāshyapa declines the Buddha's request by relating to the
Buddha how Vimalakīrti once criticized his seemingly kind intention to
beg among the poor in order to provide them with an opportunity to
accumulate merit as merely a result of his inconclusive grasp of equa-
nimity. From Vimalakīrti's viewpoint, beings, as long as they are subject
to greed, rage, and delusion, cannot escape from saṁsāric suffering. So
far as their need for release from worldly suffering, there should be no
discrimination between the rich and the poor, the privileged and the
underprivileged.

> On the first day of the eighth month
> I go into town to beg
> White clouds follow my spirited footsteps
> And an autumn wind rustles the rings on my staff . . .
> The Buddha himself taught this
> Transmitting it directly to Mahākāshyapa
> And since then it's been handed down
>   for over twenty-seven hundred years
> I, too, am a follower of Shākyamuni
> And revel in the simple majesty of a single robe and bowl
> Don't you see? Vimalakīrti said:
> "One who is impartial, receiving food of any sort,
> Has realized the impartiality of Dharma." . . .[86]

Ryōkan's use of the passages from the *Vimalakīrti Sūtra* illus-
trating mendicancy as the practice of equanimity helps explain why

Ryōkan considered begging for food an effective antidote for the problems resulting from the excessive bureaucratization of the Zen temples. Ryōkan seems to have expected the Buddhist order, rather than being the guarantor of the status quo for the privileged, to regain its function of providing a moratorium from the discriminatory conventions of the mundane world and to serve as a model for change. By forgetting the importance of begging, Ryōkan says, priests have lost their sense of gratitude to the laity, whose sincere support provides the sole legitimate grounds for the priests' authority. To repeat Ryōkan's words, "They uselessly consume the offerings of the faithful, heedless of the offenses they commit. . . . Outwardly they pretend to be superior, playing on the gullibility of old peasant women and congratulating themselves on their cleverness."

> Alas, those who practice Buddhism nowadays
> Grow old and decrepit fussing over words
> What use are all their years of idle speculation?
> Isn't the aim of our school
>   to directly realize things as they are?
> Neither delusion nor enlightenment obtain
>   in the land of nonarising
> In what aeon will you ever
>   find original nothingness?
> If you don't understand, then ask!
> My answer is: "Mañjushrī's home
>   in the east of the castle of enlightenment."[87]

In the period during which Ryōkan lived his mendicant life, Echigo was plagued by droughts, typhoons, earthquakes, and other natural disasters; farmers' uprisings were frequent; and many died of famine. A local chronicler at the village of Nakanoshima, where Ryōkan often begged, reported in 1833:

> For the six years between Bunsei 11 and Tenpo 4 (1828–1833), the crops have continued to fail. The supply of both grains and vegetables is exhausted, leading to the spread of contagious disease. . . . The lords of the local domains have decided to postpone collecting the tax; but that has not helped the people at all because there are no new harvests of grain. . . . The streets are filled with the starved and the dead; those who survive have become beggars, vying with one another for shelter under the eaves of the houses of the wealthy.[88]

Amidst such desperate conditions, Ryōkan continued for more than three decades to beg from the villagers. When the villagers were impoverished and had no food to offer, Ryōkan suffered with them. Instead of being sheltered in a large temple institution with an abundantly supplied granary, Ryōkan chose the world of suffering as the locus of his religious practice.

> In the daytime I go into town to beg
> At night I return to the shadow
>   of the mountain to practice meditation
> One robe, one bowl—a life of solitary freedom
> Ah, how precious the stream that flows
>   from the land of the Western Skies![89]

Here, Ryōkan presents his solitary life as his way of declaring that he, unlike the high priests of the powerful monastic establishment, preserves through his mendicant life the transmission of the Dharma originating in the "Western Skies" of India. Ryōkan's sense of mission in protecting the lifeline of Buddhism casts a new light on his poem "Empty Bowl."

> Will my stupidity and stubbornness ever end?
> Poor and alone—that's my life
> Twilight on the streets of a ramshackle town
> Going home again with an empty bowl![90]

Instead of the "dark, downcast thoughts" of a depressed old man suggested by Iriya Yoshitaka, this poem—once placed against the background of Ryōkan's criticism of the vitiating standard of monastic training—illustrates Ryōkan's unfaltering resolve to carry on his life of begging. Tinged with a lighthearted, self-deprecating humor, with an irony that accentuates his eccentricity, Ryōkan depicts his own lonely, stubborn commitment to mendicancy, his way of cultivating compassion and equanimity amid the sufferings of the common people.

Here Ryōkan's criticism reveals its strategy. Ryōkan was not merely seeking to hurl vitriol at the Zen establishment in order to humiliate it. He never challenged the Sōtō school in an open polemic; nor did he attempt to reform its monastic system from within. Ryōkan's strategy, instead, is playful ridicule: he quietly, yet unmistakably, juxtaposes his own life of mendicancy with the institutionalized monastic life. Ryōkan deconstructs the hegemonic authority of the monastic establishment by exposing its discriminatory posture of the privileged over the masses and by making fun of a training regimen that had lost its relevance to the life of ordinary people. Then, by way of contrast, Ryōkan presents his humble routine of begging among the villagers as a model for rectification. From the viewpoint of the institutional establishment, Ryōkan, who left monastic life without establishing himself in the Sōtō hierarchy, is a failure. But it is precisely because of his failure that Ryōkan's criticism is effective: after all, what if this failure is better than the typical Zen priest at understanding people, at showing them compassion? The more Ryōkan's daily activities—playing with children, drinking with farmers, dancing at autumn festivals—appear foolish, the further they deviate from orthodoxy, the sharper his criticism of the establishment becomes.

Ryōkan's Zen name "Great Fool" (Taigu), the name by which he was known to his patrons and remembered by his admirers, is symbolic of the unique position assumed by Ryōkan in the highly stratified society of Tokugawa Japan. In his biography of Ryōkan (written in about 1846), Kera Yoshishige states: "The Master never displayed excessive joy or anger. One never heard him speaking in a hurried manner, and in all his daily activities, in the way he would eat and drink, rise and retire, his movements were slow and easy as if he were an idiot."[91] The earliest recorded mention of Ryōkan as Great Fool appears in Ryōkan's epitaph, prepared in 1831, the year of his death, by the priest Shōgan, a regular visitor at Ryōkan's hut.[92] The epitaph also quotes the verse given to Ryōkan by his master Kokusen as proof of the completion of Ryōkan's training at Entsūji, Kokusen's monastery.[93] In the verse quoted earlier, Kokusen praises Ryōkan's carefree spirit, which can easily be mistaken for that of a fool. Almost all subsequent biographies introduce Ryōkan with this name: "Great Fool." Among these is a biography composed in 1895 by Suzuki Tekiken (1836–1896), the adopted heir of the above-mentioned Suzuki Bundai, one of Ryōkan's friends and a leading local Confucian scholar. In his biography, for which he had access to numerous Ryōkan-related documents that he had inherited as the successor to the Suzuki household, Tekiken says: "In the seventh month, the third year of An'ei [1774], at Kōshōji in Amaze . . . he took the tonsure and changed his name to Ryōkan. He was eighteen years old. He also gave himself the name 'Great Fool.'"[94] These records suggest that the name "Great Fool" embodies Ryōkan's personality both in terms of how Ryōkan regarded himself and how others saw him.[95]

What is "great" about being a "fool"? The early Tokugawa popu-

larizer of Zen Bankei Yōtaku (1622–1693) argues that the way to real-
ize nondualist wisdom is to "be stupid." "Because you've got the dy-
namic function of the marvelously illuminating Buddha Mind, even if
you get rid of discriminative understanding, you won't be foolish. So
all of you from here on, be stupid! Even if you're stupid, when you're
hungry, you'll ask for something to eat, when you're thirsty, you'll ask
for some tea. . . . As far as your activities of today are concerned, you're
not lacking a thing!"[96] The "Buddha Mind" is Bankei's way of referring
to original enlightenment: "The Buddha Mind, unborn and marvelously
illuminating, is like a bright mirror. A mirror reflects whatever is in
front of it. It's not deliberately *trying* to reflect things, but whatever
comes before the mirror, its color and form are sure to appear. . . . The
Unborn Buddha Mind is just like this. It's natural that you see and hear
things, whatever they are, when you deliberately *try* to see and hear
them; but when you see and hear things that you hadn't originally
anticipated seeing or hearing, it's through the dynamic function of the
Buddha Mind that every one of you has."[97] In a tone reminiscent of the
metaphor of water and waves in the *Awakening of Faith,* Bankei here
epitomizes Mahāyāna theory of enlightenment not as a purifying of
one's mind but as a returning to what the mind is already, originally,
and always.

Bankei underscores the notion that, intrinsically, there is no dis-
tinction between the reflecting function of the mirror-mind and the
reflected images of objects. It is the discursive thoughts of the human
mind that substantiate, or hypostatize, these objects by labeling them
with particular names and by assigning to each discriminatory values.
As these objects are established and form conventional systems of
values, the discursive function of the mind, in turn, becomes attached
to and delimited by the objects it has produced. To be enlightened, for
Bankei, is to recover one's original insight in which no duality exists
between the seer and the seen.

Within this context of original enlightenment, "being foolish"
serves as an effective method for realizing equanimity. Being crafty,
cunning, "useful," in a worldly sense is, Bankei points out, the very
reverse of being enlightened. "The fact is that those clever people
acclaimed by the world are, from the start, deluded by their own clev-
erness. They distort the Buddha Mind and obscure its marvelously illu-
minating [dynamic function], considering other people as of no ac-
count, contradicting whatever they say, slighting and insulting them.
. . . The *true* man's ideal is to show kindness to those who are foolish

and help those who are evil" (p. 81; Haskel's italics). That is to say, knowledge separates people, while the "wisdom" of foolishness, of *de*learning, brings them together. Building knowledge from the system of values consisting of dichotomous opposites may be necessary to establish and sustain social order; however, that alone would only create a society of hierarchical stratification, institutionalization, and oppressive rigidity. Ryōkan rocks this rigidity with his laughter, the laughter of a Great Fool who dares to question the most conventional, inflexible aspects of everyday life and who introduces into this institutionalization of society difference, the differential of renewal, of rejuvenation.

> Everyone eats rice
> Yet no one knows why
> When I say this now
> People laugh at me
> If they laugh, that's just fine
> Laughing is something I like, too!
> Laughing and laughing, we won't stop
> We'll welcome Maitreya here and now[98]

Ryōkan's laughing resonates well with the nonintellectualist (but not necessarily anti-intellectual) laughter of Bataille, who discloses—in contradistinction to the ordinary view of communication as intentional exchange of information between people—genuine experience of communication as the opposite of exchanging knowledge.

> If a group of people laugh at an absent-minded gesture, or at a sentence revealing an absurdity, there passes within them a current of intense communication. Each isolated existence emerges from itself by means of the image betraying the error of immutable isolation. It emerges from itself in a sort of easy flash; it opens itself at the same time to the contagion of a wave which rebounds, for those who laugh together become like the waves of the sea. . . . They are no more separate than are two waves.[99]

Ryōkan's laughter does not aim at demolishing the existing order; instead, it laughs away, or, perhaps more appropriately, laughs down, the entangling mesh of value judgments and, playfully cheating the trap of dualistic discursive convention, eliminates alienation and restores affinity. This nondualism, the "wisdom" of being a fool, because of its freedom from discriminatory views, gives rise to the compassionate perspective of equanimity that, to repeat Bankei's words, "shows kindness to those who are foolish and helps those who are evil."

It is through this curious combination of playfulness and kindness exemplified by his laughter of optimism that Ryōkan's deconstructive stance seems to escape from the danger of nihilism, a view that contemporary deconstruction is often accused of by its opponents. His eccentricity does not intend to introduce confusion or chaos to ethics by destroying conventional values. Ryōkan strives to decenter the conventionalizing force inherent in a system of values that constantly works to entrench itself in society as a discriminatory structure and a repressive authority. For Ryōkan, without the wisdom of delearning, the knowledge to reverse the conventionalizing process, there would be no hope for change, no possibility of regeneration for the underprivileged. As if to paraphrase Bankei, Ryōkan states:

> When you encounter those who are wicked, unrighteous, foolish, dim-witted, deformed, vicious, chronically ill, lonely, unfortunate, or handicapped, you should think: "How can I save them?" And even if there is nothing you can do, at least you must not indulge in feelings of arrogance, superiority, derision, scorn, or abhorrence, but should immediately manifest sympathy and compassion. If you fail to do so, you should feel ashamed and deeply reproach yourself: "How far I have strayed from the Way! How can I betray the old sages? I take these words as an admonition to myself."[100]

Ryōkan's emphasis on commiseration sheds a new light on the sense of agony expressed in many of his poems of solitude. The *Vimalakīrti Sūtra* illustrates the importance of the bodhisattva's commiseration through the root metaphor of illness. When the Buddha's leading disciples decline to visit the ailing Vimalakīrti, Mañjushrī, the bodhisattva of wisdom, comes forward and leads the assembly of disciples to Vimalakīrti's house. When Mañjushrī asks how he became ill, Vimalakīrti replies:

> From ignorance and desire come my illness. Because all living beings suffer from this illness, I, too, suffer from it. When all living beings' illnesses cease, my illness will cease, too. The reason is that a bodhisattva enters saṃsāra for the sake of living beings. When the birth and death of saṃsāra exist, there also exists the illness. . . . It is just as when a single heir to a wealthy household is afflicted by illness, so his

> parents also become afflicted. When their son's illness is
> cured, they, too, are cured.

In conclusion, Vimalakīrti declares: "The bodhisattva's illness arises out
of his great compassion."[101] As with the parents of the stricken child,
the bodhisattva is not really ill; however, out of his compassion the
bodhisattva, like the parents, suffers together with the sick. Thus, pre-
cisely because Vimalakīrti's illness is a metaphor that transgresses the
conventional distinction between the healthy and the sick, the enlight-
ened and the unenlightened, it illustrates the bodhisattva's commisera-
tion with those living beings who suffer in saṁsāra. Later in the sūtra,
Vimalakīrti explains the same point in the light of the nonduality of
saṁsāra and nirvāṇa: "the bodhisattva meditates on impermanence,
yet he never grows tired of cultivating goodness; he meditates on the
suffering of the world, yet he does not feel disgust at birth and
death.... Because of his great compassion he does not abide in
nirvāṇa; to fulfill his original vow, he does not abandon saṁsāra."[102]
Ryōkan extols Vimalakīrti's metaphorical disclosing of the illness/com-
passion:

> Mañjushrī rides on the lion
> Samantabhadra mounts the elephant
> Ghoṣa enters nirvāṇa on his jeweled seat
> And Vimalakīrti lies ill on his bed[103]

Here, Ryōkan compares Vimalakīrti's sickbed with the mounts
of legendary Buddhist teachers, symbolic of their saving activity.
Vimalakīrti's suffering from illness, described in the sūtra, is the very
proof of the bodhisattva's grasp of nonduality, his ability to transcend
the division between saṁsāra and nirvāṇa. For bodhisattvas, abiding in
the suffering of saṁsāra, which they take as the ground for generating
compassion, *is* their nirvāṇa, "nonabiding *(apratiṣṭha)* nirvāṇa."
When placed in this context of the theory of cultivating compassion—
the context in which Ryōkan places his own life of mendicancy—Ryō-
kan's poems of solitude and suffering do not necessarily presume his
secularization, just as his poems on nondualism do not have to be inter-
preted as the proof of his personal enlightenment. Because of the "ill-
ness"—that is, the ability to suffer—the practicers of the bodhisattva
path understand the nature of the suffering of the other beings. How-
ever, because their illness is metaphorical of compassion, they escape
from being consumed by it and remain optimistic about the possibil-
ity of saving others. This nonduality of distress and hope—generating

hope for understanding others in one's own *ability* to suffer—projected through the Mahāyāna theory of bodhisattva practice illustrates the continuity between Ryōkan's poems of solitary affliction, on the one hand, and those of compassionate affection, on the other.

> Lying alone and ill in my hut
> All day long I don't see a soul
> My bowl in its bag is left to hang on the wall
> My staff just sits and gathers dust
> My dreams go rambling through
>   mountains and fields
> My heart goes back to the village to play
> And there I find all the children on the street
> Just as always, waiting for me[104]

> It may seem that I have locked myself
> Away from the people of the world
> And yet
> Why is it
> I have never ceased to think of them?[105]

> If my arms draped in these black robes
> Were only wide enough
> How gladly I would shelter in them
> All the people of this floating world[106]

These poems suggest that the opposing, and seemingly contradictory, lyrical moods of Ryōkan's poems—their spiritual uplift and profound agony—derive from the figurative strategy of expressing equanimity by disclosing the relative and arbitrary nature of the duality of worldly happiness and sorrow, success and failure, dominance and subjection.

> For being obstinate and stupid
>   there's no one like me
> My neighbors have become the trees and grasses
> I'm tired of mulling
>   over delusion and enlightenment
> Seeing how old and decrepit I've grown
>   I can't help laughing at myself
> Carefree, I hoist my robe above my legs
>   and ford the stream
> My begging bag in tow
>   I go rambling with the springtime

A Poetics of Mendicancy

> I'm content just living this life of mine
> It's not that I loathe the dust of the world[107]

Clever and stupid, good and evil, masculine and feminine, young and old, enlightened and unenlightened: these discriminatory divisions of dichotomous oppositions are, from the Great Fool's non-dualist perspective, as mutable as the turbulence of waves, as transient as the reflections in a mirror. Ryōkan encourages one instead to see the very processes that give rise to the order of external objects and, through these generative processes of language—the very processes that give rise to his poetic texts—to free oneself from discriminatory conventions.

Poetry and Ryōkan's Life: An Intertextual Transposition

Despite the eloquence with which he composed his poems, Ryōkan was known as a quiet figure. Kera Yoshishige recounts: "The Master was always silent, his movements graceful and relaxed. As it's said: 'If one's mind is broad, one's presence will be imbued with grandeur.'"[108] Yoshishige's record agrees with other contemporaneous biographies in suggesting that Ryōkan never delivered lectures on Buddhism to the villagers. These sources also show that Ryōkan was extremely reserved in telling others about his past—the root cause of the difficulty in studying his earlier life. Fortunately, in his poems, Ryōkan often emerges from his reticence and provides some information on his past.

> How many winters and springs have passed
>   since my days at Entsūji?
> Outside the temple gate lay
>   a city of a thousand homes
> Yet I didn't know a single soul
> When our robes got dirty, we washed them ourselves
> When our food ran out, we went into town
> I once read in the *Record of Eminent Priests:*
> A monk should live a pure and simple life.[109]

Ryōkan's recollection of his years as a novice at Entsūji reveals the strictly maintained separation of the ecclesiastic life from the mundane world and Ryōkan's strenuous effort to complete his training within the confines of the monastic order. However, Ryōkan eventually departs from Entsūji, rejecting the segregation of the sacred from the profane symbolized here by the monastery's gate.

> One day, by a stroke of luck, I penetrated
>   my master's path
> Suddenly I took a giant leap, and that was
>   good-bye to temple life
> Enough of their rice! No more numbing routine!
>   Ah! How happy I feel!
> The twenty-eight Indian
>   and six Chinese patriarchs—
> They're all of them here, right at my side.[110]

It was around the time of his *inka* in 1790 that Ryōkan received his master's permission to study the *Eiheiroku,* a collection of writings by Dōgen (1200–1258), founder of the Sōtō school, which was a jealously guarded treasure of the school accessible only to a priestly elite.[111] However, Ryōkan suggests that reading the *Eiheiroku* only reminded him of the inconclusiveness of his religious cultivation.[112]

> Years ago, at Entsūji in Tamashima
> I recall how my late teacher instructed me
>   in the Eye of True Enlightenment
> At that time, I already had
>   some experience of awakening
> And therefore asked to read the *Eihei Record*
>   under my teacher's personal guidance
> That was when I saw that till then
>   I'd just been wasting my time
> Afterward, I left my teacher,
>   setting off on pilgrimage[113]

Ryōkan's departure from the monastery marked the beginning of his years of wandering as a pilgrim, which, in turn, ended in his return to his hometown of Izumozaki as a titleless beggar-monk. By the time Ryōkan arrived home, his parents had passed away and his younger brother, Yoshiyuki, had become head of the house of Yamamoto, in charge of the family business. However, his family was in serious decline; and Ryōkan, who had relinquished his responsibility as his father's heir, was to blame. It might have been easier if he were a high priest of a large temple or an eminent preacher, but, as a simple beggar-monk, Ryōkan had at first to endure his neighbors' prying eyes and sarcastic laughter. Returning home may have been the hardest move he could have made. What caused Ryōkan to return to his home province? And how did Ryōkan himself explain the life of mendicancy he was leading there?

Ever since quitting the temple
My life has been resolutely carefree
My staff is always at my side
My robe is worn completely threadbare
At night in my hut, through the lonely window
    I hear the falling rain
On spring days when the flowers riot in bloom
    I'm playing ball out on the street
If anyone asks what I'm doing, I say:
"The most useless man there ever was!"[114]

Streams gliding through the fields
    of distant villages brim with water
Gorgeous flowers brighten the mountains'
    green-forested slopes
That old man leading the ox, where is he from?
The boy carrying the hoe,
    I wonder whose child he can be?
The cycle of the seasons never pauses
And human beings all have their tasks
But what sort of work is there for me?
To forever stand guard at the gates of my land[115]

As his poems and essays on mendicancy demonstrate, Ryōkan took pride in his practice of begging for food, which he considered an act of preserving the authentic transmission of the Buddha Dharma. Here Ryōkan unabashedly declares himself "the most useless man there ever was," as if testifying to his dedication to the beggar's life. However, the comical, self-deprecatory note of Ryōkan's declaration does not belie the sense of shame and humility that seems always to accompany his pride. Ryōkan's depiction of himself as a gatekeeper— the one who watches over the villagers, but only passively from a distance—is also suggestive of this ambivalence. While people of the world toil from season to season for their livelihood, Ryōkan alone remains idle, helplessly dependent on others' alms.

Rags and patches, patches and rags
Rags and patches—that's my life
My food is whatever I beg by the roadside
My house is completely overrun with wild grass
In autumn, gazing at the moon
    I recite poetry all night long

> In spring, entranced by the blossoms
>   I wander off and forget to come home
> I left the temple, and this is how I've ended up—
>   A broken-down old mule[116]

Ryōkan's self-deprecating tone becomes further accentuated when one reads in his self-portrait a sense of compunction: a useless beggar, Ryōkan had to witness the fall of his Yamamoto house as members of his family sank into desperate straits. Ryōkan's hometown, therefore, provided him with the severest environment in which to test his resolve to carry on the practice of mendicancy. At the same time, this difficulty, it appears, made it necessary for Ryōkan to legitimize his eccentric life as a beggar-monk, a life that deviated not only from the ordinary life of the villagers but from the normative life of the clergy.

> I remember how it was when I was young
> The terrible hardship just staying alive
> In search of clothing and food
> I tramped hopelessly from shabby town to town
> Till on the road I found a man of wisdom
> Who explained things to me through and through
> Then I saw that all along
>   the precious jewel was in my robe
> That jewel is with me here, right now
> Having found it I've gone into business for myself
> Traveling all over with my wares exactly as I please[117]

Ryōkan in this poem recounts his life in light of the celebrated parable from the *Lotus Sūtra*. Chapter 8 of the sūtra[118] relates an episode in which there once was a young man who decided to make his living in a distant country. Before his departure, he visited a friend's house. They drank together in bidding farewell; intoxicated, the young man fell asleep. His friend then sewed an invaluable jewel inside his robe as insurance for his journey. Later, in a faraway land, the young man experienced difficulties and became impoverished, spending each day in search of food and clothing. Then his friend came to see him. Reminding the young man of the treasure he had always had in his robe, he saved him from his needless struggle. In the same manner, the sūtra explains, Shākyamuni Buddha's disciples in their previous countless transmigratory lives encountered many buddhas of the past who had similarly instructed them in the teaching of the *Lotus,* the teaching that claims to make it possible for all beings to attain buddha-hood. However, because the disciples' comprehension was not conclu-sive enough, just like the young man who fell asleep intoxicated, they did not realize that the jewel, the Dharma as revealed by the *Lotus,* had already been placed in their minds. Like the young man's friend who rescued him from his hardship, Shākyamuni Buddha teaches his disci-ples the *Lotus,* not for the first time, but to point them to the treasure they always possessed but failed to notice.

Ryōkan's poem above evokes images of his days of wandering in pilgrimage. The "man of wisdom" may be the buddha Ryōkan encoun-tered in his reading of the sūtra. Or, it is possible to understand the "ter-rible hardship" as Ryōkan's reference to his training at Entsūji, Ryōkan having realized on reading the *Eiheiroku* that at the monastery he had been "wasting time" without realizing where his goal was. If so, the "man of wisdom" who gave Ryōkan a chance to escape from his hard-ship may be Dōgen, author of the *Eiheiroku,* or Kokusen, who led Ryō-kan to study Dōgen.

Among the scriptural texts Ryōkan studied, the *Lotus Sūtra* is by far the most important source of inspiration for his poetry. In his 1817 letter to Kera Shukumon, Yoshishige's father, Ryōkan states that he per-sonally duplicated as a gift to his patron his own copy of the eight fas-cicles of the sūtra, which he always kept at his side.[119] He expressed his love of the scripture in many poems inspired by the sūtra's principal motifs. In addition, Ryōkan left two works, *Hokke ten* and *Hokke san,* both poetic devotions to the *Lotus.*[120] These verses serve as précis to the sūtra's principal chapters and are the only commentarial works Ryōkan produced on any Buddhist scripture. In contrast to such Zen favorites as the *Diamond* and *Laṅkāvatāra* sūtras, the *Lotus* is not a scripture frequently studied in the Sōtō school or in the Zen tradition generally. It is unknown why Ryōkan particularly favored this sūtra. Nevertheless, he has the personal support of Dōgen, who has de-scribed the *Lotus* as "the king of all the sūtras," because, he argues, it alone discloses the nonduality of means and goal, practice and enlight-enment, saṁsāra and nirvāṇa.[121]

The *Lotus* claims to be the ultimate revelation of Shākyamuni Buddha's enlightenment, delivered at the close of his life. The three teachings the Buddha previously preached to his disciples—the teach-ings for solitary practitioners *(pratyekabuddha),* for his immediate disciples, or listeners *(shrāvakas),* and for the bodhisattvas—are pro-visional teachings, expedients to prepare them for this ultimate teaching, which he calls *ekayāna,* or the One Unifying Vehicle. Typically, Mahāyāna Buddhism asserts that only bodhisattvas, compassionate ones, are capable of advancing to attain the Buddha's perfect enlightenment. The solitary practitioners and the listeners, those of the "lesser vehicle," or Hīnayāna, are excluded from this path because they lack the commitment to help others. The *Lotus,* however, teaches that this final revelation opens the way even for Hīnayānists to advance toward bodhisattvahood and, eventually, toward buddhahood. At the same time, it guards the bodhisattva from developing any sense of superiority toward and disparagement of Hīnayānists. The *ekayāna* frees bodhisattvas from discriminatory views because it is the integral path of the highest Mahāyāna through which all kinds of Buddhist practitioners, including Hīnayānists, can attain buddhahood.

In the sūtra, the Buddha reveals that his true identity rests not in his physical form but in the Dharma, which he shares equally with all the buddhas permeating the universe in the past, present, and future. Thus, at the profoundest level, the sūtra argues, Shākyamuni Buddha's life is eternal. The Buddha then tells his disciples that even his approaching death is provisional; it is given to them as an expedient to invoke a sense of urgency and thereby save them from the lassitude into which they would fall had the Buddha lived and taught them indefinitely. Even after his disappearance, the Buddha proclaims, the *Lotus* continues to guide all beings to the One Unifying Vehicle. Since all the buddhas of the past, present, and future teach the *Lotus* as their final instruction, all beings in the universe, through their endless transmigratory lives, have already been given opportunities to practice the *ekayāna* to attain buddhahood. That is to say, all living beings are already endowed with the potential to realize buddhahood or the possibility for enlightenment, that is, their original enlightenment.

To illustrate its central themes, the sūtra provides the reader with various parables. The episode of the gem hidden in one's robe is one of these. Another episode Ryōkan often alludes to is that of the "conjured city."[122] Suppose, the Buddha says, there is a treasure trove deep in a jungle. Because the path there is distant and dangerous, people are unable to traverse it. However, there is a guide, intelligent and well informed, who leads a group of people along this perilous path. When they have traveled over half the distance, they tell the guide that they are frightened and exhausted and cannot proceed. The guide, as an expedient, creates through his magical powers a great city, telling the people neither to be frightened nor to retrogress, because they can stay safely in this city. Believing that they have already reached their goal, the people are freed from fear and regain their strength. Only then does the guide erase the conjured city and tell the people that the actual treasure trove is near and within their reach. The Buddha explains to his disciples that he, like the guide, skillfully leads them to traverse the lengthy, treacherous path of saṁsāra. Had he preached the *ekayāna* alone, sentient beings would be discouraged by the distance they would have to travel and by the hardship they would have to endure. The Buddha preaches the three previous teachings as a conjured city in which living beings may rest, only to depart again for their ultimate deliverance. In the following poem, Ryōkan suggests that the monastery, while offering refuge from the troubles of his earlier life, like the "mountain of treasures," was only a "conjured city," a "temporary dwelling" that he must leave behind in order to continue his pursuit of the Buddha Dharma.

> Traveling and traveling
> I arrived at the mountain of treasures
> Only to realize it was none other than
> My own temporary dwelling[123]

Ryōkan thus indicates that his departure from the conjured city led to his discovery of the goal of his religious cultivation in his return to his home province of Echigo.

> How many years I spent parting wild grasses
>   to penetrate the depths
> Then suddenly I understood my teacher
>   and came back to my native place
> You go there and come back again
> Yet everything remains the same
> Clouds covering the mountain's summit
> Streams flowing by at your feet[124]

These autobiographical poems, in short, bear witness to Ryōkan's effort to understand his life in light of the nondualist perspective of *ekayāna* found in the *Lotus Sūtra*. Ryōkan strives in these poems to present a parallel between the pattern of his life—which forms an arc running away from and returning home—and the stages of Mahāyāna Buddhist training: one's initial vow to leave behind lay life, the monastic training to cultivate wisdom and compassion, and the final realization as the return to one's originally enlightened mind.[125]

This metaphorical homology between Ryōkan's life and the

Mahāyāna theory of practice provides the semantic ground for these autobiographical poems to manifest a particular implicative force. In the poems, "I" represents Ryōkan, or the characters in the parables, or a reader of the sūtra, or any practicer of Mahāyāna, and all of them at once. In the same manner, the "mountain of treasures" can refer simultaneously to the conjured city in the sūtra's episode, Entsūji, Mahāyāna training regimens in general, the dualistic perspective isolating processes from goal, and so forth. As a result of the borrowing by the poetic texts of the sūtra episodes—or, more specifically, because of the intertextual transposition of the scripture's signifying practice to that of the poems—Ryōkan's poems present themselves as polyphonic texts. They are not fixed sets of signs corresponding one-to-one with their denotative referents, but become dynamic processes with each sign producing connotations incessantly oscillating between the scriptural accounts and the events of Ryōkan's life. As Julia Kristeva asserts: "If one grants that every signifying practice is a field of transpositions of various signifying systems (an inter-textuality), one then understands that its 'place' of enunciation and its denoted 'object' are never single, complete, and identical to themselves, but always plural, shattered, capable of being tabulated. In this way polysemy can also be seen as the result of a semiotic polyvalence—an adherence to different sign systems."[126] Likewise, Ryōkan's poetic texts represent not static structures but productive movements of polysemic proliferation, which not only mediate the sūtra texts and Ryōkan's life, but coalesce each into the other in the poems' own textuality.

> To see before me,
> Brought into the present
> The days long ago
> When the Buddha preached
> How grateful I feel![127]

In this metaphorical overlapping of the events of Ryōkan's life and those described in the scriptural texts, the ambivalence in Ryōkan's self-portrait—the fluctuation between pride and shame—can be evinced as his deliberate strategy to express himself. Ryōkan in the self-deprecatory note of his poems accepts as a *fact*—that is, as a "sign" according to literal reading of his poems—that he is the eldest son of a prominent family, returned home shamefully as a beggar. However, the comic note in Ryōkan's self-portrait prevents his identity from being reduced to one signification and presents it instead as an intertextual nexus. Ryōkan's identity emerges in the mutual reflections of the diverse signs for Ryōkan—a degenerate, a beggar, the most useless man ever, the one who ran away from home and then from the monastic life, the one who returned from the "conjured city," and the one who rediscovered his home as the jewel that always remained in his robe. Through the playful interaction of these signs, each constantly sedimenting and desedimenting its meaning to that of other signs, Ryōkan expresses his carefree manner of life.

> Since becoming a monk, I've passed the days
>   letting things naturally take their course
> Yesterday I was in the green mountains
> Today I'm strolling around town
> My robe is a sorry patchwork
> My bowl a veteran of countless years
> Clear, quiet nights
>   I lean on my staff and recite poetry
> In the daytime
>   I spread my straw mat for a nap
> People may say, "He's a no-account fellow"
> Well, this is how I am![128]

Ryōkan is honest about conveying his deep distress at the solitude of his life, yet he somehow always escapes from being consumed by it. Ryōkan's pride/shame in himself as a "no-account fellow"—his simultaneously serious and comic presentation of himself—is not necessarily an indication of his irresolution, but a polyvalent sign pointing at once to his indifference to fame, power, wealth, and other worldly merits *and* to his gratitude to the ordinary people whose patronage allowed him to sustain his mendicant life.

Ever-changing Flow: Ryōkan as a Polyvalent Sign

Ryōkan left several handwritten notes, the result of his study of Japanese phonetics and grammar, which show his keen interest in language not only as a poet but as a thinker. One of them shows his effort to categorize vowels into monophthongs and diphthongs. Another note presents his knowledge of the principles governing the Japanese phonetic table, modeled on that of Sanskrit. In other notes he attempts to construct a system to illustrate diverse patterns of adjectival declension and verbal conjugation.[129] Yet another note shows studies by Ryōkan aimed at reconstructing the original usage of ancient phrases.[130] Kera

Yoshishige's record relates an episode describing Ryōkan's fascination with the mystery of language: "In the local dialect, when the rice plants ripen, people say they *'bonaru.'* Someone remarked: 'The word *bonaru* means "to roar."' Having overheard this, the Master wanted to listen to the roaring of the rice and spent all night wandering through the fields."[131]

Precisely because he had studied language and was fully aware of its power, Ryōkan was extremely sensitive about the harm that could result when this same power of words was abused. Ryōkan composed several variations of texts called "Words of Advice,"[132] each of which comprises lists of things he disliked, found distasteful, or felt to demonstrate a lack of sensitivity. Some of these lists, it seems, were written as reminders to himself; others were prepared to be given to friends.[133] In one such list, among the things Ryōkan mentions he dislikes are "people who talk too much, people who talk too fast, boisterous speech, flowery speech, talking like a know-it-all, forcing others to listen while you go on about yourself, making cheap promises." Toward the end of this list, Ryōkan remarks: "Once spoken, a word can't be called back."[134] In another list of things he dislikes, along with "people who always want to be acknowledged" and "telling others about one's distinguished lineage," one reads "pretentious talk about enlightenment, pretentious talk about academics, pretentious talk about the tea ceremony, pretentious talk about art."[135]

In these lists Ryōkan warns against the double-edged sword of language and its fictive power, which, when creatively applied, gives birth to poetry and art but, when misappropriated, becomes the source of the fictitious, illusory, and deceptive.

> Talk is always easy
> Practice always hard
> It's no wonder people try to make up for
>   their lack of hard practice with easy talk
> But the harder they try, the worse things get
> The more they talk, the more wrong they go
> It's like pouring on oil to put out a fire
> Just foolishness and nothing else[136]

Ryōkan's legendary reticence in his daily life was, therefore, an expression of his sensitivity to language. Yoshishige describes one of Ryōkan's regular visits to the Kera household:

> The Master stayed several nights at our home. Young and
> old became harmonious, and a peaceful atmosphere filled

the house for several days after his departure. Just one evening of talking with the Master made us feel that our hearts had been purified. The Master never held forth on the scriptures or classics or the importance of ethics. Sometimes he would be in the kitchen tending the fire, sometimes in the parlor practicing meditation. In his conversation he never alluded to classical poetry or ethical teachings, and his manner was indescribably casual and relaxed. It was just his own innate goodness that naturally guided others.[137]

It is hardly surprising that Ryōkan's favorite hero is the bodhisattva Never-Despising-Anyone (Skt. Sadāparibhūta; J. Jōfukyō) of the *Lotus Sūtra.*[138] In the sūtra, this bodhisattva appears as one of Shākyamuni Buddha's former transmigratory existences, having lived countless aeons before the Buddha's time. In order to help reveal the teaching of the *Lotus* to the world, he prostrated himself before everyone he encountered as proof of his respect for their intrinsic potential for enlightenment. As a result, he was often the object of ridicule and humiliation; at times he was chased off and stoned even by monks and nuns, who could not understand his teaching. However, he always returned to his practice of bowing to everyone he encountered, declaring, "I cannot despise you, since you will become a buddha." Ryōkan extols the bodhisattva in his waka:

> One who is a monk needs nothing—
> Only "Never Despising Anyone"
> For this is the unexcelled practice
>   of all bodhisattvas[139]

Ryōkan's enthusiasm for this bodhisattva is also evident in *Hokke san,* his poetic tribute to the *Lotus Sūtra.*

> Day and night you practice
>   bowing and bowing again
> You live your life simply practicing bowing
> I take refuge in you, Never-Despising-Anyone
> You stand alone, without a peer,
>   above or under heaven
>
> Some throw stones, some beat him with sticks
> He retreats, then stops and calls to them aloud
> Since this fellow has left the world
> No one has heard from him

But the wind and moonlight that fill the night
For whom do they reveal their purity?

There was no one like you in the past
There'll be no one like you in the future
Never disparaging, Never-Despising-Anyone!
Your pureness makes me forever adore you[140]

If the bodhisattva—who strives to escape from verbosity and
empty speech and to express himself with straightforward acts—served
as Ryōkan's model, that may help to explain Ryōkan's taciturnity in his
everyday life. Yoshino Hideo, a leading scholar of Ryōkan's waka,
records an oral tradition preserved in the Yamamoto family, the direct
descendants of Ryōkan's brother Yoshiyuki.

> Ryōkan's nephew Umanosuke—also known as Yasuki, Yoshi-
> yuki's first son and the heir to the declining Yamamoto clan
> —had begun to indulge in a life of dissipation and would not
> listen to anyone's advice. In desperation, his mother Yasuko
> asked Ryōkan to admonish him. Ryōkan went to the family's
> house and stayed there for three days; yet he remained
> speechless, not knowing what to say to Umanosuke. Finally,
> when the time came for Ryōkan to depart, he called Umano-
> suke to help him tie his straw sandals. Thinking that Ryōkan
> was at last about to begin preaching to her son, Yasuko hid
> behind a screen and listened. As Umanosuke was tying Ryō-
> kan's sandals, he felt a cold sensation on his neck. Looking
> up, he realized it was the tears falling from Ryōkan's eyes.
> Suddenly, Umanosuke recovered his senses. Ryōkan stood
> up and, still silent, departed.[141]

Kera Yoshishige describes Ryōkan's encounter at Yoshishige's
house with the notoriously obstreperous monk Chikai.

> Once, during the time for transplanting rice seedlings, the
> Master was staying at our home. There was a certain crazy
> priest named Chikai, whose extreme arrogance had driven
> him insane. He was always declaring, "I will found my own
> school of Buddhism in order to save sentient beings!" and
> compared himself to the eminent monks of the past, while
> disparaging his contemporaries as children. Hence, the great
> esteem accorded the Zen master Ryōkan made him seethe
> with envy.
> On this particular day, Chikai got roaring drunk and an-

nounced that he was going to help till the fields. He arrived at our home, caked with mud. When he saw the Master was there, his long-festering anger suddenly exploded, and, without a word, he started to slap the Master with his soaking belt. All of this happened entirely without warning. The Master himself had no idea what it was all about, and since he did not make any attempt to escape, the people with him were alarmed and subdued the priest. They then pulled the Master into another room and threw the priest out of the house.

At dusk, a heavy rain began to fall. The Master came out of the room and asked casually: "Did that monk have his rain gear with him?" He said nothing more about the incident.[142]

These episodes illustrate the particular way in which Ryōkan's actions deviate from social convention and, as a result, show a parallel with poetic language. Just as poetry manifests its figurative power in violating grammatical and syntactic rules, Ryōkan transgresses the tedium of everyday life to produce novelty, to reveal a surprising new perspective on the reality of daily life that makes his contemporaries marvel. Furthermore, Ryōkan's silence is replete with meanings that are not only plural but variant. In the Chikai episode, Ryōkan's subjecting himself to the crazed monk—his inexplicable defeat—is at once his victory, giving proof to his indifference not only to fame and fortune but also to misfortune, the patient detachment evoking the image of Ryōkan's bodhisattva hero in the *Lotus Sūtra.*

In the other anecdote, Ryōkan's tears falling on Umanosuke are tinged not only with pity for his nephew. If Ryōkan had not run away from his responsibility as the family's heir and had protected the house of Yamamoto, Umanosuke would not have been given the burden of restoring the house's prestige and would not have driven himself into the dissipated state; instead, however, Ryōkan became a beggar, a "no-account fellow," utterly helpless to return the family to its past glory; at the same time, Ryōkan was a monk who left the family for his religious pursuits, and it was inappropriate for him to influence affairs within the family. Ryōkan's tears show varying shades of feeling —regret, bewilderment, tenderness, compunction, shame—that highlight his deep sense of commiseration. As a polysemic sign, his tears shed in silence convey to Umanosuke their multifarious significations, which immediately redescribe the reality of Ryōkan's presence for Umanosuke: Ryōkan is no longer Umanosuke's superior urging him to rectify his behavior, but is rather his equal, a helpless being guilty of the same crime as Umanosuke, crying as if to ask for his nephew's forgiveness.

Ryōkan's legendary silence is, therefore, not necessarily the hallmark of his "enlightenment," in the sense of his aloofness from worldly affairs, as interpreted by some modern scholars. His silence as depicted in the biographies reveals traces of worry, sorrow, and distress. However, these emotions associated with Ryōkan's suffering do not necessarily bear witness to his secularization. They are rather the feelings through which Ryōkan, in conformity with bodhisattva practice, extends his compassion to and shares suffering with others. Ryōkan's taciturnity is, in short, part of the poetic—polysemic—nature of his everyday life as projected in the biographical texts.

This reminds us, students of Ryōkan, that even the Ryōkan described in his contemporaneous sources is an interpretation or, more precisely, an aggregate of diverse interpretive strategies. Just as Ryōkan's poems cannot be elucidated without their tropes, his biographies cannot be separated from their figurative intentions. The events related in the biographical texts—that is, events as figured in the texts—are already interpretations: they first happen in their texts before they are reconstructed as (or, as if) historical facts—a reconstruction that is one of many different ways of understanding what the biographical texts strive to represent through their figurations. It remains impossible to determine how much of the textual accounts corresponds to historical happenings. Instead, Ryōkan's biographies demonstrate that they are concordant with Ryōkan's poems in the figurative strategies through which they delineate Ryōkan's suffering as his cultivation of wisdom and expression of compassion. The polysemic representation of Ryōkan's life shared by both the poems and the biographies effaces the boundary between Ryōkan's poetic textuality and biographical reality—or, his poetic reality and biographical textuality.

In this problematic relationship between the text and textual representation, yet another, perhaps the most radical, aspect of Ryōkan's nondualist deconstruction is observed. Through their polyphonized signification, Ryōkan's poems create a fissure in the one-to-one correspondence between words and things in a conventional sense and dismiss it as vulgarity. For Ryōkan, external facts—"things themselves"—are not independent of the text; they are but signs, which, according to textual figurations, can be charged with a single meaning or with multiple values. As a result, for Ryōkan's poetry, too, *"there is nothing outside of the text."*[143] As Derrida notes, *"The thing itself is a sign. . . .* The so-called 'thing itself' is always already a *representamen* [that which results from representation] shielded from the simplicity of intuitive evidence. The *representamen* functions only by giving rise to an *interpretant* [that which interprets] that itself becomes a sign and so on to *infinity. . . .* The *represented* is always already a *representamen."*[144] These words recall Ryōkan's poem quoted earlier, aiming at deconstructing both nominalism and realism.

> Who was it said, "Names are the guests of reality"?
> These words have come down to us from ancient times
> But even if people know that names aren't real
> They don't see that reality itself has no root
> Name, reality—both are beside the point
> Just naturally find joy in the ever-changing flow[145]

For Ryōkan reality is no longer analogous with oneness, identity, and constancy. It is located instead in this ever-changing flow—which may be characterized as emptiness *(shunyatā)* according to Buddhist philosophy or as *différance* in the context of deconstructionalism— and in moving freely in this flow of change that erases the duality between things and words. In this flow, the world continues to regenerate itself as it is figured and refigured anew by poetic description of it. Ryōkan's waka "Tribute to Gogō-an," which refers to his thatch hut on Mount Kugami, is suggestive of this polysemic dynamism of Ryōkan's world emerging from his nondualist perspective. The poem's resonance seems to emulate and then immerse itself within the ever-changing flow, the locus—or nonlocus—of Ryōkan's life of mendicancy. The poem vibrates in its own polyvalence, interfusing the pristine stream that runs by Ryōkan's hermitage, the simple, uninterrupted flow of Ryōkan's everyday life, and Ryōkan's gentle voice uttering the poem that echoes the sound of the stream.

> The water of the valley stream
> Never shouts at the tainted world
> "Purify yourself!"
> But naturally, as it is
> Shows how it is done[146]

Commemorating Ryōkan
The Origin and Growth of Ryōkan's Biographies

Ryūichi Abé

BECAUSE of the vast amount of legendary literature, both oral and written, that has accumulated around Ryōkan since his death, it is often forgotten that the effort to document Ryōkan's life and to preserve his writings had already begun during his lifetime (1758–1831). This brief survey identifies the key primary sources for Ryōkan's biography, sketches the historical context in which the contemporaneous biographies of Ryōkan were composed, and illustrates the intertwining historical relationships that join these texts. Many of the sources exist only as unpublished manuscripts. In cases where there exist printed editions of these sources, whether partial or complete, or photo reproductions of the original manuscripts, or major secondary sources that assist in the reading of these primary records, they are cited in the notes.[1]

The earliest account of Ryōkan's life appears in the *Hokuetsu kidan* (Curious Tales of Hokuetsu) by Tachibana Konron (also known as Mochiyo), a native of Sanjō, an inland town in the vicinity of Ryōkan's birthplace of Izumozaki. Completed in 1811, the work is composed of stories relating to the history, geography, culture, and distinguished families and individuals of the Echigo (Hokuetsu) region. In spring of the following year, the woodblock edition of this text, with illustrations by the famed woodblock artist Hokusai, was published by Eijudō, one of the leading Edo publishers of the period. Fascicle 6 of the *Kidan* contains a section devoted to Ryōkan. Konron's account states that, recently, an extraordinary monk had taken residence at Gogō-an, a thatch hut on Mount Kugami, and that people all praise him for his freedom from desire, his purity, and his compassion. It is unknown whether Konron was personally acquainted with Ryōkan. Konron mentions, however, that his elder brother Genzan had studied alongside Ryōkan (then known by his secular name Bunkō) at the private academy run by Ryōkan's Confucian teacher Ōmori Shiyō, and adds that, when Ryōkan returned home after his Buddhist training and his years of pilgrimage, Genzan was among the first to identify Ryōkan as the beggar-monk who had settled in an abandoned hut on the beach of Gōmoto, on the outskirts of Izumozaki.[2]

Konron's publication of *Kidan* was not the first occasion on which Ryōkan's name was introduced to the literati in Edo. It was preceded by visits to Echigo by two prominent Edo figures who befriended Ryōkan. In 1801, Ōmura Mizue (1753–1816), a celebrated Kokugaku scholar and waka poet, arrived in Echigo.[3] Mizue's host was Abe Teichin (1779–1838), the village chief of Watabe and one of Ryōkan's principal patrons. In his *Koshiji no kikō* (Journey Along the Roads of Echigo), a selection of poems he composed during this trip, Mizue describes his visits to Ryōkan at Gogō-an and records the waka they exchanged.[4] Teichin was himself an eager student of waka and played an important role in assisting Ryōkan's study of *Man'yōshū*, the celebrated eighth-century poetic anthology, and in preserving Ryōkan's waka.[5] Teichin's ninth son, Makie Seisai (1817–1868), compiled the waka of Ryōkan collected by his father in a volume titled *Shamon Ryōkan shi kashū* (Collected Waka of the Priest Master Ryōkan).[6]

In 1809 the Edo literatus Kameda Bōsai (1754–1826), a Confucian scholar of the Eclectic school (Setchū ha), traveled to Echigo, where he remained until 1811. Bōsai was particularly renowned for his mastery of calligraphy, and over a thousand students were said to have crowded his private school at Kanda in Edo. However, during his stay in Echigo, Bōsai, hitherto known for his extremely rigorous calligraphy, was deeply influenced by Ryōkan's free-flowing brushwork.[7] The Edo historian Gamō Shigeaki observes in his *Kinsei kajin den* (Records of Waka Poets of Recent Times): "His [Ryōkan's] calligraphy impressed Bōsai as being produced by a divine hand. He immediately visited Ryōkan's hut . . . and all his doubts [about calligraphy technique] dissolved. Later, he told others: 'Having met Ryōkan, I realized the ultimate truth of grass-style writing *(sōsho)*.' "[8] After Bōsai's return to Edo, the dramatic change in his style of calligraphy was said to have inspired the following comical haiku, or *senryū: "Bōsai wa Echigo gaeri de ji ga kuneri"* (Returning from Echigo, Bōsai's characters got crooked).[9]

In 1813 yet another prominent Confucian scholar of the Setchū (Eclectic) school, Ōta Shizan (also known as Kinjō) (1765–1825), arrived in Echigo and delivered a series of lectures. It is said that Shizan, too, visited Ryōkan at his mountain hut.[10] Among Shizan's students in Echigo was the young Suzuki Bundai (1796–1870), who assisted Shizan in preparing lectures at the village of Makigahana, sponsored by Kera Shukumon, the chief of the village. In winter of the same year, Bundai composed a kanshi titled "Ryōkan zenji ni yosu" (Dedicated to the Zen Master Ryōkan).[11] In this poem Bundai states that Ryōkan had in his possession a manuscript of his own collected kanshi titled Sōdōshū (Grass Hut Collection) and that he, Bundai, borrowed this manuscript to study from time to time. It is noteworthy that as early as 1813 there existed a collection of Ryōkan's kanshi compiled by the poet himself and that the title Sōdōshū was Ryōkan's own. In the following year Bundai provided a brief profile of Ryōkan in his work Kitsuen shiwa (Stories of Poets and Poems Told While Smoking), an anthology of accounts of Japanese kanshi poets of the past and present.[12] In 1814 Bundai traveled to Edo and studied under various prominent Confucian scholars and poets, among them the above-mentioned Kameda Bōsai.[13] When he returned to Echigo in 1816, Bundai composed a preface to Ryōkan's Sōdōshū and, with the help of his brother Ryūken, began the work of preparing Ryōkan's manuscript for publication. It appears that Bundai continued this project throughout his life. In 1849 he prepared another expanded preface, detailing Ryōkan's biography and introducing colorful anecdotes concerning Ryōkan's games with the village children, his affection for the Han-shan, the collected poems of the legendary T'ang recluse-poets of Mount T'ien-t'ai, and his exchange of calligraphy with Bōsai.[14] However, despite his continuous efforts, the Sōdōshū remained unpublished during Bundai's lifetime.

In 1818, there appeared the first independent biography of Ryōkan, the Ryōkan zenji den (Record of Zen Master Ryōkan),[15] composed by Bundai's friend Ōzeki Bunchū (d. 1834), a local Confucian scholar and doctor. There survives a letter from Ryōkan to Bunchū whose content suggests that Bunchū sent his friend Nakahara Genjō (1793–1872), the doctor of the village of Akatsuka (present-day Niigata), to Ryōkan's hut to deliver the biography and solicit Ryōkan's response.[16]

The first day of the fourth month

To Ōzeki Bunchū:

I would like to thank you for kindly preparing this composition for me. However, because I have never been one to be counted among the worthies, because I find worldly praise and blame, gain and loss, a nuisance, and because my inclination is to be indifferent to people's affairs, I would like to

be excused from complying with your request. It is my wish
to meet with you once while I am alive and to express my
thoughts and feelings. Since I am old and weak, however, I
cannot make any definite promise. I found it perplexing that
Nakahara Genjō took such pains to visit me at my hut and
make this request on your behalf.

Forgive me for my lack of courtesy.

Ryōkan[17]

Because *Ryōkan zenji den* is Bunchū's only known written
work on Ryōkan, it is likely that the letter refers to Bunchū's compo-
sition of this biography. Bunchū apparently intended to ask Ryōkan
to review the work and to provide him with further information so
that he might augment and improve it. Because of the formality of
Bunchū's request, reflected in Ryōkan's letter, and because of Ryō-
kan's statement "it is my wish to meet (with) you once while I am
alive," some historians believe that Bunchū did not know Ryōkan per-
sonally at the time of his composition of the *Zenji den*. Bunchū's biog-
raphy nevertheless abounds with vivid and detailed descriptions of
Ryōkan's daily activities unavailable in previous biographical records.
It also contains a number of direct quotes from Ryōkan. To give just
one example: "Someone criticized the Zen Master's poems for trans-
gressing many phonetic regulations. The Master said, 'I simply speak
what my mind desires to express. How can I be bothered by phonetic
rules? If there are those who care about poetics, they should feel free
to go ahead and make the corrections.' Amazed, the person with-
drew."[18] Much later in his life, Bunchū became blind, and Ryōkan's
poem dedicated to the sightless Bunchū[19] suggests that their friend-
ship continued to grow after the 1818 composition of the *Ryōkan
zenji den*. It thus appears most likely that the event described in Ryō-
kan's letter took place before Bunchū's completion of the biography.
That is to say, the work by Bunchū mentioned in the letter was a draft
of the *Zenji den*, and, although it is possible that Bunchū did not know
Ryōkan at the time of Ryōkan's letter, Bunchū probably did manage to
receive Ryōkan's assistance before he completed the biography in
1818.

Around this time Sugae Masumi (1754–1829), a literary figure
and ethnographer of Akita province in northern Honshū, composed a
work titled *Koshi no shiori* (Booklet of the Northern Route), in which
he describes Ryōkan as *temari shōnin,* the Ball-bouncing Saint.

"Ball-bouncing Saint"

The Ball-bouncing Saint is a brother of Yoshiyuki of the House of Tachibana at Izumozaki. His name is Ryōkan. He dwells in the hut Gogō[-an] on Mount Kugami and lives his life composing kanshi and waka. He excels in the art of calligraphy, and even Bōsai lauds his skills. When he goes out begging, he always keeps two or three balls in his sleeve, and whenever he finds children playing ball, he takes out the balls from his sleeve and plays with them as if he were just another child. Truly, his mind is as pure as that of a child. A poem of Ryōkan:

> Spring day,
> When I play with the village children
> Under the trees at this shrine,
> Don't let the evening descend![20]

Masumi's mention of Ryōkan shows that his renown had begun to spread even to remote provinces of Japan such as Akita. By the time of Bunchū's *Zenji den,* Ryōkan had moved from his hut on Mount Kugami to another hut at the Shintō shrine of Otogo in the foothills of the same mountain. Ryōkan's correspondence, however, indicates that his daily routine, as captured by Masumi's account, remained unchanged.

One of the regular stopovers during Ryōkan's begging rounds was the house of Kera Shukumon (1755–1819) at Makigahana, a village at the foot of Mount Kugami.[21] Shukumon, the village chief, was an avid supporter of cultural activities. Those prominent literati who visited and stayed at the Kera residence as Shukumon's guests included the above-mentioned waka poet Ōmura Mizue and the Setchū school Confucian Ōta Shizan, Suzuki Bundai's teacher.[22] Among other important guests were the Kokugaku scholar Hayashi Kunio (d. 1849) and his adopted son Mikao (d. 1862). Mikao, who conducted an exhaustive search of the libraries of Ryōkan's leading patrons, Abe Teichin, Kera Shukumon, and Harada Jakusai (1763–1827), compiled the *Ryōkan zenji kashū* (Collected Waka of the Zen Master Ryōkan),[23] the most comprehensive collection of Ryōkan's waka before the advent of modern bibliographical studies of Ryōkan in the Meiji era.

In 1817 Ryōkan sent a letter to Shukumon stating that, at Shukumon's request, he had completed personally copying the *Lotus Sūtra.*[24] This letter confirms that, as stated in many of his biographies, Ryōkan was particularly fond of the *Lotus* and that a copy of the scripture was in his possession. In a traditional ritual for preserving the Buddhist

Dharma, Shukumon buried the copy of the scripture on the grounds of his residence and erected above it a stone statue of Jizō (Skt. Kṣitigarbha). Shukumon's offering was for the purpose of protecting the ancestral deities of the Kera lineage and seeking guidance for himself in his next rebirth. When Shukumon passed away two years later, Ryōkan was sixty-one years old and Kera Yoshishige (1810–1859), Shukumon's third son, only nine. Yoshishige, a regular playing companion during Ryōkan's daily rounds of begging, later wrote yet another important source for Ryōkan's biography, the *Ryōkan zenji kiwa* (Curious Accounts of the Zen Master Ryōkan).[25] A large number of Ryōkan's handwritten letters survive at Kera's house today, twenty-one of which are addressed to Shukumon and one to Shōhachi, the childhood name under which Yoshishige was then known.[26] These letters show that Yoshishige's childhood years coincide with the period in which Ryōkan was most active in composing poems in his mountain hut, begging for alms at nearby villages, and playing with the village children. It appears that Yoshishige also often ran errands for Ryōkan:

> To Shōhachi:
>
> Please bring this to Aozu.
>
> Ryōkan[27]

Adjacent to the Kera family's village of Makigahana, to the northeast, was the village of Aozu, the home of Suzuki Bundai. In his letters Ryōkan customarily refers to his friends' houses by the names of their villages, and it thus appears that Ryōkan's message requests Yoshishige to carry something to Suzuki Bundai's house in Aozu. The letter therefore shows that during his childhood Yoshishige had been acquainted with Bundai.

Because of the untimely death of Shukumon's first son and the chronic illness of his second,[28] in 1828, Yoshishige, at age eighteen, became the head of the Kera family and succeeded to the post of village chief. Yoshishige grew into an effective administrator and in 1856 was appointed to the office of *ōshōya,* head of the village chiefs of over forty villages in northern Echigo.[29] Around 1847, Yoshishige conducted a large-scale reorganization of the Kera library. All the writings of Ryōkan preserved in the Kera household—consisting of his kanshi, waka, and letters—were assembled on three scrolls, and Yoshishige requested that Suzuki Bundai compose a preface to this collection, which Bundai completed in 1847.[30]

It was during this period, about fifteen years after Ryōkan's death, that Yoshishige at age thirty-seven completed the *Ryōkan zenji kiwa.*[31] The *Kiwa* consists of brief anecdotes and episodes that record Ryōkan's sayings and sketch his daily activities, covering such diverse subjects as Ryōkan's favorite games with the children and his study of ancient Japanese phonetics. Although its presentation is not chronologically ordered, its detailed description of Ryōkan's daily life makes Yoshishige's *Kiwa* an indispensable source for Ryōkan studies.

In the *Kiwa* Yoshishige mentions another important source for Ryōkan's biography: "In Tosa, a native of Edo named Banjō shared the Master's lodging for a night. Banjō's account of this experience is recorded in his writings."[32] Kondō Banjō (1776–1848), a native of Bitchū, was a waka poet living in Edo and was known for his travel journals.[33] The work by Banjō to which Yoshishige refers is *Nezame no tomo* (A Bedside Companion), composed circa 1845. In one section of this volume Banjō recalls that, some thirty years earlier, while traveling in Tosa province on the island of Shikoku, he was caught in a heavy downpour and sought lodging at a tumbledown hut occupied by a monk. The monk had no possessions, apart from a wooden statue of the Buddha and a copy of the *Chuang-tzu.* Banjō, however, was deeply impressed by the monk's grass-style calligraphy and asked him to inscribe a fan, to which request the monk immediately responded, signing his calligraphy "Ryōkan of Echigo."

Banjō's description, if true, is critically important because there exists a dearth of information for the period of Ryōkan's pilgrimage, the years between his departure from Entsūji and his return to Echigo. Several scholars have cast doubt on the credibility of Banjō's record, which gives the wrong Chinese character for the *ryō,* using the character for "complete" instead of the correct character meaning "good." Banjō himself states in *Nezame no tomo* that, although he had forgotten his encounter with Ryōkan for many years, reading Tachibana Konron's *Hokuetsu kidan,* with its depiction of Ryōkan as a hut-dwelling beggar-monk from Echigo who excelled in calligraphy, he realized that the nameless monk he had met in Tosa was this very Ryōkan of Echigo. Konron's *Kidan,* in fact, uses the same wrong character for the *ryō* in Ryōkan's name. There is additional evidence that lends support to Banjō's record. In the Kera family library there survive two works by Kondō Banjō: one is *Nezame no tomo,*[34] the other, *Shiki zatsueisō* (Leaves of Various Compositions in the Four Seasons). The manuscript of *Zatsueisō* has a colophon written by Yoshishige himself in 1848.[35] In the colophon Yoshishige states that, on the seventeenth day of the tenth month of Kōka 3 (1846), he visited Kondō Banjō at his new residence in Kobinata, Edo, and that Banjō shared with him various reminiscences and gave him lessons in waka composition. Although the colophon does not make direct reference to Ryōkan, Yoshishige's meeting with Banjō makes it highly probable that they did discuss Banjō's encounter with "Ryōkan" when he was a young monk traveling in Tosa and that Yoshishige identified the monk described by Banjō as Ryōkan, leading to his statement in the *Kiwa* that "in Tosa, a native of Edo named Banjō shared the Master's lodging for a night."

At about the time of Yoshishige's completion of the *Kiwa*, the priest Zōun (1813–1869), the twenty-third-generation abbot of Kairyū-in, a Sōtō temple in the city of Maebashi, traveled to Echigo. Zōun had resolved to publish Ryōkan's poems when he "chanced to see his [Ryōkan's] writings and made a pilgrimage to the remains of Gogō-an on Mount Kugami, visiting one after another the elders of the villages at the mountain's foothills, meeting repeatedly with his disciple the nun Teishin, who related to me in detail her master's outlook as well as his deeds."[36] Although the task was not completed till decades after his trip to Echigo, Zōun fulfilled his resolution in 1867, with the compilation of the *Ryōkan dōjin ikō* (Writings Left by the Practitioner of the Way Ryōkan), whose woodblock edition was published by Sōkodō of Shiba, Edo.

The nun Teishin (1798–1872) appears to have been the major source of assistance for Zōun's work, the first publication of Ryōkan's kanshi. Although she knew Ryōkan only during the last four years of his life, Teishin was a frequent visitor at Ryōkan's residence, then located in quarters in the home of Kimura Motouemon in the village of Shimazaki.[37] Teishin, a devoted student who eagerly received from Ryōkan instruction in both Buddhism and waka, is remembered for her 1835 compilation of the *Hachisu no tsuyu* (Dew on the Lotus), which includes a brief preface describing Ryōkan's life, ninety-seven waka by Ryōkan, a series of waka exchanged between Ryōkan and Teishin, Ryōkan's "Words of Advice" *(kaigo),* and a letter from Teishin outlining the major events of Ryōkan's life to its addressee, Inagawa Gasai, her leading supporter.[38] There remain several letters Teishin sent to Zōun, among them the only extant detailed description of Ryōkan's funeral.[39] In another letter Teishin praises Zōun's intention of publishing Ryōkan's writings and states that she has enclosed a manuscript copy of Ryōkan's collected kanshi preserved by Henchō (1801–1876).[40] In his youth Henchō had served Ryōkan as his personal attendant on Mount

Kugami and at the Otogo shrine, and in 1826 he was appointed head priest at Gannōkaku, a Shingon temple in the village of Enmadō. Ryōkan's move from Otogo to the Kimura residence coincided with Henchō's appointment. Some historians therefore suggest that it was Henchō, who, reluctant to leave his aged master behind alone at the shrine, arranged for Ryōkan's move to Kimura's house.[41] Teishin's reference to Henchō in her letter is important because it clearly shows there existed a line of Ryōkan's kanshi manuscripts independent of Suzuki Bundai's *Sōdōshū* manuscripts.[42]

Yet another indispensable source for students of Ryōkan's biography is Ryōkan's own correspondence. Fortunately, because of his fame as a calligrapher, a large number of Ryōkan's letters have survived.[43] Although most of the letters are brief, dated, at best, with only the day and month of composition, and yielding only scattered information about the context in which they were written, as a whole they serve as an invaluable "who's who" of Ryōkan's relatives, friends, and acquaintances.

A case in point is the priest Shōgan, author of Ryōkan's epitaph, *Ryōkan zenji hiseki narabi ni jo,* composed in 1831, the year of Ryōkan's death.[44] Shōgan's epitaph played a crucial role in determining the course of development of later biographies of Ryōkan: it contains the earliest mention of Ryōkan's Zen name Taigu, Great Fool; it presents the major events of Ryōkan's life in chronological order; and it is the first record that provides information on the date of Ryōkan's death, his age at death, and the number of years between his ordination into the priesthood and his death. Nothing is known about the author, except for a single letter from Ryōkan addressed to him.

The first day of the second month

To Shōgan:

> It was my great pleasure the other day to have had such a long talk with you. Today, I gratefully received your gift of sake, rice, fermented beans, and vegetables. Please try the method of *tanden* training I described to you.

Ryōkan[45]

This letter indicates that Shōgan knew Ryōkan personally and was probably his friend, sufficiently acquainted with Ryōkan to discuss the meditative technique of concentrating one's inhaled breath in the *tanden,* the center of one's vital breath in the lower abdomen.

Ryōkan's letters are also important because they provide the reader with a list of the texts Ryōkan studied. Most such references to texts appear in letters in which Ryōkan asks his friends to lend him a particular volume for study. Elsewhere, Ryōkan speaks of books he owns, of whose publication he has learned, or of which he has made copies for his friends. Ryōkan's reading covered a wide range of fields, from calligraphy textbooks to works on poetics, from Buddhist texts to treatises on Chinese phonetics.[46] There are, for example, several letters that testify to Ryōkan's rigorous study of the *Man'yōshū*, the earliest collection of waka, compiled by Ōtomo no Yakamochi (716-785). In 1819, at the request of his poet friend Abe Teichin, Ryōkan inscribed in vermilion ink in Teichin's copy of the twenty-volume *Man'yō wakashū* a detailed annotation of the text and a transliteration of the original Chinese characters into *kana*.[47] The *Man'yōshū* was originally recorded in *man'yō gana*, Chinese characters deprived of all semantic value and, thus, representing purely phonetic qualities. Because of the shifts in phonetic practices in Japanese throughout the medieval period, reconstructing the original pronunciation from the *man'yō gana* characters is a complicated task. Ryōkan accomplished it with the help of the *Man'yō ryakuge*, a comprehensive commentary on the *Man'yōshū* by the Edo scholar Tachibana Chikage (1735-1808). Ryōkan borrowed the *Ryakuge* from Miwa Gonbei, a friend and patron in the village of Yoita, who already had acquired the twenty-scroll text, composed by Chikage during the years between 1791 and 1800 and published in thirty volumes between 1786 and 1812.[48] Ryōkan's study of the *Man'yōshū* crystallized in his work *Akinono* (Autumn Field),[49] a selection of Man'yō poems transliterated in plain *kana* characters. Kera Yoshishige also testifies to Ryōkan's special emphasis on the *Man'yōshū*:

> I asked the Master: "To learn about poetry, what work should I read?" The Master told me: "You should read the *Man'yōshū*," "I can't understand the *Man'yōshū*." I said. The Master replied: "Then just stick to whatever you *can* understand." On another occasion, the Master said: "The *Kokinshū* is relatively acceptable. But the poetry collections composed after that aren't worth reading at all."[50]

Ryōkan's enthusiasm for the study of ancient phonetics never abated. In 1827, at age sixty-nine, he borrowed from Kodama Rihei, a wealthy Izumozaki trader, the *Kanji San'onkō* (On the Three Phonetic

Systems of Chinese Characters) by the famed Kokugaku scholar Motoori Norinaga (1730–1801).[51] Ryōkan's study of the *San'onkō* might have been an outgrowth of his study of the *Man'yōshū*. Tachibana Chikage was first inspired to study the *Man'yōshū* when he came across Norinaga's celebrated 1779 work *Man'yō tama no ogoto* (A Little Jeweled Harp of the Man'yōshū) and its innovative interpretations of *man'yō gana*. Resolved to continue the project launched by his teacher Kamo no Mabuchi (1697–1769) in his uncompleted work *Man'yōkō*, Chikage began the composition of the *Ryakuge*, which he undertook in frequent consultation with Norinaga. Because of Ryōkan's acquaintance with the Kokugaku scholar Ōmura Mizue, a disciple of Mabuchi, and other Edo intellectuals such as Kameda Bōsai and Yamada Kinjō, it is highly probable that Ryōkan was aware of the cooperation between Chikage and Norinaga.

Again Kera Yoshishige offers a further explanation of Ryōkan's keen interest in the study of phonetics, an interest that derives not only from Ryōkan's instincts as a poet, but from his conviction that the act of helping others originates in one's proper use of language:[52]

> The Master made an exhaustive study of Japanese phonetics, thoroughly mastering their essentials. In our province, the works of Motoori and Mabuchi were unknown, so the Master was truly a pioneer. When I was young, I asked the Master about this, and he showed me the principles of declension. . . . Only when the student had truly mastered the principles of grammar would he go on teaching him. How I regret that I was too young to grasp the essentials of the Master's instructions![53]

Finally, a reading of Ryōkan's correspondence shows that nearly all the contemporaneous biographies of Ryōkan were composed by authors who not only knew Ryōkan personally but supported him in his mendicant's life and literary activities. Modern scholars often consider Ryōkan's composing of poetry to have been a solitary act carried out in isolation from society. Yet Ryōkan's composition of poetry was inherently related to his reading of various texts, many of which were made available by the people around him, people who encouraged his literary creation and commemorated in their writings both Ryōkan's life and his art. It is from this curious intertwining, this link between Ryōkan and his supporters, that the primary sources of Ryōkan's biography emerged. The value of these records as historiographies rests not in the objective observation historians may expect to find in their descriptions of Ryōkan's life, but in the relationship these documents themselves evidence between Ryōkan's writing of poetry and the biographers' writing about Ryōkan. These primary sources not only describe Ryōkan's life but stand as testimony to the historical conditions in which Ryōkan's literary production developed. These texts, together with Ryōkan's poetic texts, remain open-ended, projecting to us, as students of Ryōkan, the world in which Ryōkan lived with his friends, a world whose door opens to those who would introduce new approaches to the understanding of Ryōkan's life and art.

Translations

Translators' Note

RYŌKAN has frequently suffered from being presented in one-dimensional terms. Because of his fame as a poet and a calligrapher, for example, Ryōkan is sometimes treated primarily as a literary figure. But to many ordinary Japanese, Ryōkan is above all a cultural hero, a teacher in the broadest sense of the word, one who has something to say not simply about poetry, but about life itself. This is the "Ryōkan san" familiar to millions of Japanese who may never even have attempted Ryōkan's poems. Indeed, Ryōkan lived his life as a Zen Buddhist beggar-monk, and his poetry and other writings express his Buddhism in a personal manner that is neither sectarian, doctrinaire, nor abstract.

In arranging the translations in this book, we have sought to present Ryōkan not simply as a literary figure but as a teacher of Buddhism. For this reason, the translations open with the *Curious Accounts of the Zen Master Ryōkan (Ryōkan zenji kiwa),* an early record of Ryōkan's daily life composed by Kera Yoshishige (1810–1859), who as a child had been one of Ryōkan's playing companions. The Kera were *nanushi,* or hereditary chiefs, of Makigaha˷a, a local village where Ryōkan often begged. Yoshishige's father, Shukumon, was Ryōkan's close friend and faithful supporter, and the Master was a regular house guest at the Kera mansion. Heir to the Kera household, Yoshishige was well trained in the Chinese classics and Japanese poetry, and proved to be an able administrator. In 1856, he was appointed to the office of *ōshōya,* the head of the chiefs of over forty local villages. Yoshishige began his composition of the *Curious Accounts* at around age thirty-five, some fifteen years after Ryōkan's death, and completed it within the next two years. The work as a whole presents a vivid picture of the Master that lends coherence to the self-portrait that emerges from Ryōkan's poems. Our translation is based on the photographic reproduction of the original manuscript

preserved in the Kera household, edited by Harada Kanpei (Sanjō, Nii-
gata, 1979), and the transcription in Tōgō Toyoharu's *Ryōkan zenshū,*
which remains among the most authoritative and comprehensive edi-
tions of Ryōkan's works (2 volumes; Tokyo, 1959).

The selection of Ryōkan's poems includes both *kanshi,* poetry
composed in classical Chinese and recited in Japanese transliteration,
and *waka,* poetry composed in *kana,* the characters of the Japanese
syllabary. Roughly half the kanshi collected in Tōgō's *Zenshū* are trans-
lated in this volume.

We have grouped the kanshi under separate topics—begging,
meditation, friendship, nature, and so forth—to illustrate the varied
dimensions of Ryōkan's life and the character of his religious experi-
ence. The section titles ("Playing with the Children," "Strolling without
a Care," and so on) are our own, although many are borrowed directly
from Ryōkan's poems. Most of Ryōkan's kanshi do not have original
titles. Titles that do accompany individual poems are Ryōkan's own
and are displayed in italics.

The approximately one thousand waka composed by Ryōkan
are faithful to a Japanese poetic tradition in which emotion is subtly
expressed through key words suggesting seasonal change *(kigo),* with
many poems composed as reflections and variations on celebrated
waka of the past *(honka).* We therefore limited our selection of waka
to those poems that speak to us directly about Ryōkan's life and
thought and can be readily understood without the need for lengthy
commentary. As in the case of the kanshi, Ryōkan's original titles, as
well as any accompanying explanatory phrases in the original manu-
scripts, appear in italics. (For a detailed examination of the various
original manuscripts of Ryōkan's waka, see Tōgō's *Zenshū* 2, pp. 1–
33.) Included are selections from *Dew on the Lotus (Hachisu no
tsuyu),* a collection of poems exchanged between Ryōkan and Teishin,
a young nun who was close to Ryōkan in his final years. Nearly all the
waka included in this section are *tanka,* traditional short poems of thir-
ty-one syllables in alternating five- and seven-syllable phrases that form
a 5-7-5-7-7 pattern. The only exception is a single *chōka,* or long
poem, a form consisting of indefinitely repeated alternating five- and
seven-syllable phrases ending with two consecutive seven-syllable
phrases. Romanized Japanese readings are supplied for all the *tanka.*

Supplementing the poems is a selection of Ryōkan's letters to
various friends and supporters. The letters testify to the generous sup-
port Ryōkan received from his neighbors around Mount Kugami, sup-

port that enabled him to maintain his way of life. The translations close with Ryōkan's miscellaneous reflections on Buddhism, including his views on the decline of the authentic Zen tradition in Japan, his stern criticism of the contemporary Buddhist establishment, and the words of advice *(kaigo)* he composed for the lay men and women of his native area. Although observing Chinese poetic form, the two opening works in this section, "Invitation to the Way" and "The Priesthood," are intended to be extended essays and have therefore been rendered in prose.

Unless otherwise indicated, the translations of Ryōkan's poems, both kanshi and waka, as well as the translations of his letters and other writings, are based on Tōgō Toyoharu's *Ryōkan zenshū,* mentioned above. The location of kanshi and waka in the original sources is noted in the "finder's lists" at the end of the volume. The location of other works is given in the introductory remarks accompanying the translations.

Curious Accounts of the Zen Master Ryōkan

by Kera Yoshishige

Despite Ryōkan's enduring reputation as a poet and calligrapher, it is above all the character of his daily life, its essential naturalness and simplicity, that earned him the affection of the men, women, and children of his native Echigo and continues to attract Japanese of all ages and backgrounds. Our principal firsthand source for Ryōkan's day-to-day existence is *Ryōkan zenji kiwa* (Curious Accounts of the Zen Master Ryōkan), a short document composed around 1845 or 1846 by Kera Yoshishige (1810–1859), the son of Ryōkan's friend and supporter Kera Shukumon (1765–1819). Ryōkan was a frequent guest in the Kera household, and from childhood, Yoshishige was in close personal contact with the Master, even receiving lessons from him in Japanese poetry. Although only twenty-one when Ryōkan died in 1831, Yoshishige remained devoted to his memory. In the *Kiwa*, he recorded various accounts of Ryōkan's life, based on his own experience with Ryōkan, on stories and details he had garnered from other friends and associates of the Master, and on anecdotes Ryōkan had personally related to him. As Yoshishige admits, the collection is strung together haphazardly, but this very quality imparts to the *Kiwa* a rustic authenticity, and it is regarded by Japanese scholars as our most reliable testimony to Ryōkan's actual way of life. The original manuscript is still in the possession of the Kera family and remained unpublished until 1959. Numbering of the sections follows that in Tōgō Toyoharu's *Ryōkan zenshū*, vol. 2, pp. 522–523. No numbers appear in the original manuscript.

1. The Master was always silent, his movements graceful and relaxed. As it's said: "If one's mind is broad, one's presence will be imbued with grandeur."[1]

2. The Master always loved to drink, yet I never saw him drink to excess. Whether it was farmers or woodcutters, he enjoyed exchanging cups with them. They'd pay for his drinks, he for theirs: "This

one's on you; this one's on me . . ." and so on, always making sure that, by the end, each had exactly the same number of drinks.

3. The Master also loved to smoke. At first, he did not have his own pipe and tobacco,[2] and would always borrow other people's. But later, he acquired his own.

4. When the Master went visiting, he invariably left behind all sorts of personal belongings. Someone suggested: "Make a list of everything you have with you and, before leaving, just read it through." The Master said: "Fine idea!" After that, he would write a list of his belongings and before he left would make sure to read it through. Such a list is still preserved.

> A similar list, itself said to have been forgotten by Ryōkan and still preserved at the home of his friends and patrons the Suzukis, includes the following items: head rest, hand towel, handkerchief, fan, coins, ball, playing stones, straw hat, leggings, hand guards, arm guards, cane, short robe, miscellaneous articles of clothing, tung oil, begging bowl, and bag. It closes with the note: "I must be sure to read this when I leave. If I don't, it's going to land me in trouble!"[3]

5. The Master always said: "I hate entertaining guests."

6. The Master said: "Whenever I visit someone's home and they ask me where I'm from, I just tell them: 'None of your business!' "

7. The Master's voice was clear and melodious. When he chanted the sūtras,[4] the sound carried straight into people's hearts and naturally aroused faith in those who listened.

8. The Master was always joining the village children in their games, playing ball, matching playing stones and picking spring vegetables. When the Master passed the Jizōdō[5] post station, the children would rush after him. First they would shout at him: "Master Ryōkan, one *kan!*"[6] The Master would recoil, bending back in alarm. Next they would shout: "Master Ryōkan, two *kan!*" causing the Master to bend back still farther. As they continued in this way, increasing the amount from two *kan* to three and so on, the Master would bend back farther and farther, till he would nearly lose his balance and fall, at which point the children would burst into peals of delighted laughter.

When I[7] was a child, the superintendent of the post station, Tomitori Kurata,[8] visited our house. As it happened, the Master was also staying there, and said to him: "The children of your town are real little rascals. Don't let them do that to me any more. I'm old, and it's getting awfully hard for me."

I was sitting beside them and remarked to the Master: "Why do you put up with all this to play with them? Why don't you just stop?"

The Master replied: "I can't just stop what I've been doing for years."

The story behind this was that one year some people held an auction near the post station, and the Master came by to watch. One of the vendors shouted a price at him so loudly that the Master recoiled in alarm, bending all the way back, and ever since, the local children would pester him to play this game.

9. Wherever the Master went, he would join the children in their games. When playing with the children of a certain village, the Master would always pretend to be dead and lie down by the side of the road. The children would cover the Master with grass and leaves and play that they were burying him, laughing with delight.

One day, a crafty child came and, as soon as the Master began to play dead, squeezed the Master's nostrils shut with his fingers. Finally, the Master could stand it no longer and suddenly "revived."

The Zen Master seems to have done all this as part of his practice of breath control.[9]

10. The Master would go begging in my village, Makigahana.[10] When he stood before the gate of the first house, someone would come up and say: "This place is Hanbei's," and the Master would tiptoe away. When he came to the place next door, it was the same thing: someone would tell him, "This is Hanbei's home," and the Master would slink off. In this manner, the Master would have to pass up the next ten houses, coming away empty-handed.

The story behind this is that a man called Hanbei had once attacked the Master in a drunken rage, so that the name Hanbei made the Master tremble, leading people to play this trick on him. It seems the Master never thought it suspicious that Hanbei had so many homes.

11. Once, during the time for transplanting rice seedlings, the Master was staying at our home. There was a certain crazy priest named Chikai, whose extreme arrogance had driven him insane. He

was always declaring, "I will found my own school of Buddhism in order to save sentient beings!" and compared himself to the eminent monks of the past, while disparaging his contemporaries as children. Hence, the great esteem accorded the Zen master Ryōkan made him seethe with envy.

On this particular day, Chikai got roaring drunk and announced that he was going to help till the fields. He arrived at our home, caked with mud. When he saw the Master was there, his long-festering anger suddenly exploded, and, without a word, he started to slap the Master with his soaking belt. All of this happened entirely without warning. The Master himself had no idea what it was all about, and since he did not make any attempt to escape, the people with him were alarmed and subdued the priest. They then pulled the Master into another room and threw the priest out of the house.

At dusk, a heavy rain began to fall. The Master came out of the room and asked casually: "Did that monk have his rain gear with him?" He said nothing more about the incident.

12. When I was a child, I was temporarily in residence at Hōtō-in in Sanjō,[11] studying calligraphy. The Master also came and stayed there. At that time, I had what was popularly referred to as a *hariko-robashi*.[12]

I told the Master: "Paint me a picture of Lord Sugawara.[13] If you refuse, this thing will turn into a ghost and come get you at night!" The Master looked at it and appeared frightened. He then painted me the picture of Lord Sugawara, including Sugawara's title and a dedicatory verse. It remains in our home to this day.

13. When anyone asked the Master for a sample of his calligraphy, the Master would say: "After I practice and become good at it, I'll write something for you." At other times, in the grip of inspiration, he would toss off one sheet of calligraphy after another. He never complained about the quality of his materials. The Master would write his poems from memory, and that's why there were sometimes missing characters and some small variations in wording, so that there is no definitive version of his poems.

14. The Master loved grass-style calligraphy[14] and is said to have studied Huai-su's *Tzu-hsü-t'ieh*[15] and Sukemasa's *Akihagichō*.[16] While at his hut at Kugami, the Master still seems to have had supplies of brushes, inkstones, and paper, and it is said that visitors also saw scrap

paper on which he practiced. But after moving to Shimazaki,[17] he ran out of supplies and, whenever he had the chance, would go to people's homes in order to do calligraphy. No doubt, this is the origin of the comic verse the Master composed: "Yesterday at the temple, today at the doctor's."

Yoshishige is apparently referring to a Japanese poem by Ryōkan:

How pitiful, having neither brush nor ink!
Yesterday I went to the temple
Today I'll go to the doctor's

There is another poem in a similar vein:

Not even a brush—how pathetic I am!
This morning again I take my staff
And knock at the temple gate

15. When the Master was staying in his hut at Kugami, he kept next to the hearth a small jar containing some soy extract. Whenever he had any leftovers from his meal, he'd place them inside the jar. He would eat this mixture even on summer days and, when guests came, would offer it to them as well. No one else could bring himself to eat it. But the Master did not mind and seemed oblivious to the stench. "Maggots may breed in this," he said, "but when you scoop some into a bowl, they just crawl away on their own. So there's really no harm in eating it."

16. When my elder brother was married, the Master arrived carrying an old box containing a fan[18] and delivered a formal speech of congratulation. My grandfather asked the Master: "Who taught you this kind of worldly thing?" The Master answered innocently: "The wife of Hokusen of Jizōdō,[19] *she* taught me."

17. The Master loved to play *go*. Losing, however, upset him. Once he played *go* with a certain Tomitori, headman of Jizōdō, winning nearly every game. His host, pretending to be angry, said: "It's unforgivably rude to visit someone's home as a guest and then beat him. I forbid you to come here any more!" Devastated, the Master left.

On his way back, the Master stopped at our home. He seemed very dejected, as if deeply troubled by something. When my grandfather asked what was the matter, the Master told him: "I have been cut off by the Master of Jizōdō." "How terrible!" my grandfather said. "I'll go and apologize for you."

Next day, they went together to the Tomitori home. My grandfather pretended to apologize for the Master's rudeness the day before. All the while, the Master stood outside, not daring to come in. Only when he was formally invited did he finally enter. What's more, I understand that no sooner had the Master stepped through the door than they started playing again!

This took place before I was born, but I learned of it from the late priest Kankoku.[20]

18. The Master would sometimes play *go* for money, and people would often let him win. It seems, however, that when the Master accumulated a lot of money, he had nowhere to keep it. He once declared: "People always worry about not having enough money, but I worry about having too much!"

In the town of Izumozaki, Ryōkan's birthplace, a legend survives of a *go* contest between Ryōkan and Sekigawa Mansuke (n.d.). Mansuke was a close friend of Ryōkan's, and people who sought samples of Ryōkan's calligraphy would often employ Mansuke as a middleman.

One clear autumn day when Mansuke was picking persimmons in the garden behind his home, he turned to find Ryōkan standing there, gazing up dreamily. When Mansuke climbed down from the tree, Ryōkan said: "Let's play *go* today."

Go was Mansuke's favorite pastime, and he immediately brought out his *go* board. But first he had an idea: "Just playing plain *go* is no fun. Why don't we bet something instead?" he proposed. "If you win—"

It's getting cold," Ryōkan said, "so you can give me a quilted robe."

"And if I win?" asked Mansuke.

"I have nothing to give you," Ryōkan admitted.

"Then why not do some calligraphy?" suggested Mansuke, glancing toward the paper he had piled high on his desk.

"All right," agreed Ryōkan, having no choice.

They began to play, but Mansuke was Ryōkan's superior at *go* and quickly beat him. He then insisted that Ryōkan do some calligraphy, and reluctantly Ryōkan took a fan from the desk, on which he wrote:

> Picking persimmons
> My balls feel the chill
> Of the autumn wind

Mansuke read the poem and smiled bitterly. He went on to win the next round as well, and Ryōkan wrote out the same poem again. After this had been repeated three times, Mansuke could finally bear it no longer.

"Three times for that same poem about balls is too much!" he protested.

"Well," Ryōkan replied, "you won the same game of *go* three times, didn't you? So I wrote the same poem three times, too."

19. The Master never displayed excessive joy or anger. One never heard him speaking in a hurried manner, and in all his daily activities, in the way he would eat and drink, rise and retire, his movements were slow and easy, as if he were an idiot.

20. On the Master's personal belongings, such as his bamboo hat, he would write: "This is mine; really, it's mine!" In our family home is a copy of the *Muyūshū*[21] that the Master carried with him, and this, too, is inscribed: "Really mine."

21. Inoue Kirimaro[22] greatly revered the Master and often visited his hut at Kugami. He once asked the Master about the virtuous men of the present day, and the Master told him about my father. From then on, Kirimaro became a regular visitor at our home.

22. The Master often cared for those who were ill, doing everything he could, helping them to eat and drink, to sit up and lie down. He was also skilled at massage and applying moxa.[23] People would ask him: "Please come tomorrow and give me a moxa treatment." But the Master would not make any promises, telling them: "We'll see about tomorrow tomorrow." Was this because he felt that casually promising things showed a lack of sincerity? Or was it, perhaps, that one cannot really be sure whether tomorrow one will be dead or alive?

23. The Master would never slander others or utter empty praise. Once when a village headman erected for himself a grand residence, however, the Master was heard to remark: "This is what it means when they say that being greedy makes you foolish."

24. Once the Master was ill with a cold, resting at the home of someone in Na'nokaichi.[24] The following morning, he awoke to find that a folding screen had been placed around his bed. The Master said: "No wonder I'm sick—they've put up a screen covered with Kōsai's[25] calligraphy!"

25. The things the Master hated were the calligraphy of calligraphers, the poems of poets, and thematic poetry contests.[26]

26. When anyone presented the Master with special calligraphy paper or poem cards[27] and asked for his calligraphy, he would simply write out Chinese or Japanese poems any way he pleased, with no rules governing the way in which he formed and arranged the characters. It was as if he was oblivious to the standards then in vogue for writing poetry.

27. At one time, the Master attended a formal tea ceremony, a so-called *koicha*.[28] The Master drained the entire tea bowl, then realized that another guest was sitting next to him. So he spit the tea back into the bowl and offered it to the man. The guest, praying for the Buddha's protection, drank the tea.

28. On the same occasion, the Master picked a piece of dried snot from his nose, and, trying not to attract any attention, went to place it beside him on his right. The guest there pulled back his sleeve in disgust. So the Master tried to place it on his left; but the guest there also recoiled. Realizing that he was stuck, the Master simply placed the snot back in his nose.

29. At one time, the Master traveled through a certain post station. As he passed by a brothel, a prostitute grabbed his sleeve and began to cry. The Master could not understand the reason for her behavior. It seems that when only a child, she had been sold and taken to this distant place, so that she never knew her parents and always thought longingly of them.[29] The night before, her father had visited her in a dream, and seeing the Master, she had mistaken him for her father. The Master himself told this story. I was very young and did not grasp all the details, but later heard the story from someone who knew.

30. The Master stopped to rest on top of a mountain. Without realizing it, he took the same road down again and proceeded to beg at a nearby house. Recognizing him, someone exclaimed: "Why, that's the same monk who was just here!" The Master was taken aback and fled home.

31. The Master stayed the night at the home of a certain Yamada in Yoita.[30] In the house was a screen decorated with a painting of an animal that the Master particularly liked. Once, seeing that no one was about, he placed himself in front of the painting, imitating the animal's

pose. Without being noticed, the lady of the house came and observed him. When the Master saw her, he asked: "Do you know what I'm doing?"

"Your Reverence is imitating the animal in the picture," she replied.

"My, you're smart!" the Master exclaimed in amazement. "But please don't tell anyone. I don't want to upset the servants!"

32. At midsummer, it was the local custom for everyone to dance through the night. It was as if people had all gone mad, and the Master loved it. He would wrap a towel around his head and, pretending to be a woman, mingle with the crowd and dance. One man recognized the Master and, standing near him, remarked: "What an attractive young woman! I wonder whose daughter she is."

When the Master overheard this, he was thrilled. He bragged to people: "Someone saw me and wanted to know whose daughter I was!"

33. When I went to visit the Master at his hut in Shimazaki, he measured the width of the opening of his iron tea kettle with a piece of straw and then went out, taking the straw with him. After a while, he returned carrying a bottle of sake, which he then placed inside the kettle and heated. The Master had calculated that unless the bottle was the right size to fit the opening of the kettle, he would not be able to warm the sake.

34. I asked the Master: "To learn about poetry, what work should I read?"

The Master told me: "You should read the *Man'yōshū*."[31]

"I can't understand the *Man'yōshū*," I said.

The Master replied: "Then just stick to whatever you *can* understand."

On another occasion, the Master said: "The *Kokinshū*[32] is relatively acceptable. But the poetry collections composed after that aren't worth reading at all."

35. The Master made an exhaustive study of Japanese phonetics, thoroughly mastering their essentials. In our province, the works of Motoori and Mabuchi[33] were unknown, so the Master was truly a pioneer. When I was young, I asked the Master about this, and he showed me the principles of declension. He would give the first declension, and then if the student could not come up with the rest, he would remain silent. Only when the student had truly mastered the principles

of grammar would he go on teaching him. How I regret that I was too young to grasp the essentials of the Master's instruction! Now I bitterly realize what I missed.

36. The Master said: "I spent an entire winter at my hut studying phonetics and mastered their true essence."

37. When the Master was at his hut on Mount Kugami, bamboo shoots sprouted in the outhouse. Using a candle, he tried to burn holes in the roof so the shoots could keep growing but ended by burning down the outhouse.

38. When the Master carried firewood on his back, he passed the rope that bound the wood under his crotch.[34]

39. Hearing people say, "It's such fun to find money!" the Master threw some of his own coins on the ground and tried picking them up. But it did not give him any pleasure. "They were just trying to trick me," he thought. After throwing his coins away like this several times, the Master finally forgot where he'd dropped them. Searching and searching, he found the coins, and then at last felt happy. "They weren't deceiving me after all!" he exclaimed.

40. In the local dialect, when the rice plants ripen, people say they *"bonaru."* Someone remarked: "The word *bonaru* means 'to roar.' " Having overheard this, the Master wanted to listen to the roaring of the rice and spent all night wandering through the fields.

41. In farming villages, after the autumn harvest, the unhulled rice was wrapped in straw bundles, which were hung from the rafters.[35] The rice would ferment slightly inside the straw, making it feel warm. The Master went back to his hut and tried hanging an empty straw bundle from his own rafter.

42. On summer evenings in the stables, the grooms would twist together bundles of straw and hang them from the rafters with rope. When the horses were bitten by mosquitoes, they would rub against the straw, and the mosquitoes would be driven off. Seeing these bundles, the Master asked what they were for and was told they were used for driving away mosquitoes. He promptly returned to his hut and hung one up himself.

43. The Master was caught in a downpour and took shelter from the rain beside a stone Jizō[36] equipped with a straw rainhat. A passerby recognized the Master and brought him to his house, where he asked

for a sample of his calligraphy. The Master then wrote out in large char-
acters twelve copies of the "Alphabet Song."[37]

44. A certain Manzō, owner of a confectionary in Niigata,[38] was
a great admirer of the Master's calligraphy and wanted the Master to
draw the characters for his shop sign. Carrying paper and brushes, he
pursued the Master and finally caught up with him at the house of a
certain person near the Jizōdō post station. Manzō pleaded so earnestly
that the Master finally agreed to do what he asked. Later that day, the
Master remarked to someone: "Today, I ran into disaster!"

This year, I passed through Niigata and noticed that the Master's
shop sign still hangs outside the confectionary. As the memories of that
time came rushing back, I found myself wandering alone from place to
place.

45. There was a thief who broke into the Master's hut at Kugami.
Finding nothing to steal, he pulled at the Master's sleeping mat,
attempting to remove it without waking him. Pretending to be asleep,
the Master rolled over, allowing the thief to pull the mat out from
under him and carry it off.

46. There was a certain doctor named Shōtei, who asked the
Master: "I want to be rich. How can I get more money?"

The Master told him: "Just be a good doctor and don't be
greedy."

47. On another occasion, when someone asked the same ques-
tion, the Master said: "If you borrow money, be sure to pay it back on
time."

48. The Master stayed several nights at our home. Young and old
became harmonious, and a peaceful atmosphere filled the house for
several days after his departure. Just one evening of talking with the
Master made us feel that our hearts had been purified. The Master
never held forth on the scriptures or classics or on the importance of
ethics. Sometimes he would be in the kitchen tending the fire, some-
times in the parlor practicing meditation. In his conversation he never
alluded to classical poetry or ethical teachings, and his manner was
indescribably casual and relaxed. It was just his own innate goodness
that naturally guided others.

49. The Master once spent the night in the home of a family
belonging to the Nichiren school.[39] When he began to recite a sūtra,

one of the members of the household tugged at his sleeve and demanded that he stop. When he told me this, the Master laughed.

50. The details of the Master's everyday life are fully revealed in his poems, so I have not had to repeat them here, recording only certain items of exceptional interest.

51. In the Master's entire life, there was nothing that could be considered miraculous or supernatural, apart from a single episode. Several days after the Master had died and been placed in his coffin, a nun arrived. Unable to bear her terrible grief, she begged to be allowed one last look at the Master, and finding it impossible to refuse her, they were finally obliged to open the coffin. The Master's posture was still perfectly erect, and his appearance dignified, just as if he were alive.

52. The Master exuded a divine energy, and his appearance was that of a hermit-immortal. He was tall and spare, with a prominent nose and shining eyes, warm and gentle, yet strict and fair, without any trace of sanctimoniousness. His lofty virtue was quite beyond my own limited vision. Now as I reflect on the Master's character, I find none to compare with him. Kameda Bōsai[40] said: "His like has not been seen since the priest Kisen.[41]"

53. The Master was given lodging for a certain period at Kanshōji,[42] in our village. Since I was too young, however, it was not possible for me to meet him at that time.

54. There was a haiku poet named Hajō,[43] who lamented the poor quality of his calligraphy. The Master chanced to hear of this and told him: "Don't be tormented by envy of others. Your own calligraphy will naturally perfect itself." From that time, Hajō found that his writing came more easily. This was told me by Hajō's disciple Jakusui.

55. The Master traveled on pilgrimage through other provinces before settling at Gogō-an on Mount Kugami and afterward in a hut in the same village in the precincts of the Otogo shrine. In old age, he went to live behind the Notoya[44] family home in Shimazaki. His reason was to escape the burdens of gathering firewood and drawing water.

56. In Tosa,[45] a traveler from Edo named Banjō[46] shared the Master's lodging for a night. Banjō's account of this experience is recorded in his writings.

57. The items I have recorded here were set down simply as they came to mind. They are not arranged in chronological order.

58. I do not know the reasons for the Master's originally becoming a Buddhist monk. I must ask the priest Henchō.[47]

59. Story of the bamboo shoot thief; essay on the precepts; discussions on waka and kanshi; episode of Kengi's folding screen; story of Master Bundai's question; poetry exchange with Bōsai; story of Suibara Kakusho.[48]

60. One day, the Master picked chrysanthemums from the garden of someone's home near the Yamada station. The owner, who was watching, accused the Master of being a flower thief. "However," he told the Master, "if you paint me a picture of this and add an inscription in your calligraphy, I'll let you off." The Master then took a brush and wrote: "Image of the Monk Ryōkan making off with a flower in the morning. In the expectation that it will be preserved for later generations. . . ."

61. This was the poem given Master Ryōkan by his master[49] and cherished by him all his life:

To the Hermitage-Master Ryōkan

Ryōkan! How nice to be like a fool
    for then one's Way is grand beyond measure
Free and easy, letting things take their course—
    who can fathom it?
I therefore entrust to you this staff of wild wisteria
Whenever you lean it against the wall
Let it bring the peace of a noonday nap

Kanshi (Poems in Chinese)

My Poems Aren't Poems

The first day of summer
I lazily pull on my robes
By the water's edge
    willows have turned a deep green
On the opposite bank
    peach and plum blossoms
    scatter in the morning breeze
I amble along, plucking blades of wild grass
And casually knock at a brushwood gate
Butterflies cavort in the garden in the south
Turnip flowers choke the bamboo fence in the east
Here, in an atmosphere of perfect ease
    the long summer days stretch endlessly
So remote a spot is naturally striking
Easily moved by beauty—such is my nature
I take a few phrases
    and they just turn into poems

Who says that my poems are poems?
My poems aren't poems at all
When you understand
   that my poems really aren't poems
Then we can talk poetry together

Inspiration

Shaving my head, becoming a monk
I spent years on the road
   pushing aside wild grasses
   peering hard into the wind
Now, everywhere I go
   people just hand me paper and brush:
"Do some calligraphy!" "Write me a poem!"

At Saitō's Country House

Five or six miles from town[1]
I fall in with a woodcutter
Green pines stand erect lining the roadside
From across the valley
    drifts the fragrance of wild plum blossoms
Coming here, it always seems as if I'm expected
The moment I set down my staff, I feel at home
In the old pond, fish are busily swimming
The forest is silent;
    the spring day stretches endlessly before me
What's in the house?
One long table piled with books of poetry
Utterly at ease, I loosen my belt and robes
And picking a few phrases, try to make up a poem[2]
At twilight when I step out the door for a stroll
Spring quail are startled into the air

The stone stairs are bright with fresh layers of moss
A breeze carries the aroma of cedar and pine
It seems the rains are over at last
I send one of the children to buy some country wine
And after I'm drunk, toss off a few lines of calligraphy

Midwinter, the eleventh month
The season for wet, heavy snow
A thousand peaks, a single hue
Myriad paths with scarcely a traveler
Yesterday's wanderings seem like a dream
Deep in retreat in my thatch hut
All night long I burn pieces of roots
And quietly read the poems of long ago

I love the remoteness of this place
And taking my staff, traveled straight here
A cold sky, between the eighth and ninth months
A garden grove after the rains
The dog remembers me from last year
On the eastern fence, autumn arrives
    with flowering chrysanthemums
The people here are plain, like those long ago
So secluded a spot is serene of itself
In the house, what does one find?
Books of poetry and prose covering the floor
By nature I shun the clamor of the world
When I come here to visit, I like to stay
The mind of poetry, the mind of Zen
Come together effortlessly

*   *   *

With My Begging Bowl

Begging

When the spring weather begins to turn pleasant
I take my staff and walk east into town
In the gardens, the willows are tinged deep green
Duckweed drifts on the surface of ponds
From my begging bowl comes the aroma of rice
    the offerings of a thousand homes
My heart has forsaken splendor and glory
Following the path of the buddhas of old
I beg my way from door to door

On the first day of the eighth month
I go into town to beg
At dawn, the doors of a thousand homes are flung open
The smoke of a myriad hearths slants through the air
Last night's rain has washed the road clean
And an autumn wind rustles the rings on my staff[3]
I take my time begging
The universe is vast without end

Shelter from the Rain

Today, out begging, I'm caught in a shower
And take shelter for a while inside an old shrine
Laugh at me if you will, caught like this
    with nothing but a water bottle and begging bowl
But mine is a life of poetry
    with worldly cares all left behind

The warbler sings so tranquilly
The spring day stretches lazily on
I sit and meditate inside
But the mind of spring naturally won't stay still
So I take my begging bag and staff
And set off carefree down the road[4]

Begging, I arrive at your house
In the refreshing cool of early autumn
The garden is sparse
    with spiny chestnut burrs scattered about
In the chilly air, the cicadas' voices are stilled
My nature is to be free of attachment
Whatever I do, my thoughts are at ease
I sit and read the *Lotus Sūtra*[5]
Rolling and unrolling its eight scrolls
    which I keep always by my seat

My makeshift hut stands beside the Kannon temple[6]
A thousand green trees my only companions
Now and then I put on my robe
    take my bowl and go into town
I walk all over, begging for food
And offer it respectfully to myself!

Empty Bowl

Clear skies ring with the honk of wild geese
On deserted hills, leaves whirl in the wind
Twilight on a smoky village road
Carrying an empty begging bowl and walking home alone

Will my stupidity and stubbornness ever end?
Poor and alone—that's my life
Twilight on the streets of a ramshackle town
Going home again with an empty bowl

At daybreak, I take my staff
And go into town to beg
The town is no longer as it was
Hills and ponds seem to have changed
My face is lashed by a bitter wind
    harsh with the frost's lingering chill
My begging bag weighs on my aged shoulders
I walk past the places where I used to play
But all I find is pines and cedars
    locked in icy mist

One begging bowl holds the rice of a thousand homes
A thin robe, and my whole body feels light
Having eaten my fill, what's left for me to do?
Grow old in the great peace, soaring calm and free

All day I gaze on smoky villages
Walking and walking, begging as I go
Night falls, and the long mountain road stretches before me
The wind bitter enough to tear out your whiskers
My threadbare robe trembles like swirling fog[7]
My wooden begging bowl grows
    ever stranger with age
I've never minded hardship, hunger, and cold
Such has always been the lot of people like me

How many years since I came to this place?
How many changes have there been?
When I see people now, I don't know who they are
And they don't know me
To them, I'm just another beggar at the crossroads

On the first day of the eighth month
I go into town to beg
White clouds follow my spirited footsteps
And an autumn wind rustles the rings on my staff
At the crack of dawn
    the doors of a thousand homes are flung open
Noon finds me at the edge of town
    passing among banana plants and bamboo
I wander freely, east or west
A wine shop, a fish shop—what difference does it make?
By looking at things squarely, I can make even
    the Mountain of Swords[8] crumble to dust
By just taking a stroll, I can dry up the
    boiling cauldron of hell[9]
The Buddha himself taught this
Transmitting it directly to Mahākāshyapa[10]
And since then it's been handed down
    for over twenty-seven hundred years
I, too, am a follower of Shākyamuni[11]
And revel in the simple majesty of a single robe and bowl
Don't you see? Vimalakīrti said:
"One who is impartial, receiving food of any sort
Has realized the impartiality of Dharma"[12]
You must grasp this directly for yourself
Otherwise you'll spend donkey's years
    just mired in the same old rut

Autumn Twilight

What quiet loneliness fills the autumn air!
As I lean on my staff, the wind turns cold
A solitary village lies shrouded in mist
By a country bridge, a figure passes
    bound for home
An old crow comes to roost in the ancient forest
Lines of wild geese slant toward the horizon
Only a monk in black robes remains
Standing motionless before the river at twilight

*   *   *

In My Hut

A Visit from Chikukyū Rojin

The cicadas buzzing in the treetops
The stream cascading down the ravine
The rain last night that left the air
    cleansed of every speck of dust
Don't say my hut has nothing to offer
Come and I will share with you
The cool breeze that fills my window[13]

Gogō-an

It's plain and simple, Gogō-an[14]
Inside, a room that's utterly bare
Beyond the door, a forest of cedars
A few sūtra hymns[15] are placed on the walls
The rice pot often gathers dust
The steamer simply sits unused[16]
Only the old man from the village to the east
Now and then knocks at my door in the moonlight[17]

The days and months move on, and now as
    the year draws to a close
Heaven sends down a chastening frost
Across a thousand hills, trees stand bare
On myriad paths, scarcely a traveler
I burn dried leaves
The long night passes, broken
    now and then by the sounds
    of wind and rain
As I think back, everything gone by
Is just a picture in a dream

The end of the year
The whole world reels
   with the hustle and bustle of delivering gifts[18]
Only my thatch hut remains peaceful and calm
What kind of thanks can I offer the Buddha?
One stick of incense, one period of meditation

As a child, I studied literature
   but lacked the desire to become a scholar
As a young man, I studied Zen
   but never passed the teaching on
Now I live in a thatch hut
   and serve as caretaker of a Shinto shrine[19]
I'm part shrine priest, part Buddhist monk

I make my home deep in the forest
With each passing year, the green creepers advance
Here, no worldly troubles intrude
Now and then I hear a woodcutter singing
Basking in the sun, I mend my robes
Gazing at the moon, I recite hymns
A word to you who practice the Way:
Those who find the meaning of Mind are few

It's quiet, my little three-mat hut
The whole day long not a soul to be seen
I sit and meditate by my lonely window
The only sound, the endlessly falling leaves

How long has it been since I came to this place?
With no one to tend them, the grounds have run wild
My begging bag and bowl just sit gathering dust
A solitary lantern lights the bare walls
Evening rain patters on my lonely door
Every detail is complete
Ah! What else is there that I need?[20]

A riot of fallen petals covers the deserted stairs
The songs of lovely birds
    mingle in a gorgeous brocade
Soft and languid, sunlight pours through my window
A slender column of smoke
    floats above the open hearth

Raindrops on the Banana Leaves

When you're old and decrepit
    the slightest thing wakes you
My lamp flickers, an evening shower passes
I smooth my pillow and, in silence
    listen to the rainwater
    falling through the banana leaves
With whom can I share the feeling of this moment?

Impromptu Verse

This poem is said to have been written to Ryōkan's prized buddha
statue, a small stone image of the bodhisattva Jizō, which, accord-
ing to legend, Ryōkan used as a pillow when he napped. The statue,
known as the "Pillow Jizō," is still preserved at the Ryōkan Museum
in Izumozaki.

We sit face to face, and you don't say a word
Yet your silence reveals the timeless essence of things
Open books lie strewn about the floor
And just beyond the bamboo shade
   a gentle rain soaks the flowering plum

In my thatch hut, with nothing but the four bare walls
Relying on others, I live out my remaining years
Sometimes an old friend comes to stay
And we sit up together listening
   to the music of the bell-ring insects[21]

Green mountains on every side
White clouds to the east and west
Even if a traveler passed right by
He'd never know anyone was here

Looking back over these fifty years and more
Good-and-bad, gain-and-loss
    are only a dream
Toward midnight in my mountain home
    the early summer rain
Falls quietly outside my lonely window

Rising from My Sickbed

Alone and ill, I was confined to bed
But my dreams kept returning to my old haunts
This morning, at last, I managed to rise and
    stand beside the river
An endless trail of peach petals
    drifting down the stream

All spring I lie ill and alone in my hut
A visitor comes and asks for calligraphy
In my thoughts, it's last year's spring
Playing with the children
    at the Hachiman shrine
Not even noticing the sun go down

Who is there to pity this life of mine?
A pepper tree props up the brushwood gate
Mugwort obliterates the narrow garden path
On my bamboo fence dangles a solitary gourd
Across the valley
    I hear the sounds of trees being felled
And spend the clear morning
    with my head on the pillow
A mountain bird trills a few notes as it passes
As if trying to console me in my solitude

Lying alone and ill in my hut
All day long I don't see a soul
My bowl in its bag is left to hang on the wall
My staff just sits and gathers dust
My dreams go rambling through
     mountains and fields
My heart goes back to the village to play
And there I find all the children on the street
Just as always, waiting for me

There were problems where I used to be
So I've come back to this ramshackle town[22]
By day I suffer the pranks of troublesome kids
At night I endure the neighbors' racket
My room is empty, completely bare
The hearth has been cold for who knows how long
Enough! Why go on complaining like this?
Everything is just cause and effect

A Thief Visits

Making off with the backrest[23] and cushion
A thief has struck my tumbledown hut
How can I refuse him?
All night, by the window
    I sit alone in the stillness
The drip-drip of fine rain
    filling the forest of bamboo

After begging all day
I come back home and close the brushwood gate
In my hearth I build a fire
    of branches still covered with leaves
And quietly recite the poems of Han-shan[24]
A wind from the west brings an evening squall
Driving the rain, which softly brushes the thatch roof
At times like this
    I lie down and stretch out my legs
What is there to worry about
    what is there to trouble me?

My dwelling stands on the slopes of Mount Kugami
I subsist on the coarsest tea, the plainest food
A Zen monk at the end of his days, dogged by bad luck
The only people I see are those
    who come gathering leaves in the empty forest

In my cold hearth
    I poke at the deep-piled ash
My single light has finally burned out
In perfect silence
    midnight comes and goes
Through the walls
    the sound of the distant valley stream

The sun goes down
    and a freezing wind tears through my robe
The forest is bare, stripped of leaves
The chrysanthemums nearly gone
But the faithful bamboo outside my window
Remains forever pure and green
Waiting for me when I return

Impromptu Verse

How cold the hearts of men have grown!
I don't know where I can live
Last night in the village below
They were beating and beating the warning drum
A mob of bandits, I heard
    had broken into people's homes

Late spring, with its darkness and showers
My robes become clammy and never dry out
The path is overrun with mugwort
Wisteria bores through the bamboo fence
My tongue is still there, but it's heavy as a hammer
Completely forgotten, the gate just stays locked
All day, beneath the thatch eaves of my hut
I sit and meditate alone, prey to gloomy thoughts

Impromptu

In my hut, toward midnight, the rain has stopped
As I return from my dreams
A solitary lamp shines quietly in the room
Outside, the plop-plop of rainwater dripping from leaves
Against the wall, my old staff
    displays its hidden ridges and furrows
The hearth is cold, there's no more charcoal
    but whom have I to entertain?
Books lie on my bare floor
    but I'm not even tempted to stretch out my hand
The flavor of this night is known only to me
Hours later, days later
    how can it ever be described?

In Answer to Your Poem on My Broken Wooden Bowl

Ryōkan's literary friend Harada Jakusai (1763–1827) composed a poem titled "To Dharma Master Ryōkan's Broken Wooden Bowl," in which he gently teases the impoverished Ryōkan for having come into possession of an apparently fine, albeit damaged, objet d'art. What follows is Ryōkan's reply.

One fine morning I went for a stroll
Hitching up my robes
   and tramping over the eastern hills
I found it, poking about with my staff
   in a dense thicket of bamboo
Then carried it down to the valley with me
   to wash in the clear spring
I use it for burning incense
I fill it with my morning gruel
In it, I prepare my meals
   and serve my dinner at night
It may not be in prime condition
Yet anyone can tell, it is a work of quality

When young, I abandoned worldly learning
Determined to follow the Buddha's path
With only my water bottle[25] and begging bowl
I wandered on pilgrimage, as spring followed spring
Finally I came home to the shadow of the mountain
And quietly laid out my simple retreat
The songs of the birds are my music
The passing clouds, my next-door neighbors
At the foot of the cliff is a crystalline spring
    where I can go to wash my robes
On the rocky summit are cedars and pines
    which keep me supplied with firewood
Free and easy, free and easy—
Thus I make these days go on and on

*   *   *

Playing with the Children

Early spring
The landscape is tinged with the first
    fresh hints of green
Now I take my wooden begging bowl
And wander carefree through town
The moment the children see me
They scamper off gleefully to bring their friends
They're waiting for me at the temple gate
Tugging from all sides so I can barely walk
I leave my bowl on a white rock
Hang my pilgrim's bag on a pine tree branch
First we duel with blades of grass
Then we play ball[26]
While I bounce the ball, they sing the song
Then I sing the song and they bounce the ball
Caught up in the excitement of the game
We forget completely about the time
Passersby turn and question me:
"Why are you carrying on like this?"
I just shake my head without answering
Even if I were able to say something
    how could I explain?
Do you really want to know the meaning of it all?
This is it! This is it!

Having finished begging in the middle of town
I stroll over toward the Hachiman[27] shrine
When they see me, the children call to each other:
"The crazy monk from last year is back!"

Dueling Grasses

Here I am with the children again
 tugging at looped blades of grass[28]
Over and over, a hundred times
The harder we play, the more absorbed we grow
At dusk the townsfolk have all gone home
And a solitary moon, round and bright
Rules the pristine autumn

The Ball

In my sleeve is a ball of colored silk thread
    worth a thousand pieces of gold
I'm a great player—the best there is!
Do you want to know my secret?
It's this:
One! two! three! four! five! six! seven![29]

My lower robe is too short, my upper robe too long
But my stride is high-spirited and energetic
The moment the children in the street see me
They clap their hands and, all together,
    break into the ball-playing song

Retiring and awkward, careless and lazy
I lack what it takes to succeed in this world
My begging bowl comes with me wherever I go
My begging bag, too, makes a perfect companion
Arriving here at the temple gate
I run into the children
There's nothing like this life of mine
Just passing the days, soaring calm and free

Hair wild and unkempt, ears sticking out
My threadbare robe trembles like swirling fog
At twilight I make my way home from town
As the children tug at me from every side

Every day, day after day
I spend at my ease playing with the children
In the sleeves of my robe, two or three balls
A useless fellow, yes
But I know how to make myself drunk
   sipping my fill of the peaceful springtime

*   *   *

Mountains and Mists

No bird flies past these distant peaks
The deserted garden fills
   with steadily falling leaves
Standing in the lonely autumn wind
A solitary figure in a black robe

Don't envy me living apart from the world of men
If you're content, you'll naturally be at peace
Who can say that amid the green hills
Are not lurking the wolves and tigers of the mind?[30]

Early Autumn Composition

All night the tumbledown village
    was drenched by rain
And this morning the oppressive heat
    is gone from my hut
Through my window are the green hills
    freshly cut jade
Beyond my door the river unwinds
    a glistening ribbon of stretched silk
The burbling of the pure spring beneath
    the cliff cleanses my ears
In the treetops, the song of the last cicadas
    punctuates the autumn stillness
My monk's staff is ready—let's go for a stroll!
From here on, nature will be at her loveliest

Carrying firewood on my shoulders, I descend the
    mountain's green-forested slopes
The path down the hillside is rugged and steep
From time to time I stop to rest
    in the shade of a soaring pine
And quietly listen to the songs of spring birds

Departing Spring

As spring draws to a close
    fragrant grasses grow rank
Scattered peach blossoms drift lazily
    on the surface of the stream
I've always been innocent of the wiles of men
Nature's beauties still sweep me off my feet

Turning and gazing from the summit of Mount Kugami
A half-set sun lingers in the frozen sky
Can that blue-green patch of shadow be the place
Where yesterday I was drawing water, picking berries?

Seated in meditation on a flat rock
Chin held erect, I gaze across
   banks of mist and cloud
A pagoda glistens in the morning sun
Below lies the well of the Dragon King
   whose waters can cleanse
   the face of the mind
Above stand pines a thousand years old
   whose whispers all day
   are carried on the refreshing breeze
Who will forsake the cares of the world
And linger here with me?

A solitary path among myriad trees
A thousand hilltops wrapped in fog
It's not yet autumn, but already here
   leaves have begun to fall
It hasn't rained
   but the boulders are always wet
Carrying my basket, I go hunting for mushrooms
Or fill my water bottle at a spring
   that bubbles from between the rocks
No one ever finds this place
Only those who've lost their way

Outside a woven bamboo fence linger a few stalks
    of yellow chrysanthemums
Winter crows flutter
    among the bare limbs of soaring forests
A thousand peaks, ten thousand hills
    bathe in the light of the setting sun
I pack up my bowl
    and follow the river valley home

*   *   *

Wandering

With grass for my pillow
I bed down in an open field
The only sound
    the shriek of a bird of prey
Kings, commoners—
Just fragments of an evening's dreams

On my journey home, I had come as far as the Itoi River,[31] when I fell ill and had to stay the night at a certain home. As I listened to the rain, I suddenly felt a shiver run down my spine and composed this poem.

A robe and bowl are everything I have in the world
Forcing my ailing body on, I burn incense
    and sit in meditation
All night, a gentle rain fills the darkness outside
My long years of hard travel are over at last

It's two or three years since I left and went away
Now I've come back to Otogo shrine[32]
But there's something I want you to understand:
My travels haven't changed me a bit
My eyeballs are still where they were before—
    right underneath my eyebrows

On the road to Mount Kōya,[33] I want to buy a new robe, but can't
come up with the money

I don't shrink from making a distant journey with
    only my water bottle and begging bowl
But my robe has become so desperately worn
    it's almost like wearing nothing at all
I know I haven't a thing in my purse
And all because nature's beauties led me astray!

Coral grows in southern seas
Purple mushrooms sprout on northern peaks
Everything has its natural place
It's always been so, it's not just today
In the vigor of youth, swinging my staff
I tramped across a thousand miles
Knocking at the doors of countless teachers
How many years wandering place to place?
I was determined to spread the Buddha's teaching
Even at the risk of losing my life
But I can't keep up with the advancing years
Enough! Why go on complaining?
I've come home to live in
    the shadow of the mountain
And harvest the bracken for my meals

In this back alley, lined with dreary huts
I sit up all evening with an old woman
    chanting the *nenbutsu*[34]
Don't think it's only a penniless monk
    looking for somewhere to spend the night
We're all just traveling through this world—
    and how long, really, can we stay?

When I was young, I abandoned my father
    and ran off to other domains
I struggled hard to paint a tiger
But couldn't even come up with a cat
If anyone asks about my realization, I'll say:
"Just the same old Eizō."[35]

Delayed by Showers on the Road to Ise:
Two Poems

I

Already twelve days since I left Kyoto
And not one day it hasn't poured
How can I help feeling concerned?
Even the wild goose must be dragging its wings
Blushing peach blossoms droop lower and lower
At daybreak, ferrymen abandon their crossings
Travelers at dusk find the paths washed away
My journey isn't even halfway done
I think of how far I still must go
    and anxiously knit my brows
Autumn last year, the wind
    blew without stop for three days
Strewing great trees by the sides of the road
Tossing thatch roofs into the air
As a result, the price of rice soared
And this spring, it's the same again
If things keep going on this way
How in the world can people live?

II

Staying the night at a deserted temple
My solitary lamp
    summons up thoughts of icy misery
How will I dry my traveling robes?
Reciting lines of poetry
    puts me somewhat more at ease
But all night the sound of rain fills my ears
And keeps me tossing on the pillow till dawn

Arriving at Entsūji,[36] I see the temple signboard forbidding liquor[37]
and thereupon compose a poem to present to Master Shakuan
Soun[38]

Seven years I've been gone
And I find the temple water clock
    dry and half-rotted away[39]
These days, it seems, no one here has
    any feeling for a drunk
So I'll just pay my respects at the altar
And remember the way things used to be
    when the old master sat in his chair

On the Road to Yonezawa

Lines of wild geese fly screeching southward
I turn and look back
An unbearable melancholy
    suffuses the autumn landscape
Wind and rain have stripped the mountains bare
A lonely village huddles in the evening sun[40]

Night's Lodging at Tamagawa Station

Late autumn with its cold, stormy winds[41]
And the traveler frets over the hardships of the road
Through the long night, time and again
    I'm startled from my dreams
Mistaking the sound of the river
    for pouring rain[42]

I lived here once in quiet retreat
And now, without intending to, I've come back
    wandering alone
The latticework fence has fallen in
    making a pathway for rabbits and foxes
The well has long since run dry
    nearly overgrown by tall bamboo
Across the window where I'd sit and read
    a spider has come to stretch its web
The seat where I'd practice meditation
    is covered by a blanket of dust
Autumn weeds bury the garden steps
Underfoot, a cricket chirps up at me
I linger aimlessly
    unable to bring myself to leave
Shivering as I watch the sun go down

Night's Lodging

Staying the night at an old temple
All evening I gaze out the lonely window
It's too cold to sleep
I sit in meditation and wait for the gong at dawn

Admiring the Midautumn Moon

This evening the moon shines, pure and white
A magpie shrieks and shrieks in alarm
The lonely sound makes me think of home
But where, oh where, can I return?

Two Nights' Lodging

Shivering in the autumn wind
I find shelter for two nights
    in a pious home[43]
One robe and one bowl
This is my life, simple and pure

Visiting Matsuno-o

I arrive here early in the ninth month[44]
Geese honk in soaring autumn skies
The chrysanthemums are in full bloom
Young and old go strolling together
        then depart
Leaving the pine forest
        stretching for miles, undisturbed

*   *   *

Meditations

Finished begging my food in a ramshackle town
I return to my home among the green hills
The evening sun drops behind the western peaks
A pale moon lights the stream that runs by my door
I wash my feet, climb onto a rock
Burn incense and sit in meditation
I am, after all, a Buddhist monk
How can I let the years just drift uselessly by?

A rain-filled sky
    mountains and forests blurred in mist
Then the fog clears, clouds and haze vanish
    no one knows where
On the surface of the swollen stream
    water birds bob playfully
I'm going for a walk through the gorges
    and do some meditation

How many years I spent parting the wild grasses
    to penetrate the inmost depths
Then suddenly I understood my teacher
    and came back to my native place
You go there and come back again
Yet everything remains the same
Clouds covering the mountain's summit
Streams flowing by at your feet

Yesterday was different from today
Tomorrow morning will be different
   from this morning
The mind responds according to its past karma
But this changes, too
   as new things come along
So if you know the problem
   better correct it at once
No matter how right it seems
As soon as you attach to something
   truth disappears
Can you wait and watch by the same old stump
   till your hair turns white with age?[45]

Looking back over these seventy years and more
The human world of good-and-bad
   completely dissolves before my gaze
A late-night snowfall blurs
   the footsteps of the last passersby
I light a stick of incense
   and sit and meditate beside my old window

Walking along
    I followed the drifting stream to its source
But reaching the headwaters left me stunned
That's when I realized that the true source
    isn't a particular place you can reach
So now, wherever my staff sets down
I just play in the current's eddies and swirls

I close my eyes as darkness falls across
    a thousand peaks
And the countless woes of human life grow empty
Resolute, I sit cross-legged in meditation
A silent figure before a lonely window
In the long, black night
    the incense stick has burned away
And a layer of frosty dew settled on my thin robe
I get up from meditation
    and take a stroll around the garden
To find the full moon of autumn risen to its zenith

After two or three years wandering
     over foggy seas and cloud-capped peaks
Today I've returned to my old shrine[46]
Well, you may ask
     now that you're back
Give us a verse to express your thoughts
"I hang the tip of my staff on the moon
The ground feels light beneath my feet"

Through the still night
     in my tumbledown hut
I practice meditation draped in my robe
Navel and nostrils in a line
Ears directly over the shoulders[47]
My window brightens, the moon appears
The rain has stopped
     yet water keeps dripping everywhere
This precious moment
     permeated by silence
Something known to me alone

Hired Laborer

My home is in a ramshackle village
    four walls that can barely stand
My days are spent toiling here and there
    a hired laborer[48]
I think back over my years of traveling
    on pilgrimage
Fired with determination
    spirits soaring to the skies—
Ah, what a diligent fellow I was!

Because of the finger
    you can point to the moon[49]
Because of the moon
    you can understand the finger
The moon and the finger
Are neither different nor the same
This parable is used only
To lead students to enlightenment
Once you've really seen things as they are
There's no more moon, no more finger

Even if you've read through countless books
You're better off sticking to a single phrase
If anyone asks which one, tell him:
"Know your own mind just as it is"[50]

A thousand peaks locked in freezing cloud[51]
Myriad paths without a single traveler
Each day I just sit in meditation
Now and then hearing the snow
    softly drift against my window

I want to ask you: in this whole world
What is the most profound
    most wonderful thing?
Sit erect and meditate right to the end
As you meditate, you'll find a clue
And everything will naturally become clear
Keep your concentration
    don't miss your chance
After a while, your mind will be pure
    your wisdom ripe
Then you won't have to fool yourself any more

I remember how it was when I was young
The terrible hardship just staying alive
In search of clothing and food
I tramped hopelessly from shabby town to town
Till on the road I found a man of wisdom
Who explained things to me through and through
Then I saw that all along
    the precious jewel was in my robe[52]
That jewel is with me here, right now
Having found it, I've gone into business for myself
Traveling all over with my wares, exactly as I please

Rainy Night

Worldly success is fickle as a cloud
Over fifty years
    I've spent living in a dream
In my hut the whisper of gentle rain
    fills the night
Quietly I put on my black robe
    and settle myself by the lonely window

This staff of mine
Has been passed down through
   no one knows how many generations
Its surface has long since worn away
Leaving only the hard inner core
Once I used it to test the waters' depths
As together we faced countless dangers
But now it rests against the eastern wall
Letting the years drift idly by

Delusion and enlightenment
   two sides of a coin
Universal and particular
   just parts of one whole
All day I read the wordless scriptures
All night I practice no-practice meditation
On the riverbank, a bush warbler
   sings in the weeping willow
In the sleeping village, a dog bays at the moon
Nothing troubles the free flow of my feelings
But how can this mind be passed on?

Impromptu

Alas, those who practice Buddhism nowadays
Grow old and decrepit fussing over words
What use are all their years of idle speculation?
Isn't the aim of our school
    to directly realize things as they are?
Neither delusion nor enlightenment obtain
    in the land of nonarising
In what aeon will you ever
    find original nothingness?
If you don't understand, then ask!
My answer is: "Mañjushrī's home
    in the east of the castle of enlightenment"[53]

The sun sets, and all living things cease to stir
I, too, close my brushwood gate
A few crickets begin to chirp
The color of grasses and trees has faded
Burning stick after stick of incense
    I meditate through the long autumn night
When my body gets cold, I put on more clothes
Practice hard, fellow students of Zen!
Time is gone before you realize

How can a true monk spend his days in idleness?
Shouldering my water bottle
   I left my first teacher
Spirited and determined, abandoned
   my native place
By day, I scaled the summits of lonely peaks
Nightfall found me ploughing
   the waters of murky seas
I swore that unless I reached my goal
I'd never give up, as long as I live!

Everyone eats rice[54]
Yet no one knows why
When I say this now
People laugh at me
But instead of laughing along with them
You ought to step back
   and give it some thought
Think it over, and don't let up
I guarantee the time will come
When you'll really have something worth laughing at

Everyone eats rice
Yet no one knows why
When I say this now
People laugh at me
But instead of laughing along with them
You'd better just stop fooling yourselves
Stop fooling yourselves and then you'll know
Just how wonderful my words are!

Everyone eats rice
Yet no one knows why
When I say this now
People laugh at me
If they laugh, that's just fine
Laughing is something I like, too!
Laughing and laughing, we won't stop
We'll welcome Maitreya[55] here and now

In the daytime I go into town to beg
At night I return to the shadow
    of the mountain and practice meditation
One robe, one bowl—a life of solitary freedom
Ah, how precious the stream that flows
    from the land of the Western Skies![56]

Buddha is a conception of your mind
The Way isn't anything that is made
Now that I've told you this
    take it to heart
Don't let yourself be misled
If to reach Yüeh[57] you point your cart north
When can you ever hope to arrive?

How many winters and springs have passed
   since my days at Entsūji?[58]
Outside the temple gate lay
   a city of a thousand homes
Yet I didn't know a single soul
When our robes got dirty, we washed them ourselves
When our food ran out, we went into town
I once read in the *Record of Eminent Priests:*[59]
A monk should live a pure and simple life

One day, by a stroke of luck, I penetrated
   my master's path
Suddenly I took a giant leap, and that was
   good-bye to temple life
Enough of their rice! No more numbing routine!
   Ah, how happy I feel!
The twenty-eight Indian
   and six Chinese patriarchs[60]—
They're all of them here, right at my side!

Kannon: Two Verses

I

Having so long forsaken the Pure Land[61]
You've immersed yourself
   in the world of defilement
Meeting a tree, you're a tree
Meeting a bamboo, you're a bamboo
You give yourself completely
   spring after spring, for aeons and aeons
The golden lotus beneath your feet
   is soaked in the mire of sentient life
The jeweled crown upon your head
   collects the dusts of the world
Long ago at the Laṅkāvatāra Assembly[62]
The Buddha had Mañjushrī rank
   all the bodhisattvas, and among
Those twenty-five eminent bodhisattvas
You alone were singled out for praise
I now prostrate myself in devotion
May you have pity upon us and embrace us
   O savior of the world!

II

The wind has stopped
   and still a blossom falls
A bird sings
   and the hills grow yet more silent
The power of Kannon's marvelous wisdom:
Ah!

All these monks traveling on pilgrimage—
    what a pitiful lot!
Unless you've studied at the great temples[63]
    they say
You can't call yourself a real Zen monk
That's why students leave their original teachers
Grab their staffs and take to the road
    wandering from place to place
Summer at one temple, winter at another
They spend their whole lives idly parroting masters
But meet one of these monks
    surprise him with a question
And he's just as pitiful as he was at the start!

Of the twelve divisions of the Buddha's teachings[64]
Each and every one embodies the pure truth
As the east wind carries with it a night of rain
That brings fresh life to all the forest
There is not one of the teachings of the Buddha
    that does not deliver sentient beings
Not a single flowering branch
    that does not proclaim the arrival of spring
So grasp their underlying meaning
Don't waste your time trying to decide
Which sūtras are the most authentic
    the least authentic

Troubled and confused is life in the three worlds[65]
It's not just the way things are today
Things have always been like this
Because you fail to realize the truth
You spend a lifetime chasing about
Reading the Buddhist scriptures, you become
    caught up in names and forms
    and never return
Practicing Zen, you become attached to nirvāṇa
    and end by being mired there
It reminds me of Master Tung-shan's apt words:
"The moment you set foot outside the gate
Grasses are sprouting everywhere"[66]

Reading the Eihei Record

Late on a spring night,
   with the world covered in darkness
A gentle rain mingles with the snow
   trickling through the bamboo in my garden
I try to assuage my loneliness
   but nothing seems to help
In the gloom I fumble for the *Eihei Record*[67]
And burning incense and lighting a candle
   quietly begin to read
Each word, each phrase is a priceless gem
Years ago, at Entsūji in Tamashima
I recall how my late teacher[68] instructed me
   in the Eye of True Enlightenment[69]
At that time, I already had
   some experience of awakening
And therefore asked to read the *Record*
   under my teacher's personal guidance
That was when I saw that till then
   I'd just been wasting my time
Afterward, I left my teacher
   setting off on pilgrimage
Ah, what mysterious affinity
   joins me with the *Eihei Record?*
Why is it, wherever I turn, I meet
   the Eye of True Enlightenment?
I've read it over and over
   I don't know how many times
But in it there's scarcely a thing one could fault
Having studied under teachers of every school

In the end I came back to the *Eihei Record*
    finding myself at one with its words
Alas, what can be done?
Everywhere today confusion reigns
People can't tell a rock from a jewel
For five hundred years, it's been gathering dust
Because no one has eyes to discern the truth
For whom was this monumental work proclaimed?
I'm consumed with longing for the past
    racked with despair for the present age
All night I sit before my lamp
Crying and crying
    till the Eihei Record of the ancient buddhas
    ends up soaked completely through
Next day, the old man who's my neighbor comes to visit
"Why are these volumes all wet?" he asks
I try to tell him, but I can't, and it tears at my heart
It tears at my heart, but I just can't explain
For a while I bow my head in silence
    searching for the right words
Finally I say:
"Last night the rain came in and soaked all my books"

On an Autumn Night, at Play with the Moon

Every season has its moon
But this is the moon that I prize above all
Mountains in autumn soar, waters are limpid
In a cloudless sky stretching ten thousand leagues
    spins a solitary mirror
Originally its brightness does not exist
    nor do the objects it illumines
When brightness and objects are both forgotten
Who is it that remains?
In the chill autumn air
    the heavens seem boundless
I take my staff
    and roam the mountains' green-forested slopes
Everywhere I look, the world is vast, clear
    without a trace of dust
I see only the autumn moon
    growing in brightness
Who is it tonight watching this moon?
Who is the autumn moon shining upon?
Autumn after autumn it goes on shining
Men stand before it and stare
    yet enlightenment passes them by
The Buddha's sermon on the Vulture Peak
    the Sixth Patriarch's pointing to the mind
All these reveal the wonders of moonlight[70]
Immersed in my poem beneath the moon
    the night has deepened
In every eddy of the deep-flowing stream
    the moon appears
        as if in a forest of dewdrops

Somewhere the heart of a traveler
    fills with autumn melancholy
Somewhere a garden's hills and ponds
    lie flooded in moonlight
Don't you recall that evening long ago
    when Kiang-hsi,[71] admiring the moon
Declared that P'u-yüan alone had returned
    to the transcendental world?
Don't you remember Yüeh-shan's[72] great laughter
    exploding on the summit of the mountain?
From that moment, the fame of these men
    spread through the land
Their renown will endure for ages to come
Yet in vain does the moon let ordinary passersby
    gaze on its endless waxing and waning
I, too, have long been enraptured
    by these ancient truths
And here, tonight, at play with the moon
The tears fall and dampen my robe

How many times since I came to this place
Have I seen the leaves green and then gold?
Wrapped by vines, the old trees have turned dark
The bamboo have grown tall
    even in the valley's shade
My staff has rotted from the night rain
My robe frayed from the years of wind and frost
In the vast silence of the universe
For whom do I meditate each morning and night?[73]

*   *   *

Neighbors and Friends

Traveling, I come to a rustic home
Just as dusk begins to fall
Sparrows gather in the groves of bamboo
Chirping as they dart one past the other
The old farmer returning from the fields
Greets me like a long-lost friend
He calls his wife to strain some cloudy wine[74]
Picks some greens and lays them out, too
We sit and pour each other drink after drink
Talking and laughing as one—what a marvelous time!
Together we get happily drunk
Until we no longer care

Midwinter, the eleventh month
A cool dawn swallows clouds and mists
The morning sun climbs the green hills
Its rays glinting on lofty towers
Children play beside the gate
Sparrows chatter at the edge of the eaves
I burn some incense in my censer
Sit in meditation and find myself
    thinking of old friends
I reach for my staff. Where shall I go?
My thoughts drift back across the long years

The sūtra scroll falls from your hands
Your head droops, you begin to doze
On my meditation cushion
    I sit and study the old patriarch[75]
Now far off, now close at hand
    the ceaseless croaking of frogs
Behind the rough bamboo shade
    my lamp flickers on and off

Insects buzz noisily in the grass
Bonfires light up the entire landscape
People pass the long autumn night
    seated around brushwood fires
Weaving straw mats and preparing for spring
The whole family gathers in a cozy circle and chats
No squabbles here over who's right and who's wrong
How different from the officials in the towns—
Wasting their lives
    bowing and scraping before the mighty!

Autumn Poem

At the year's end, I moved to this temporary retreat
On the outskirts of a ramshackle town
In the soft, cold rain
Fallen leaves have buried the deserted steps
I page intently through the scriptures
Or recite my own poetry
And now, suddenly, here are the farmers' children
To bring me to a village feast

It's not the same this year as last
Things now aren't what they were
I wonder where my old friends are?
New friends already have begun drifting off
It's worst of all at this time of year
    now when the leaves are scattering down
When mountains and streams turn somber again
Nothing anywhere seems to please
Everything I see
Fills me with icy loneliness

We meet, we part
Free as white clouds that come and go
All that remains
 are the fugitive traces of brush and ink
The world of human bonds
 is not the place to find what we seek

Begging for Rice

A solitary three-mat hut
A pitiful, worn-out old body
It's worse still now, in the depths of winter
My suffering can't be described
I pass the cold nights sipping gruel
Counting the days till spring
Unless I can beg a measure of rice
I'll never be able to make it through
I've thought it over carefully
 but just can't see any way to survive
So I sit down and write this poem
And send it to my old friend

Evening of the Sixteenth Day of the New Year

Late on an early spring evening[76]
I wander aimlessly past my brushwood gate
A dusting of snow cloaks the pines and cedars
A solitary moon rises over distant peaks
I think of you far away beyond rivers and mountains
My brush is poised to write
But a thousand memories crowd my mind

On the second day of the twelfth month, I received a gift of sweet potatoes and pears from Kera Shukumon,[77] and composed this poem to express my gratitude

I climbed the mountain to gather firewood
And returned to find the sun already setting
Who could have come and left these pears and yams
    on the ledge beneath my window?
The pears were placed in a bag
    the yams wrapped in straw
Next to these a note, which bore your name
Living here in the mountains
    my meals never vary
Occasionally I get hold of some vegetables
    but nothing more unusual than turnips
I ran to my pot and threw in the yams
    along with some miso and salt

Going into my empty belly
   the broth went down like hot sugar syrup
Only after swallowing three bowlsful
   did I start to feel I'd had enough
My only regret is that you, my poet friend
   failed to include a bottle of wine
I put the leftovers in the larder
   under the kitchen floor
And, patting my belly, went out for a stroll
The commemoration of the Buddha's enlightenment[78]
   is only six days off
And I was at a loss
   what to give to express my devotion
My neighbors here are too poor
   to afford anything in the way of offerings
So I usually end up asking at the temple nearby
   or going into town
In town at the end of the year, however
   prices are ten times what they normally are
Even if I put together everything I owned
   it wouldn't fill a bamboo basket
This year, thanks to your presents, my friend
I can make a proper offering to the old Indian sage[79]
How will I go about it, you ask?
The pears I'll offer him as sweets
And the yams will make a nice hot stew![80]

Staying a while at your home
Just as spring draws to a close
Bees wander off in search of flowers
Songbirds swoop past the eaves
When a poem comes to me, I share it with you
      my dear friend
Otherwise I'm absorbed in our game of go[81]
Does anything resemble this life of mine?
Letting things naturally take their course
I maintain my foolishness

My hut sits on a lonely peak
But my body is free as a drifting cloud
A riverbank village, a lovely moonlit night
Walking alone, I knock gently at your gate
Here, one is far from the affairs of the world
In the center of the room, steam from a teapot
      rises heavily through the air
Together we let the long autumn evening
      trim and trim the candle's wick
      beneath the southern window

At Dusk, I Come to Stay at Kankan-sha

Ever since leaving my family and home[82]
I've spent the years wandering north and south
Now, with nothing but a robe and bowl
I come calling at your house
You've got me, and this weather, too—
   a bitter wind mixed with freezing rain

Happily Drinking with Yoshiyuki

At last we brothers meet again[83]
Two old men with dangling white eyebrows
But for now let's enjoy this peaceful world
Drunk like idiots every day

This Evening

This evening the world is lovely and still
Plum blossoms brush the roof of the veranda
A crescent moon hangs in the sky
Inspired by the occasion, our host
   has prepared his finest room
The guests wield their brushes
   bending over inkstones
I've spent the years a lonely skiff
   drifting in a dream of rivers and lakes
Tonight I find myself in the intimacy of your home
   celebrating together with music and wine
But if anyone asks about me tomorrow, just say:
"A penniless beggar on the street!"

With your monk's staff, you come flying on the wind
To find my hut buried
   under a silver canopy of frost and snow
We're old hermit companions, you and I
Untroubled by the poverty here within
   our peaceful enjoyment goes on and on

Yesterday: I go into town
   begging here and there
My bony shoulders feel the weight of my bag
My single robe sags with the heavy frost
Where have they gone, my old companions?
It's rare that I meet anyone new
Passing the places where we frolicked
All that remain are pines and cedars
   filled with the soughing of the wind

Today, by good luck
I've got money in my bag
And come to see my friend
   the little sleeping dragon
For a long time now
   I've been meaning to drink with you
But when we'd meet
I was always broke

Ancient vines strangle the trees
Mountain torrents rush helter-skelter through ravines
Of ten paths I take, nine end up leading nowhere
But the old man who lives in the hills
     still remembers me from long ago
And kindly sees me all the way to my hut

A Visit from Jizen Shōnin and Nisen Rōjin [84]

My home lies at the foot of Mount Kugami
I open the gate and before me
     rise the mountains' green-forested slopes
If you are not averse to solitude
Come knock at the door of my woodland retreat

On the first day of summer
I take my staff and go walking alone
An old farmer suddenly recognizes me
And drags me along with him for a drink
Straw mats serve for seats
Paulownia leaves make do as plates
After a few cups of wine in the open air
I'm pleasantly drunk and, with the ridge
Of the furrow for my pillow, fall fast asleep

Visiting the Layman Ugan

The hermitage is silent, its door shut
Falling leaves fill the sky
Sparrows chatter at the edge of the eaves
The afterglow of a setting sun
     bathes the ramshackle village
Thinking of you, I crossed mountains and rivers
Traveling here staff in hand
Looking back, it seems
     we've been friends a thousand years
The waters of the stream flow by
     always fresh and clear[85]

*Watching the Flower Petals, I Arrive at
Tanomo-an*

Peach blossoms, like mist
    cover the banks of the stream
Blue as indigo, the river in spring
    flows off till it meets the sky
I stroll along
    watching the petals swept by the current
And find myself at your home
    on the eastern strand

Staff and sandals beckon me
    to the road of a village by the water's edge
It's the second month, when spring winds blow
A warbler shifts among the tall treetops
    its song still hesitant and unformed
Snow clings to the low garden fence
Shoots of grass push up here and there
By chance I run into a friend
    and we talk of the beauties of valleys and hills
Quietly we pore over books
    our chins resting in our hands
Tonight with the world turning lovely and mild
Each thing enhances the other—
    the plum flowers in bloom and the feeling of poetry

    *   *   *

Butterfly Dreams

Without intending it
   the flower attracts the butterfly
Without intending it
   the butterfly seeks out the flower
When the flower opens, the butterfly comes
When the butterfly comes, the flower opens
I'm the same
I may not know other people
And they may not know me
But without knowing one another
We naturally follow the universal law

Where did my life come from?
Where will it go?
Meditating by the window of my tumbledown hut
I search my heart, absorbed in silence
But I search and search and still don't know
     where it all began
How will I ever find where it ends?
Even the present moment
     can't be pinned down
Everything changes, everything is empty
And in that emptiness, this "I" exists
     only for a little while
How can one say anything is or is not?
Best just to hold to these little thoughts
Let things simply take their way
     and so be natural and at your ease

What was right yesterday
Is wrong today
How do you know what's right today
Wasn't wrong the day before?
Right and wrong aren't something fixed
You can't tell in advance the pros and cons
The foolish are stuck on a single note
So wherever they go, they're out of tune
The wise penetrate to the source of things
And pass their time roaming free and at ease
Forget about knowledge and ignorance both
And you can call yourself one who has the Way

Arriving at the path by the foot of the mountain
I come upon a heap of old gravestones
Night and day
    winds moan through the evergreen forest
The names on the stones have gradually worn away
Not even their descendants recall
    who lies buried in this place
I'm choked with tears, unable to speak
I pick up my staff and start back home

Dream Dialogue

Going into town to beg
I meet a wise old man on the road
He asks me: "Master, why do you live there
　　in the mountains, among white clouds?"
"And you," I ask him:
"Why do you live out your days
　　here in the world's red dust?"[86]
We both start to answer, but then remain silent
And the dawn gong startles me from my dream

Who was it said, "Names are the guests of reality"?[87]
These words have come down to us from ancient times
But even if people know that names aren't real
They don't see that reality itself has no root
Name, reality—both are beside the point
Just naturally find joy in the ever-changing flow

In my house live a cat and a mouse
Both creatures have furry skins
But the cat eats his fill
    and dozes in the noonday sun
While the mouse starves
    and scurries about in the dark of night
What makes the cat so good?
He watches carefully for his prey
    and almost always hits his mark
What makes the mouse so bad?
He gnaws holes in things
    which is surely to be deplored
Yet something with a hole can always be repaired
While one who is dead will never return
And so, weighing the seriousness of their crimes
Judgment must fall against the cat

People's minds aren't all the same
Any more than people's faces
Everyone clings to his own point of view
Incessantly arguing over right and wrong
"If you think like me, you're right
   even if you're wrong"
"If you don't think like me, you're wrong
   even if you're right"
Whatever is right to you is right
Can't you see that's wrong?
From the start, right and wrong are both in you
But the Way itself isn't like this at all
Only a fool would even attempt
To fathom the ocean with so clumsy a pole

Under the heavens lives a man
Whom no one has ever reviled
Visit him and he won't show his face
Instead his servant comes out and
   conveys his words
He twirls empty space to form
   mountains and valleys
Folds rocks to conjure churning waves
At times he turns up on the bustling streets
Holds out his hand and begs for a coin

A forest of masts
Ships from every corner of the land
   disgorging their cargo onto the docks
The boatmen chanting *"Ai! Oh!"*—
   impromptu music of the piers
Yesterday I went to a temple in the mountains
But there, too, it was just
   butterfly dreams in spring[88]

Where you have beauty
   you have ugliness, too
Where you have right
   you will also have wrong
Knowledge and ignorance are each other's cause
Delusion and enlightenment produce one another
It's always been so
It didn't start now
You get rid of this, then grab hold of that
Don't you see how stupid it is!
If you're determined to find the innermost truth
Why trouble about the changing face of things?

With my staff I go for a solitary stroll
Walking to the foot of the northern slope
Day and night, winds moan
    in ancient evergreen forests
Old corpses lie buried under the earth
What can they expect to find through that long night?
Foxes and wolves lurk in the dusky underbrush
Horned owls hoot on wintry branches
A thousand years from now
    ten thousand years from now
Is there any of us who won't be resting here?
Aimlessly, I linger a while
    unable to bring myself to leave
A cold shiver runs down my spine
Teardrops fall and stain my robe

Sitting alone in my empty room
My mind restless and downcast
I saddle my horse and ride far, far away
Climb to a height
And gaze out over the distant scene
A whirlwind springs up, shaking the earth
In no time at all, the sun sinks in the west
Broad rivers churn with foaming waves
Fields stretch endlessly past the horizon
Black monkeys call to their companions
With melancholy cries
    geese wing their way south
A hundred cares line my brow
Ten thousand troubles rend my heart
I want to return
    but I've lost the way back
Here it is, the end of another year
What am I to do?[89]

Though I've grown old living in this world
The world itself seems always the same
But when I look for people
like those long ago
Hardly any can be found
Monks, laymen—
All rush headlong down the same
    treacherous slope
Never pausing, night or day
And of the safe, level road, alas!
Nothing remains but rank-growing weeds

Colophon for a Painting of a Skeleton

Everything that arises from conditions will cease
   when those conditions come to an end
But from where did those conditions arise?
From previous conditions, of course
Then how about the first condition—
   where does *it* come from?
When you arrive here, words fail you
   thinking is simply no use
I brought all this to the old woman
   who's my neighbor to the east
But the old woman didn't like it at all
So I told it to the old man
   who's my neighbor to the west
And the old man just frowned and walked away
I tried writing it down on a rice cake
   and feeding it to a dog
But even the dog wouldn't take it
My choice of words must be bad, I thought
My language must be a bit confused
So I rolled arising-and-ceasing into one big whole
And gave it to the skeleton lying in the field
Instantly, the skeleton stood up
And started to sing and dance for me
Its song went on and on, resonating through the past
   the present, the future
Its dance's subtleties revealed
   all the realms of sentient life
Three times the song was repeated
   three times the dance performed

And then it stopped
The moon had sunk below the horizon
And I heard the midnight bell
   tolling in the city of Ch'ang-an[90]

*   *   *

Strolling without a Care

All night, carried on the eastern wind
A spring rain soaks my hut's thatch roof
The master of the house sleeps soundly through it all
Oblivious to affairs in the floating world
In the first light of dawn, green mountains stand forth
And spring birds twitter on their branches
I, too, leave my shelter
   strolling along without a care
Streams gliding through the fields
   of distant villages brim with water
Gorgeous flowers brighten the mountains'
   green-forested slopes
That old man leading the ox, where is he from?
The boy carrying the hoe
   I wonder whose child he can be?
The cycle of the seasons never pauses
And human beings all have their tasks
But what sort of work is there for me?
To forever stand guard at the gates of my land

I was not originally a denizen of
   mountains and forests
But who wants to pursue an official career?
My begging bowl comes with me wherever I go
My begging bag, too, makes a perfect companion
Arriving here at the temple gate
I run into the children
What use is there in such a life?
Allow me humbly to explain:
This is how I spend my time!

The weather at last is turning mild
Swinging my staff
   I set off for a spring outing
Streams burble in the valleys and gorges
Mountains and forests ring
   with the trilling of birds
I may go walking with a monk
Stop at a friend's and rest a while
There's nothing like this life of mine
A boat that's slipped its moorings
   bobbing on the waves

Song of the Wide-Open Spaces

All alone, leaning against a solitary pine
Together with the tree again
   letting the time slip by
Is there anyone in this whole wide world
Who'll come along with me?

With early autumn the cold air arrives
And the wild geese begin to fly south
I, too, gather my robe and bowl
And cheerfully descend
   the mountains' green-forested slopes
Wild chrysanthemums perfume the air
Mountains and streams shimmer and glow
Human beings are not metal or stone
As the seasons change
   my heart can't help but respond
Who can shut himself up in a corner somewhere
Sitting stiffly in meditation
   till old age dangles its silver threads?

An Answer to Your Poem

For being obstinate and stupid
　　there's no one like me
My neighbors have become the trees and grasses
I'm tired of mulling over
　　delusion and enlightenment
Seeing how old and decrepit I've grown
　　I can't help laughing at myself
Carefree, I hoist my robe above my legs
　　and ford the stream
My begging bag in tow
　　I go rambling with the springtime
I'm content just living this life of mine
It's not that I loathe the dust of the world[91]

Since becoming a monk, I've passed the days
　　letting things naturally take their course
Yesterday I was in the green mountains
Today I'm strolling around town
My robe is a sorry patchwork
My bowl a veteran of countless years
Clear, quiet nights
　　I lean on my staff and recite poetry
In the daytime
　　I spread my straw mat for a nap
People may say, "He's a no-account fellow"
Well, this is how I am!

I've never bothered about getting ahead
But just gone leisurely along
    letting things take their way
In my bag are three measures of rice
A bundle of firewood sits by the hearth
Who cares about delusion and enlightenment?
What use is there in fame and fortune?
In my hut, I listen to the evening rain
And stretch my legs without a care in the world

Desire nothing, and you're content with everything
Pursue things, and you're thwarted at every turn
Wild greens can stave off hunger
A simple robe serves to cover the skin
Going for a solitary stroll
    I fall in with the deer
When the children from the village sing, I join
    right in at the top of my lungs
I cleanse my ears in the sound of water
    tumbling over rocks
And gladden my heart with the whisper of pines
    high on the mountains' peaks

Rags and patches, patches and rags
Rags and patches—that's my life
My food is whatever I beg by the roadside
My house is completely overrun with wild grass
In autumn, gazing at the moon
   I recite poetry all night long
In spring, entranced by the blossoms
   I wander off and forget to come home
I left the temple, and this is how I've ended up—
   A broken-down old mule

Ever since becoming a monk
I've been drawn to the country's clouds and mists
I spend my time with fishermen and woodcutters
Or join the children in their games
What is the glory of kings to me?
Even the immortality of gods holds no appeal
Wherever I happen to be is home
It's no different from Bodhidharma's Mount Sung[92]
Riding the changes each new day brings
I live out the years soaring calm and free

How many winters and springs have passed
Since I came to live in this secluded place?
My only vegetables are bean leaves and wild spinach
For rice, it's whatever I can beg from the neighbors
My greatest joy is to have so few worldly concerns
I've never minded the poverty of a hermit's life
Since coming home I've grown uncommonly lazy
I sit, I lie down, I do just as I like

To the Blind Man of Magari

In the forest of Otogo[93]
   on the slopes of Mount Kugami
Stands the thatch hut
   where I spin out my remaining years
Crimson gates, golden pavilions[94]—
   I can't bear it for long in lavish surroundings
Here, the clear breeze and bright moon are my family
I run into the children and together we play ball
Seized by inspiration, I set down poem after poem
One day, my learned friend, you'll ask me:
"What happened to that ridiculously strict
   Zen monk I used to know?"

Think about the past—it's already gone
Think about the present—it's the same
Time keeps moving, leaving no traces
Who is foolish, who is smart?
Just pass the days letting things take their course
And abiding in your own true self
    wait for life to draw to a close
I drifted to this place quite casually
And twenty years later, here I am

A Buddhist monk of the old Indians' school[95]
I hid myself on Mount Kugami
    I don't recall how many springtimes ago
I've worn out countless pairs of robes
But my staff has never left my side
Following the mountain streams
    I wander singing along distant paths
Or sit and watch the white clouds
    billowing from jagged peaks
Pity the traveler in the floating world
    of fame and fortune
His life spent chasing after specks of
    swirling dust!

The rain clears, the clouds clear
   then the air clears, too
When the mind is pure, the whole universe is pure
I gave up the world, gave up my station in life
   became an utter good-for-nothing
Now at last I can live out my days
   companion of the flowers and the moon

For Suzuki Ryūzō

A useless life in which nothing gets done
On Mount Kugami I've made my home
If anyone ever wants to know
   the sort of fellowship we share
Tell him: "Ours is a friendship
   of mountain scarecrows" [96]

How long has it been since I came here to live?
When tired, I stretch my legs for a nap
Inspired, I put on my sandals and go for a walk
People in the world can think what they like
Laughter or praise, it's all the same
My mother and father gave me this life
I'm naturally happy, whatever comes my way

Ever since I quit the temple
My life has been resolutely carefree
My staff is always at my side
My robe is worn completely threadbare
At night in my hut, through the lonely window
    I hear the falling rain
On spring days when the flowers riot in bloom
    I'm playing ball out on the street
If anyone asks what I'm doing, I say:
"The most useless man there ever was!"

*   *   *

Waka (Poems in Japanese)

Playing ball
With the children in this village
Spring day, never let the shadows fall!

konosato ni temari tsukitsutsu kodomora to
asobu harubi wa kurezutomo yoshi

Oh! my poor begging bowl!
I left it behind
Picking violets by the roadside

michinobe ni sumire tsumitsutsu hachinoko o
wasurete zo koshi aware hachinoko

I was on my way to beg
But passing by a spring field
Spent the whole day
Picking violets

    iikou to waga koshi kado mo haru no no ni
    sumire tsumitsutsu toki o henikeri

In spring rain, in summer squalls or
   autumn drought
I go out begging
Wishing peace to all the world

    haru wa ame natsu wa yūdachi akiwa teri
    yononaka yokare ware ii kowam

Because the Dharma Path
Carries truth in all directions
You can simply drift at ease
Coming or going, west or east

    nori no michi makoto wakatam nishi higashi
    yuku mo kaeru mo nami ni makasete

You abandoned this life
For the sake of the Dharma
So it will never succumb
To earthly decay

    itsumade mo kuchiya senamaji mihotoke no
       minori no tame ni suteshi sonomi wa

My words cannot hope to match
The Buddha's exquisite teaching
My sermon:
This gardenia from the mountains[1]

    taenaru ya minori no koto ni oyobaneba
       motekite tokam yama no kuchinashi

To see before me,
   brought into the present
The days long ago
   when the Buddha preached
How grateful I feel!

    mihotoke no shiroshimeshitsuru inishie o
       imani utsushite miru ga tōtosa

One who is a monk needs nothing—
Only "Never Despising Anyone"[2]
For this is the unexcelled practice
   of all bodhisattvas

    sō no mi wa makoto wa irazu jōfukyō
    bosatsu no gyō no shushō narikeri

In my begging bowl
Violets and daisies mixed together
Let's make an offering
To all the buddhas in the three worlds[3]

    hachinoko ni sumire tampopo kokimazete
    miyo no hotoke ni tatematsuritena

In the autumn field
Breaking off pampas grass[4] to add to the bush clover
We've made an offering
To all the buddhas in the three worlds

    aki no no no hagi ni susuki o orisoete
    miyo no hotoke ni tatematsuritem

I visit Saigyō's[5] grave and offer flowers

> Forgive me
> If the flowers I plucked
> Have begun to fade
> I can offer you
> Only my heart

> > taorikoshi hana no iroka wa usukutomo
> > awaremitamae kokoro bakari wa

During the Master's lifetime, [a certain woman named] Yoshiko asked him to give her a poem as a keepsake.[6]

> What have I to leave as a keepsake?
> In spring, the cherry blossoms
> In summer, the warbler's song
> In autumn, the maple's crimson leaves

> > katami tote nanika nokosam haru wa hana
> > natsu hototogisu aki no momijiba

> If not for Amida's inconceivable vow[7]
> What then would remain to me
> As a keepsake of this world?

> > fukashigi no mida no chikai no nakariseba
> > nani o konoyo no omoide ni sem

What joy to know that
Just because I am a hopeless soul
I've found Amida Buddha's vow!

> orokanaru mi koso nakanaka ureshikere
> mida no chikai ni au to omowaba

Afterward, if someone should ask:
"Did Ryōkan leave a final verse?"
Just say: *"Namu Amida butsu!"*

> ryōkan ni jisei aruka to hito towaba
> namu amida bu(tsu) to iu to kotaeyo

Clouds billow upward
Skies are clear
I go out to beg
And receive heaven's gifts

> kumo ideshi sora wa harekeri takuhatsu no
> kokoro no mama ni ten no atae o

It's not that I don't care
To mingle with others
Only that I'm better
At amusing myself

> yononaka ni majiranu to niwa aranedomo
> hitoriasobi zo ware wa masareru

In the shadow of the mountain
Like the water that trickles
    through the moss-covered rocks
Thus do I live
Quiet, unnoticed
But free of impurity

> yamakage no iwama o tsutau kokemizuno
> kasuka ni ware wa sumiwataru kamo

Tribute to Gogō-an

The water of the valley stream
Never shouts at the tainted world
"Purify yourself!"
But naturally, as it is
Shows how it is done

       nigoru yo o sumetomo yobazu waga narini
         sumashite misuru tanigawa no mizu

Who would ever have known it was there
Beneath the duckweed
That chokes the water by the shore:
The full moon[8]

       ukikusa no hauru migiwa ni tsukikage no
         ari to wa koko ni dareka shiruram

The lotus flowers vying
   in the freshness of their blooms
Lustrous with morning dew
Such is the preciousness of those
Untainted by the dusts of the world

       asatsuyu ni kioite sakeru hachisuba no
         chiri ni somazaru hito no tōtosa

It may seem that I have locked myself
Away from the people of the world
And yet
Why is it
I have never ceased to think of them?

    yononaka ni kado sashitari to miyuredomo
      nadoka omoi no tayuru koto naki

If my arms draped in these black robes
Were only wide enough
How gladly I would shelter in them
All the people of this floating world

    sumizome no waga koromode no yutanaraba
      ukiyo no tami ni ōwashi mono o

Go ahead, plant the seed!
There isn't a village
Where flowers won't grow
The very notion of being "lowborn"
Only comes from people's minds[9]

    uetemiyo hana no sodatanu sato mo nashi
      kokoro kara koso mi wa iyashikere

Someone recited a poem that read:

> The breath going out, the breath coming in
> Over and then over again
> Only leaves me to reflect
> What a fleeting world this is

> > izuru iki mata iru iki to bakari nite
> > yo o hakanakumo omooyuru kana

To which the Master replied:

> The breath going out, the breath coming in
> Over and then over again
> Know that this is itself the proof
> That this world never ends

> > izuru iki mata iru iki wa yononaka no
> > tsukisenu koto no tameshi to zo shire

Once, inspired by the beautiful autumn evening, the Master was strolling through a sweet potato field. A farmer, thinking he was bent on stealing the crops, surprised him and struck him with his fist. Not content with this, he then tied the Master to a pine tree and continued to pummel him with blows. Begging forgiveness, the Master declared: "I never intended to steal!" The farmer, shocked to recognize the Master's voice, promptly untied him, apologizing profusely. The Master broke out laughing.[10]

> The one who beats
> And the one who is beaten
> Recognize one another to be
> As ephemeral as a drop of dew
> Or a flash of lightning across the sky[11]

> > utsuhito mo utaruru hito mo morotomo ni
> > nyoro yaku nyoden ōsa nyozekan

Mind itself is the mind
That leads the mind astray
When you ride the mind-horse
Never loosen the reins!

    kokoro koso kokoro madowasu kokoro nare
      kokoro no koma no tazuna yurusuna

The reason why I left my home—
Let it permeate my heart
Deeply as the color
That dyes the sleeves of my black robe

    naniyue ni wagami wa ie o ideshi zo to
      kokoro ni someyo sumizome no sode

Let's go out to beg, to cut firewood
And draw the clear water
  that bubbles from beneath the moss
Now, before the passing showers return

    iikowam mashiba ya koram kokeshimizu
      shigure o ame no furanu ma ni ma ni

I forget my staff while visiting Hoshi Hikozaemon in Takemori[12]

A pathetic old man—
　　But whom can I tell?
Having forgotten my staff
　　I trudge home at dusk

　　　oigami no aware o dare ni kataramashi
　　　　tsue o wasurete kaeru yūgure

Here at last!
　　The spring days
When I play with the children
　　Under the shrine grove's trees

　　　konomiya no mori no koshita ni kodomora to
　　　　asobu harubi ni narinikerashi mo

If someone asks
　　About this monk's mind
Say: "The answer is arriving
　　in his letter—
The wind that races through the
　　great sky"

　　　kono sō no kokoro o towaba ōzora no
　　　　kaze o tayori ni tsuku to kotaeyo

Poem on the hurricane of the fifth month of the first year of Tenpō (1830)

On my dwelling's garden fence, I grew
Bush clover, acanthus, cosmos, daisies
    pinks and chrysanthemums[13]
I pulled up demon weeds, carried water
Built an awning to shade my plants from the sun
They thrived, obliterating the garden path
I found myself going there morning and evening
When I was about to leave the house or when I returned
I'd stand there, looking at my plants
It was then, just as I was thinking
    how lovely autumn was going to be
On the evening of the twenty-fourth day of
    the fifth month
That storm winds began to blow, as if racing
    one against another
Everything was dashed to the ground
Thrown into disorder and scattered by the rain
I went inside, closed the door
And just lay down,
    rubbing my legs together anxiously
Ah, what's to be done!

The plants I'd
    cared for faithfully:
Abandoned to the mercies of the wind!

        te mo suma ni uete sodateshi yachigusa wa
            kaze no kokoro no makasetari keri

In my grass hut
I lie awake all night
As hailstones
Brush the needles of the cedars

      yomosugara kusa no iori ni ware oreba
        sugi no ha shinugi arare furu nari

Distant villages hidden
  in the evening mist
I return along the road
  to my hut
Surrounded by towering cedars

      yūgiri ni ochi no satoba wa uzumorenu
        sugi tatsu yado ni kaeru sano michi

Dew on the Lotus

Ryōkan's last years were brightened by his relationship with the young Buddhist nun and poetess Teishin. The two first met in 1827, at a time when Ryōkan's failing health forced him to abandon his beloved Mount Kugami and accept the hospitality of his old friend and supporter Kimura Motouemon in Shimazaki. Teishin became a frequent visitor at Ryōkan's cottage in the Kimura compound and helped to nurse the Master during his final devastating illness. Ryōkan and Teishin's devotion to one another is revealed in the many poems they exchanged, collected and edited by Teishin after Ryōkan's death under the title *Dew on the Lotus (Hachisu no tsuyu).* In her introduction to the work, dated 1835, Teishin writes:

> I could not bear to see these poems buried here and there like dead trees moldering in a valley, and so avidly collected them from every corner, adding to these the poems I exchanged with the Master in my visits to his hut. I always have the collection by my side as a keepsake of the Master. Every morning and evening, I take it and read it as a way to recall those events of the past.

The following poems are excerpted from Teishin's collection (*Zen-shū* 2, pp. 490–499).

Having heard that the Master was always playing ball, I offered this poem:

> Playing in the Buddha's Path
> You never tire of bouncing your ball
> This, just this—
> The inexhaustible Dharma
>   (Teishin)

> korezo kono hotoke no michi ni asobitsutsu
> tsukuya tsukisenu minori naruram

The Master replied:

> Now you try:
> One two three four five six
> Seven eight nine ten—
> And after ten, you start again!
>   (Ryōkan)

> tsukitemiyo hi fu mi yo i mu na ya koko no tō
>   tō to osamete mata hajimaru o

> Your mind, the bright moon at the mountain's summit
> Sheds a clarifying light
> But the thin haze of my doubts
> Still lingers below the mountain's peak
>   (Teishin)

> yamanoha no tsuki wa sayaka ni terasedomo
>   mada hareyaranu mine no usugumo

The Master replied:

> There are those like you who give up
>   their lives
> To save the people of the world
> But I am only
> Seeking peace in a thatch hut
>   (Ryōkan)

> mi o sutete yo sukuu hito mo masumono o
>   kusa no iori ni hima motomu towa

Awakened, there is no longer
Darkness or light
Only the moon at dawn
Illumining the road of dreams
　　　　　　　(Teishin)

　　samenureba yami mo hikari mo nakarikeri
　　　　yumeji o terasu ariake no tsuki

The Master replied:

Better than all the jewels
All the gold on earth
Is your first visit
In the spring
　　　　　　　(Ryōkan)

　　amegashita ni mitsuru tama yori kogane yori
　　　　haru no hajime no kimi ga otozure

[So bare is my hut]
I can stretch out my hand
Without touching a thing
Yet this, just this
Is the Dharma Way
　　　　　　　(Ryōkan)

　　te ni sawaru monokoso nakeru nori no michi
　　　　sore ga sanagara sore ni ariseba

I replied:

> The deep mountain snow is
> Melting in the spring breeze
> But the water of the valley stream
> Still waits trapped between the rocks
>   (Teishin)

>   harukaze ni miyama no yuki wa tokenuredo
>   iwama ni yodomu tanigawa no mizu

The Master answered:

> Once the deep mountain snow
> Has begun to melt
> No water should remain
> Trapped in the valley stream
>   (Ryōkan)

>   miyamabe no miyuki tokenaba tanigawa ni
>   yodomeru mizu wa araji to omou

I wrote:

> "From where does spring come?" I ask
> The plum flowers do not reply
> But in their midst
> A warbler sings
>   (Teishin)

>   izuko yori haru wa koshi zo to tazunuredo
>   kotaenu hana ni uguisu no naku

If not for you
I would have counted to one hundred, to one thousand
And yet never understood what it means
Each time I count to ten
Ten times to make one hundred
                    (Teishin)

      kimi nakuba chitabi momotabi kazou tomo
         tō zutsu tō o momo to shiraji o

The Master replied:

It's time to go
I'll stop at nine, bouncing the ball
Now that you understand what it means
Each time you count to ten
Ten times to make one hundred
                    (Ryōkan)

      iza saraba ware mo yaminam koko no mari
         tō zutsu tō o momo to shirinaba

When it was time to leave, the Master wrote:

Forget it not
The pledge before the Buddha on Vulture Peak[14]
No matter how much time may pass
                    (Ryōkan)

      ryūsen no shaka no mimae ni chigiriteshi
         koto na wasure zo yo wa hedatsu tomo

I replied:

No, however much time may pass
I'll not forget
The pledge before the Buddha on Vulture Peak
                    (Teishin)

ryūsen no shaka no mimae ni chigiriteshi
    koto wa wasureji yo wa hedatsu tomo

Letters

Numerous letters by Ryōkan have survived. The majority of these are "thank you" notes for an assortment of foodstuffs, clothes, and household articles, as well as tobacco and medicine supplied by Ryōkan's many friends and patrons. The following selection focuses on those letters that reveal the character of Ryōkan's daily life and of his social relations. Certain letters note the name and village of the recipient, others only the month and day (never the year) on which they were composed. Bracketed numbers refer to numbers in Tōgō Toyoharu, *Ryōkan zenshū* 2, pp. 321–392; sources for letters not included in the Zenshū are noted in parentheses.

Fourth day of the first month

To Kera Shukumon:[1]

My greetings on the occasion of the New Year. I was fortunate in welcoming the year in good health. Toward the close of last year, I received your year's-end gift[2] with deep gratitude. How have you fared in the recent cold weather? . . .

Ryōkan
[57]

Eleventh day of the second month

To Kera Shukumon:

My cold returned the day after you visited me in my hut, but in the past day or two I have recovered. I am enclosing for you the copy that I made of the *Lotus Sūtra*. Since I was ill, my brushwork is lacking in strength, so I hope you will forgive me. I have used up all my paper and am returning the brushes.

Sincerely,
Ryōkan
[58]

Twelfth day of the sixth month[3]

To Shukumon:

How are you faring in the heat? I am enjoying some temporary relief from my own aches and pains. This is to acknowledge receipt of the silk fabric that you sent.

> I count them off—
> Already sixty years buried in the forest
> I live out my remaining days
>   with one wooden box, one gourd flask
> People may envy worldly honors and riches
> But now is the bamboo shoot season
> And I haven't time to bother
> about such things

[70]

Fifth day of the tenth month

[To Kera Shukumon:]

Many thanks for your letter, which I received the other day. I'm delighted to hear you are keeping well in this cold weather. I myself am fine.

The money and rice that I received from my begging and then lost have turned up. I'm now preparing myself to burrow in for the winter. But next spring, let's be sure to get together at the earliest opportunity.

That's all.

> Burning brushwood
> I hear the sound of a passing shower
> Night has fallen

[59]

Sixteenth day of the eleventh month

To Kera at Makigahana:

How are you faring in the cold weather? I am fine. Please send me the rice I left at your place before. This time I won't be returning the mosquito netting to you, but you don't have to worry about thieves, as I've arranged to store it at Hōjū-in's.[4]

[73]

Twenty-sixth day of the twelfth month

To Kera Shukumon:

Many thanks for the New Year's presents, which I received the other day. The tobacco also arrived. Recently, due to the cold weather, I suffered an attack of lumbago. I had to bake yams for myself to eat every night, and now I'm fully recovered.[5]

Still eagerly awaiting the return of spring,

Sincerely,

Ryōkan

[60]

New Year's Day

[To Kera Shukumon:]

The bearer of this message is a person from my area. Her husband had gone to another province to work as a miner,[6] but, whatever happened, last winter he failed to return. She has many children, all under the age of ten. They are spending this spring begging their way from village to village. I wanted to give them something myself, but being an impoverished monk, there was nothing I could do. Please offer them some assistance, whatever you can manage.[7]

[71]

Twenty-second day of the eleventh month

To Kera Shukumon:

It has been some time since I heard from you, and I wondered how you were. As for myself, these days I'm finally feeling well again. My thanks for the soy beans, which I received the other day. I've been getting rice from here and there, so that this year, too, I'm quite well supplied. Just so you'd know.

Your son's departure for Edo in this weather must be causing you concern. How is your own health? After your treatment, you should be fine. You must be careful about eating and drinking and not let things upset you. Only a few days are left to this year, so when it's time to pick spring greens, I'll come visit and we can have a refreshing chat.

That's all.

Ryōkan

[61]

Twelfth day of the fifth month

To Kera Magouemon:[8]

It has been some time since I saw you. How have you been faring? This spring, both your grandfather and your father have been in particularly poor health. They pray day and night for your return. You had better accompany this messenger now and come home. Otherwise you may never see your father again. Is it not deplorable to abandon yourself to momentary pleasures and so forfeit forever your rightful station in life? Once you have alienated yourself from the Buddha's mercy and incurred the punishment of heaven, repentance will be useless.

As I observe the variety of living beings, it is clear that they all have some purpose in their lives. Even if you are young in years, I am sure you have some idea of what I am saying. I have thought long and hard over your situation but can see no way other than for you to make up your mind to come home.

That's all.
Ryōkan
[75]

[Date unknown]

To Kera Magouemon:

My thanks for your letter the other day. I would like to come see you—so much that I could almost fly there. But, sadly, I'm recovering from illness and must avoid all travel. Next year, perhaps—provided I'm still alive. Please send a bit of rice.

Your servant,
Ryōkan
[76]

Thirteenth day of the New Year

To Kera:

It was a pleasure to see you again the other day after such a long time. Speaking of which, I left my copybook of Tōfū's calligraphy[9] at your home and am extremely anxious about it. I'm sorry to bother you, but could you please find it and return it to me with this messenger.

[Here Ryōkan sketches a picture of the cover of the book and writes out the text's opening lines]

In case the head of the household is out, please use the above as a guide and look for the item for me.

> That's all.
> Your servant,
> Ryōkan
>
> [72]

Fourth day of the first month[10]

To Abe Teichin:[11]

Thank you for the New Year's gifts, which I received with gratitude. As you were traveling before the close of the year, I imagine you must have been quite busy. Today your messenger is in a hurry, so I am not able to include my poems in reply to the poems you sent me, but I will do so next time.

> Sincerely,
> Ryōkan
>
> [19]

Twenty-ninth day of the tenth month

To Abe Teichin:

I have finished copying the *Man'yōshū,* so please return it to Ōsaka-ya.[12] I would like to borrow the next volume and have discussed this in detail in the enclosed letter. Please send it to me by tomorrow if possible. My supply of red ink is nearly exhausted, so could you send me some? I also need thongs for *geta* and a brush.

> Sincerely,
> Ryōkan
>
> [30]

Sixteenth day of the New Year

To Teichin in Watabe:

This winter you sent me a sack of red peppers, and I'm still enjoying them.

Here's a poem:

> Living in a rustic hut
> High among the mountain fields:
> Yesterday and again today
> No one's come to visit me

Ryōkan

[52]

Twenty-fifth day of the twelfth month

To Teichin:

As you'd advised, this winter I've come to stay at the Notoya's in Shimazaki.[13] I must say it's hard for me to live confined like this. But once the warm weather is here, I can be on the move again.

My thanks for the sake, tobacco, and greens.

That's all.

Ryōkan

[54]

[Date unknown]

To Abe Teichin:

My gratitude for the New Year's Day gift of liquor. I enjoyed all the New Year's Day poems you sent. Let me offer one of my own:

> I believe there is no one
> Who is not celebrating this day
> Which begins the peaceful world under heaven

Ryōkan

[49]

Twenty-second day of the twelfth month

To Teichin:

The flavor of this miso is fine, but its saltiness is too pronounced. Please send a replacement.

That's all.

Ryōkan

[51]

First day of the seventh month

[To Abe Teichin:]

I sincerely appreciate the rice and vegetables you sent me the other day. I haven't been able to get out with my begging bowl in this heat, but at the Toyamas in Teradomari, I've laid away a good supply of rice from begging, so please don't worry.

That's all.
Ryōkan
[24]

First day of the eighth month

[To Abe Teichin:]

I'd like to come to your breakfast[14] on the morning of the ninth. But living alone as I do, if anything should force me to change my plans, I have no one I can send to let you know. On top of which, these days I'm old and sickly, so I'm sure you'll understand. As for tomorrow, I have an appointment and won't be able to join you.

> I came here intending to beg for food
> And discovered the drain beneath the eaves
> Filled to bursting with bush-clover flowers

Ryōkan

PS: My sincere appreciation for the basket of eggplants, the small barrel of sake, and the prepared vegetables.

[26]

To Tokō:[15]

Thank you for the dance scarf,[16] which I recently received.

> All together
> We danced the autumn night away
> I even forgot
> That I was ill!

Ryōkan
[103]

Eighth day of the twelfth month

To Yamada Tokō in Yoita:

The earthquake was truly terrible.[17] Thankfully, my hut was spared and no one in my family was killed.

> If I die without warning. . .
> But spared, I go on living
> Sorrowful witness
> To untold misery

Yet, when it's time to face disaster, it's best to face it. When it's time to die, it's best to die. This itself is the wonderful method for *averting* disaster.

Respectfully,
Ryōkan

[107]

The Shūzō referred to in the following letter was the eldest son of Ryōkan's friend Kimura Motouemon. Shūzō's conflicts with his father led to his being disinherited, and though Motouemon refused all other attempts to intercede for his son, he seems to have finally accepted Ryōkan's apology on Shūzō's behalf and forgiven him.

Heirs to wealthy merchant families like the Kimura were the objects of great concern as they would ultimately assume responsibility for the firm's prosperity and for the welfare of family members and employees. Consequently, punishment for an erring first son could be harsh. In Ryōkan's day, there were, generally speaking, three increasingly severe measures by which a father could disown his son: initially, the son could be expelled from the household but allowed to take shelter with relatives; next, he could be formally disowned at a family conference and all family members forbidden to help him; finally, in the most extreme case, the father could have the local authorities strike the son's name from the family register, making him a permanent social outcast. It is the second of these sanctions that Shūzō seems to have suffered.

Fourteenth day of the fourth month

To Shūzō:

Regarding your expulsion from the family: Everyone tried to intercede, but your father would not forgive you. I also became involved, joining the others in making apologies on your behalf, and your father is now ready to offer you forgiveness. You should return home immediately. But after your return, you must make sure there is no more bad behavior. To begin with, you must get up early in the morning, not disobey your parents, and work just as hard as you can. In everything else, too, you must be absolutely scrupulous. And remember: if you ever do anything like this again, apologies will be useless.

That's all.
Ryōkan

(Tōgō, Shinshū Ryōkan, p. 297)

An anecdote that forms an epilogue of sorts to this letter is recorded by the early modern Ryōkan scholar Nishigori Kyūgo. According to the story, on the morning of Shūzō's return home, Ryōkan arrived beforehand and entered the Kimura house. As he waited, he noticed the figure of Shūzō approaching awkwardly from across the road. Ryōkan then rushed to the front entrance and held the door shut, pressing the door's panels firmly together to keep Shūzō from entering. His plan was to suddenly let go and, when Shūzō fell inside, shout "Surprise!" and welcome him home.

Shūzō thought it strange that the door would not open, but finally decided to simply walk around and enter by the back. When he reached the main entrance, he found Ryōkan, sweating profusely and holding the door shut, but because Shūzō felt so awkward, he remained silent.

Anticipating that Shūzō would be famished, the family had laid out a meal for him on the bench in the vestibule.[18] Ryōkan, meanwhile, unaware of what was happening, continued vigorously pressing the door shut. But it no longer felt as if Shūzō was on the other side, and suddenly Ryōkan turned and saw him seated at the bench, holding his chopsticks and about to start eating. Realizing his prank had been foiled, Ryōkan laughed and returned to his hut, having at any rate succeeded in leavening the tense atmosphere surrounding Shūzō's return.

Twenty-sixth day of the tenth month

To Nakamura Gon'uemon:[19]

I would like to borrow the *Kojiki* (The Record of the Ancient Affairs)[20] to look over for twenty days or so. Please remove the cotton padding from the quilted vest I left with you this fall. I want to make it into an unpadded jacket.

Ryōkan
[119]

[Date unknown]

To Shichihiko:[21]

I trust you have survived the winter without difficulty and are looking forward to spring. Have you actually been practicing what it says in the biography of Hakuyū?[22] I myself have been doing those practices, and maybe that's why I have gotten through this winter so easily.

A poem:

> Don't go clambering wildly after things
> Just keep quiet and guard your tongue
> Eat when your stomach starts to growl
> Click your teeth together when you wake up[23]
> I studied the record of Hakuyū
> And grasped something of the art of preserving life[24]
> If you always have your vital force
> filling you within
> How can you be overrun
> by evils from outside?

Ryōkan
[109]

Eleventh day of the fifth month

To Shichihiko at Na'nukaichi:

My deep appreciation for the lily bulbs,[25] which I received before the end of the year.

> Everything in this world changes
> Only your heart
> Remains ever the same
> Straightforward as the bamboo

Ryōkan
[110]

Twenty-second day of the second month

To Master Ryūzen:[26]

The other day I sent you a letter. Did you receive it?

I had wanted to climb the mountain, but anticipated that your temple would be bustling at that particular time and so decided not to come after all. I still have some of the sake left over from the other day. Having my wits fully about me again,[27] everything I eat or drink tastes simply marvelous. I'm recovering day by day, so you mustn't worry about me.

That's all I wanted to say. When you have the chance, please also convey this to Hōju-in[28] for me.

That's all

Ryōkan

[125]

Fourth day of the tenth month

To [the Abbot of] Dairenji:

This is to let you know that I received the ball you kindly sent. It has a particularly beautiful design, and I'm delighted to have it.

Sincerely

[127]

Ryōkan mentions Dairenji in an interesting handwritten fragment in the possession of the Abe family, descendants of Ryōkan's friend and patron Abe Sadayoshi. The account, written in Japanese, has sustained some insect damage, and brackets in the translation below represent missing characters:

On around the tenth day of the eleventh month, on my way back from Makigahana, a storm suddenly blew up, filling the air with dust, while from the northwest [   ] rain and hail fell like small stones. When I glanced up toward Mount Kugami [   ] fearsome clouds had gathered, and there was a rumbling of thunder; in the distance, villages faded from view. That day, I was barely able to reach a town called Nakajima.

At Dairenji was a monk of my acquaintance, whom I asked for lodging. The storm had left me soaked to the skin, and seeing the state I was in, the village women took pity on me and brought me a change of clothes. They took turns, each woman removing an item of clothing and, with her own hands, hanging it out to dry.

They vie to take them and
    hang them out to dry
My traveling clothes
Sodden from the rain and hail

[Zenshū 1, pp. 515–516]

Twenty-first day of the first month

To the Owner of Chikiriya:[29]

    I'm delighted with the new ball you sent me, which arrived safely.

With the new ball you sent
I've passed
The whole day
Bouncing and counting[30]

[154]

[Date unknown]

To the Owner of Muramatsuya:[31]

    Last winter, after you had returned home, I found some writing paper left in my scrap pile. I thought I would send it back to you now, but I've searched everywhere and just can't seem to find it. I'm really getting old! Whenever I do get my hands on the paper, I'll return it to you.

Since I live in a hut
In the shade of the grove of Otogo shrine
The sound of the iron prayer bell
Tells me a visitor has come

Ryōkan

[153]

In Japan, spherical iron bells, known as *nude* or *sanagi,* are generally hung over the entrance to Shintō shrines. Worshipers, or even those simply passing through the shrine's precincts, will pull the bell-rope, ringing the bell and signaling their presence to the shrine's god, or *kami.* Ryōkan's poem implies that the place where he lives is so remote that the ringing of the shrine bell invariably announces a visitor to his hut. In a sense, the shrine god functions as Ryōkan's gatekeeper.

                                    At Teradomari,[32] end of the third month
To Kuwahara Yūsetsu:
    What a pleasure the other day after such a long time to behold
your august visage. And by the way, I seem to have left behind my
undershirt. If you have it there, I would appreciate your giving it to this
messenger.

                                                    That's all.
                                                    Ryōkan

    The opening sentence of this letter to Kuwahara Yūsetsu (n.d.), a
    local physician and friend of Ryōkan's, is comically respectful in
    tone. The undershirt was presumably misplaced during an exami-
    nation by the doctor.

                        [Tōgō, *Shinshū Ryōkan,* p. 280]

                                                    The eleventh month
To Kashiwasaki:[33]
    I have felt very unwell of late and, even if people expressly ask
me, am not doing any calligraphy.

                                                    That's all.
                                                    Ryōkan
                                                    [169]

                            Twenty-eighth day of the eleventh month
To Niigata:[34]
    I don't know if this scroll is authentic or not. In any case, I don't
find it particularly interesting. Perhaps you'd better show it to someone
else.

                                                    That's all.
                                                    Ryōkan
                                                    [172]

                                    Eleventh day of the second month
[Recipient unknown]
    Following your visit the other day, I caught another cold but
after a day or two, was finally well again. Stuck indoors with my hair

still long,[35] I've used the time to copy out the *Lotus Sūtra*. Enclosed is the result. Because I've been ill, there's no power in my brushwork, so please excuse the appearance of the characters.

Ryōkan

[161]

Fourth day of the seventh month

[Recipient unknown]

Even though you sent a messenger here in the snow, the fact is that lately I'm unable to do any calligraphy. All my brushes are worn out. And even if I had a brush, I wouldn't be able to lift it. No matter who comes asking, my reply will be exactly the same.

That's all.

Ryōkan

[158]

Ryōkan disliked being badgered for samples of his calligraphy, and popular legend suggests that letters such as this one, refusing to comply with collectors' requests, resulted from the ingenuity of the collectors' agents themselves. According to these accounts, if Ryō-kan was unwilling to do any brushwork, the agent would beg him to state this in writing so that his employer would not berate him for returning home empty-handed. The kind-hearted Ryōkan invariably complied, thus being tricked into supplying a piece of his calligraphy after all.

Fifth day of the tenth month

[Recipient unknown]

How are you faring in this cold weather? I am well. By the way, I find myself in need of cotton clothes. I earnestly entreat you to have two rolls of cotton dyed black and sent to me.

That's all

Ryōkan

[171]

Tōgō Toyoharu has suggested that this letter is associated with the following Japanese poem and introduction by Ryōkan:

In the tenth month, a traveler with only a straw raincoat stood begging at the gate of my hut. I removed my old robe and gave it to him. That night, there was a storm, accompanied by blisteringly cold winds:

> At whose village is the traveler sleeping
> Now at midnight
> As the winds of the storm
> Blow colder and colder?

[*Zenshū* 2, no. 430]

Forgeries of Ryōkan's calligraphy seem already to have appeared during his lifetime, as revealed in the following excerpt from a letter sent by Ryōkan's friend and patron Kimura Motouemon. It was composed about 1830, shortly before Ryōkan's death, in response to a request for examples of Ryōkan's calligraphy by the Echigo writer Suzuki Bokushi.[36]

Even though there are pieces of calligraphy attributed to Master Ryōkan on the market, I would caution you not to purchase them carelessly. Recently, a messenger brought from Mr. Yamada in Yoita two pieces said to be by Master Ryōkan: a verse attached to a painting of Kanzan and Jittoku[37] and a poem with which I was familiar copied on writing paper. Both were for sale, but Mr. Yamada could not tell if they were genuine and wanted to ask [Ryōkan's] advice. When Master Ryōkan examined them, he kindly wrote me, saying: "Both are fakes." So, if I may, in light of the above, I would humbly advise you not to purchase such items.

. . . As to Master Ryōkan's health, since the beginning of the eighth month, he has been unwell, and has not yet recovered from his diarrhea. However, he has no problem in getting about, so that we do not need a nurse. If he survives till the warm spring weather, a visit from you would be welcome indeed. You know how Master Ryōkan is: with people he knows well, he does not make any particular effort to be hospitable. But just come to visit, nevertheless, and let him see your face.[38]

We have virtually no verifiable documentation for Ryōkan's period of *angya*, or pilgrimage. An exception is the following letter from the nun Teishin to her colleague the Monk Zōun (1813–1869). The letter describes the young Ryōkan's visit to the Master Taiji Sōryū (d. 1789, reading uncertain), an Echigo Sōtō Zen teacher.

The Zen Master Sōryū was surely an accomplished teacher, according to a story I heard from Master Ryōkan. At that time, the Master was traveling on pilgrimage, and hearing of the Zen master Sōryū's great reputation for wisdom and virtue, he determined to meet him. The Master [i.e., Ryōkan] visited his temple, but Sōryū, having retired from his official duties, was living at a nearby hermitage and almost never received visitors. There was no question of rashly intruding, and the Master sought out the help of one of Sōryū's monk attendants. The attendant, however, was unable to do anything for him, and the Master found himself spending the days in vain, having come all the way there for nothing. Since his attempts to have the attendant intervene on his behalf showed no signs of promise, he determined to appeal directly to Sōryū himself, and having written a letter to this effect, he stole out one evening at midnight and went to Sōryū's hermitage. The hermitage, however, was surrounded by a high wall, and the Master could find no way to scale it.

"Well, what shall I do?" he thought, and then, glancing around, noticed that a branch of the pine tree in the garden protruded over the wall. Delighted, he grabbed the branch and easily lowered himself into the garden, only to find the sliding doors [of Sōryū's quarters] locked shut. Unable to get in and filled with regret at the prospect of returning unsuccessfully after having come this far in his quest, he stood there wondering what to do. Looking around, he noticed outside the sliding doors a basin for washing the hands. "This is the perfect place!" he exclaimed. "He's sure to come out and wash his hands at daybreak, and when he does, he'll see my message!" The Master then placed a written message on the lid of the washbasin and retreated to the foot of the wall. It suddenly occurred to him, however, that a wind might blow the message away. So he came back and, picking up a stone, placed it on the note.

The Master had barely returned to the temple when the morning services began.[39] Halfway through the chanting of the twenty-fifth chapter of the *Lotus Sūtra*,[40] a monk was seen approaching along the passageway that led from Sōryū's hermitage, holding a paper lantern to light his way. People were curious and wondered what sort of business could bring someone to the temple at such an hour. The monk announced: "Among you is a monk named Ryōkan. [Sōryū] has sent me as a messenger to invite you to join him."

"The others were all shocked and amazed," the Master recalled, "but I was overjoyed." He immediately went to meet Sōryū, who told him: "From now on, you don't have to ask to be admitted. Just come any time you please."

Thereafter, the Master frequently visited Sōryū and discussed Buddhism. This is the story that he told me. How I now regret never having asked him for the details of those dialogues!

[*Zenshū 2*, pp. 501–502]

Reflections on Buddhism

Ryōkan was critical of the Buddhist temple establishment of his day, regarding it as degraded. Yet, as the following works reveal, he remained committed to Buddhism itself and to the monk's vocation. "Invitation to the Way" (Tōgō Toyoharu, *Ryōkan zenshū* 1, no. 1) is a summary of the history of Buddhism, and Zen in particular, in which Ryōkan assesses the current situation of Buddhism in Japan. "The Priesthood" (*Zenshū* 1, no. 2) presents Ryōkan's criticism of the contemporary Buddhist clergy. "On Begging One's Food" (*Zenshū* 1, no. 102) explains Ryōkan's views on the importance of the monk's begging practice. Ryōkan believed that this practice embodied the essence of the Buddha's teaching and felt that, through his own simple and independent way of life, he was striving to revive the authentic Zen of the early masters.

Invitation to the Way

With each passing year, the ways of the world grow more depraved. People's hearts grow ever more unsettled, while the patriarchs' teaching grows dimmer and dimmer. Teachers of Buddhism promote their particular schools, and their students parrot their example. Both stick together like lacquer and glue, stubbornly holding to their position, never giving even an inch. If Buddhism required separate schools, why didn't the ancient worthies establish them? People set up various schools; but where does someone like me fit in? So I want you all to keep quiet for a while, and listen to my Invitation to the Way.

Of course, the teaching of the Way had a beginning, when the Buddha was asked to preach on the Vulture Peak.[1] The Buddha was supreme among even the gods. No one could challenge the truth of his teaching. But five hundred years after the Buddha entered nirvāna, people began to elaborate on what he taught. The Sage Nāgarjuna[2] appeared in the world, composing commentaries of the greatest subtlety. But if you just follow the Way itself, you needn't fight over which teachings are right and which wrong.

Buddhism traveled to the East, establishing itself first at the White Horse temple.[3] The patriarch Bodhidharma journeyed to China, and immediately all other teachings yielded to his. His school flourished during the great T'ang dynasty,[4] its glory unequaled since that time. It guided the priesthood and the people, with each teacher of Zen becoming a leader of Buddhism. The Sudden and Gradual schools[5] were provided for people of differing spiritual capacity, but the Northern and Southern schools had not yet diverged. Toward the close of the Sung dynasty,[6] the first cracks began to appear in the white wall of Zen. The five houses[7] turned to fighting among themselves, the eight schools[8] vied with one another for supremacy. The consequences of these events are still with us, and the situation is now nearly hopeless.

Here in Japan, we had the Master of Eiheiji.[9] He stood at the forefront of the patriarchs' teaching. Having received his teacher Ju-ching's[10] sanction, he proclaimed the teaching throughout our land. Eminent priests and learned scholars are dwarfed by the grandeur of his *Shōbōgenzō*.[11] So successfully did he labor to spread the teaching through this work that no student of Zen, however benighted, can fail to receive its light. Everything in it that needs pruning has been pruned; everything that needs adding has been added. But in the years since the teacher left this world, the brambles of heresy have overgrown the lordly temple halls, while the fragrant grasses of true Buddhism lay smothered by weeds. Who among us can sing your lofty melody? Today vulgar songs fill the streets. How sad to have been born into such an age! A great house stands on the brink of collapse. I am but a single rafter—how can I support it alone? In the stillness of the night, I toss restlessly and, unable to sleep, compose this poem.[12]

The Priesthood

You shave your head and become a monk, begging for food, living from hand to mouth. Just look at yourself: that's how it is. So why not simply face the truth?

I see those who have become monks thoughtlessly raising their voices night and day. Only concerned with filling their stomachs, they spend their lives pursuing externals. For a layman to lack dedication to the Way may be excused; but for a monk to be like this is obscene.

When you shave your head, you sever all attachment to the

three worlds.[13] When you don the monk's robes, you destroy the world of appearances. Casting off all bonds of affection, you enter the realm of the unconditioned, indifferent to "right" and "wrong."

Wherever one goes in the world, men and women have their allotted tasks. Without weaving, how can one make clothes? Without tilling the fields, how can one feed oneself? Those who nowadays call themselves Shākyamuni Buddha's disciples have neither practice nor enlightenment. They uselessly consume the offerings of the faithful, heedless of the offenses they commit. Instead, they band together and talk big, going on like this from morning till night. Outwardly, they pretend to be superior, playing on the gullibility of old peasant women and congratulating themselves on their cleverness. Alas! Will they ever come to their senses? A monk would sooner walk among mother tigers than tread the path of fame and fortune. Let the smallest lust for fame and fortune enter the mind, and all the waters of the ocean will not wash it away. What have you been doing with your time since your father sent you to become a monk? You may burn incense or pray to the gods and buddhas that your dedication to the Way will always be firm; but if you remain as you are today, your path will be blocked at every turn.

The three worlds are but a temporary abode and human life as fleeting as the morning dew. A good opportunity is easily lost, the true teaching hard to encounter. You've got to make a fresh start! Don't wait for me to tell you again and extend a helping hand. I'm pleading with you earnestly now, but for me it's a cheerless task. From here on, I want you to reflect carefully and change your ways. Strive hard, you successors of the Buddha, that you may have no regrets!

On Begging One's Food

The practice of begging one's food is the very lifeblood of the tradition of monkhood. That is why there exist the particular forms for begging and for eating with the wooden bowl. With the pure rice from the Buddha of Fragrance, Vimalakīrti was able to feed the vast assembly;[14] Cunda offered the Buddha his last meal and was thus able to receive Shākyamuni's illuminating wisdom.[15] When Prince Siddhartha[16] undertook ascetic practice in the Himalayas, he first studied with the teacher Ârâda Kālāma,[17] subsisting on a daily ration of only one hemp seed and one grain of millet. Yet this difficult and painful practice was of no benefit in his search for enlightenment. Seeing that this practice was not the true Dharma, he abandoned it, and realized the Way.

The practice [of begging] is common to all the buddhas. Know that all the buddhas practiced begging in realizing the Way. The successive generations of patriarchs, too, practiced begging in transmitting the torch of the teaching. Therefore it is said that a monk should receive food obtained in the proper manner and should not receive food obtained in a manner that is improper. It is further said that over-eating makes one drowsy and slothful, while eating too little deprives one of the energy to pursue enlightenment.

The *Last Admonition Sūtra*[18] says: "O monks, receive offerings of food and drink just as you would medicine. Whether [the food] is good or bad, your response must not differ."[19] It is also said: "During those periods when eating is allowed, you should nourish yourself in a pure fashion and endeavor to dispel all afflictions. You must not be greedy and thereby destroy good intentions (i.e., both your own and those of the food's donors). Just so, one who is wise knows what load his ox can bear and will not let it exhaust itself."[20] The *Vimalakīrti Sūtra* says: "Once Mahākāśyapa, as a deliberate act of kindness, went begging in a poor village. Vimalakīrti upbraided him, saying: 'You should beg from all alike. For one who is impartial, receiving food of any sort, has realized the impartiality of Dharma.'"[21]

The *Rules for Zazen* state: "In winter, do not allow yourself to become cold; in summer, do not allow yourself to become hot. If it is bright, lower the shade; if it is dark, open the window. Be moderate in eating and drinking, and sleep during the assigned periods."[22] The *Five Meditations on Received Food*[23] states: "In receiving this food, first, be aware of all the effort involved in providing the food; second, be aware of the source of the food; third, be aware of your own degree of dedication [as a monk] when receiving offerings; fourth, [bear in mind that the food you receive is only] meant to sustain you—nothing more; fifth, be aware that the food is provided you in order to realize your practice of Buddhism."[24] All these testify to [the importance of] receiving food [as part of the monk's life].

Unless [a monk] receives food, his body will not be in proper order; if his body is not in proper order, his mind will not be in proper order; if his mind is not in proper order, it will be impossible to practice the Way. Is this not why we praise the Buddha as the Great Charioteer?[25] A man of old said: "Man's mind is filled with dangers; the mind

of the Way is subtle; make your mind pure and dedicated and adhere to
the Mean."[26] There are those who grow their nails long, whose hair is un-
kempt, who do not bathe all year. Some expose themselves to the
scorching sun, others fast and avoid eating grains. Such men follow the
way of the heretical teachers,[27] not the way of the Buddha. And even
for those who do not follow precisely these practices but only similar
ones, know that these remain heretical teachings, not to be accepted
or practiced.

There are those who leave behind the family ties that doom one
to ignorance, sitting in meditation in a rustic hut, walking in meditation
beneath the trees, who take as their companions the valley streams and
the color of the hills, following in the footsteps of the old sages and
becoming models of religious devotion.

I once heard from a learned priest that many of the ancient wor-
thies lived in retreat deep in the mountains and valleys. Far from any
town, they always had difficulty in begging their food. When the op-
portunity presented itself, they would gather mountain fruits or wild
vegetables to sustain their diet.

Nowadays, one finds practitioners who subsist exclusively on
trees. They live right in the towns, and yet refuse to eat any cultivated
grains. What kind of teaching is that! It seems like Buddhism, but it's
not; it resembles the heretical teachings [of the Buddha's day], but it
isn't even that. It is nothing more than a display of eccentric behavior
that deludes sentient beings—unless they've just gone crazy practicing
Buddhism. Nevertheless, laymen revere these people as if they were
arhats with the six supernatural powers.[28] And seeing themselves so
highly revered by laymen, they, too, begin to consider their practice
superior. How shameful! The blind leading the blind, and all of them
falling together into a great pit!

The ancient worthies, for the sake of the Dharma, surrendered
their lives, renounced selfish existence, relinquished all craving for
fame and fortune, devoting themselves only to seeking the Way. For
this reason, they received the offerings of heavenly beings, revered
even by devas and nagas.[29] The men of today perform difficult and
painful practices, in vain debilitating the body they received from their
parents. What a pity! [A monk,] it is true, should never struggle desper-
ately to preserve his life, and yet how can it be correct to deliberately
endanger it? Such behavior goes even beyond fanaticism! What I want
people to understand is that endangering your physical health is not
difficult. What is difficult is thoroughly to realize [the Dharma]. That is

why it is said: "The hardest thing is to persevere." I respectfully address these words to all who practice the Way, in hope that they will carefully reflect upon and take them to heart.

                                                                    The Monk Ryōkan

Fragments

> The following is a fragmentary essay in which Ryōkan discusses the principles for studying with a teacher (*Zenshū* 1, no. 154).

If you're going to study with a teacher, above all, you've first got to grasp his realization. What does it mean, to grasp his realization? If your view is different from his, for the time being, you must cast your own view aside and devote yourself to penetrating his teaching. Once your understanding conforms to his, then you can calmly reflect:

Where do his strengths and weaknesses lie? Where is he right? Where is he wrong? Then, abandon the areas of weakness, affirm the areas of strength. Abandon what is wrong, and affirm what is right. And going along step by step like this, you'll arrive at the wisdom of enlightenment.

> The following "admonition" in Ryōkan's hand is in the collection of the Kimura family, descendants of Ryōkan's patron Kimura Motouemon (*Zenshū* 1, p. 505).

When you encounter those who are wicked, unrighteous, foolish, dim-witted, deformed, vicious, chronically ill, lonely, unfortunate, or handicapped, you should think: "How can I save them?" And even if there is nothing you can do, at least you must not indulge in feelings of arrogance, superiority, derision, scorn, or abhorrence, but should immediately manifest sympathy and compassion. If you fail to do so, you should feel ashamed and deeply reproach yourself saying: "How far I have strayed from the Way! How can I betray the old sages? I take these words as an admonition to myself."

                                                                    The Monk Ryōkan

> Ryōkan copied out the following passages from the *Last Admonition Sūtra,* a short Buddhist text purporting to be the Buddha's last instructions to his disciples before his passing and an important text in the liturgy of the Zen school.[30] Ryōkan then reduces the passages

to six capsule phrases and rearranges them in his own numerical order, evidently as a kind of reminder in his daily practice. The manuscript, brushed in Ryōkan's finest *kaisho,* or standard-style, calligraphy, was discovered by Tōgō Toyoharu in a private family collection (*Shinshū Ryōkan,* p. 111).

In his final instructions, the Buddha said:

Always keep control of your mind. The mind is fearsome as a poisonous snake, a wild animal, or a murderous brigand. It is hard to restrain as a mad elephant without a chain or an ape free to leap among the treetops. It must be promptly subdued and not allowed to run wild.

Whatever sort of food you receive, receive it as if it were medicine. Whether it is pleasing or displeasing, your attitude should remain the same. Accept only what you need to sustain your body, and so stave off hunger and thirst.

A sense of shame is the greatest adornment. Shame is like an iron hook: it can restrain a person's wrong conduct. Therefore one must always preserve a sense of shame and never lose it for even a moment. One who is without shame is no different from a beast.

Even upholding the precepts and practicing austerities cannot compare with the virtue of forbearance. One who truly practices forbearance deserves to be called mighty.

If you would obtain the joy of absolute peace, you must avoid commotion and live alone in a quiet place. One who dwells in a quiet place will be worshiped by Indra and all the gods.[31]

If you indulge in idle talk, your mind will become agitated.

1. Guard your tongue!
2. Keep your mind in control!
3. Know shame!
4. Forbear!
5. Always live alone!
6. Be moderate in eating!

These are the admonitions bequeathed by the Buddha to be upheld by practitioners. Never treat them lightly! Human life is like the morning dew. The Buddha Dharma[32] is difficult to meet with. Strive hard!

Words of Advice

Ryōkan composed various pieces in which he expressed his view of human foibles, often in the form of lists offering the reader "words of advice," or *kaigo*. Taken literally, the characters for *kaigo* may be read "words of the precepts"—the precepts *(kai)* being rules of conduct administered by a Buddhist teacher in accepting a person as his disciple. The giving of the precepts is, as a rule, a formal procedure, conducted in a temple and often involving elaborate ritual. But here Ryōkan merely presents a series of personal notes and reflections, his own characteristically simple and straightforward means of instruction.

There is considerable similarity among these compositions, with many repeated or nearly identical items, so that only three of the lists (I, II, and IV) are translated here in their entirety, accompanied by selected translations from others (III). Ryōkan's distaste for "empty" or unnecessary talk is a frequent theme of the "lists." A Chinese poem he composed articulates his feelings on the perils of thoughtless speech:

> Talk is always easy
> Practice always hard
> It's no wonder people try to make up for
>   their lack of hard practice with easy talk
> But the harder they try, the worse things get
> The more they talk, the more wrong they go
> It's like pouring on oil to put out a fire
> Just foolishness and nothing else[33]

Although at times the order of items is not strictly logical—mixing things Ryōkan dislikes with bits of homely advice and casual observation—the lists are presented in their original formats except for the editing of some redundant portions.

I

Some things I find disturbing:

People who talk too much
People who talk too fast
Boisterous speech
People who talk to themselves
Gratuitous remarks
Flowery speech

People who never learn
People who are two-faced
People who start to speak before others have finished
Inappropriate remarks
Lecturing others about losing their tempers
Lecturing others when you lose your temper
People who make a fuss over nothing
Exposing things people wish to conceal
Playing the fool
Toadyism
Answering people without understanding what they've told you
Words spoken in passing
Fight stories
Political scuttlebutt
People who swindle children
People who make children worldly-wise
Drivel
People who like to use words they don't understand
Miracle stories
Bewailing things that can't be helped
Treachery
If something trivial is said, just ignore it
It's not easy to be a good listener
Idle chatter
Telling a story properly from beginning to end is no easy
    matter
Constantly regretting what's already past
Bragging about one's exploits
Knowing something isn't so, yet insisting it is
Irritating chatter
People who get together and talk raucously after everyone else
    has gone to sleep
People who speak without first taking account of others'
    feelings
People who are always correcting others
Talking like a know-it-all
Forcing others to listen while you go on about yourself
Replying to people without understanding what they're saying
Discussing the gods and buddhas in a casual manner
Giving too many orders at once
Giving too many orders at once and not explaining them fully

Piling on extra demands

Making discouraging remarks

Perversely refusing to heed advice

Flattering others

Mistakenly scolding people

Making cheap promises

Speaking in a vulgar manner

Before you finish speaking about one thing, moving on to another

Telling people things through second parties

Speaking to others with feigned sympathy only leads them to hate you in the end

Casually promising someone things only leads in the end to breaking your promise

You can say what you want behind someone's back, so long as you can say it to their face

Explaining something to others that you don't fully understand yourself

Acting as if you know something you don't know

Be sparing with words as if each one were precious

If one word can't say it all, explain further

Once spoken, a word can't be called back

Verbosity is unappealing[34]

II

Things that show a lack of feeling for others:

Amusing oneself by deceiving children

Amusing oneself by teasing the blind

Amusing oneself by using false flattery

Using rude speech when giving orders to servants

Speaking harshly to beggars

Careless speech

Telling people how you're going to give something to them before you do it

Telling people how you gave something to them after you do it

Giving people directions for things with which you yourself are unfamiliar

Leading people to believe false information

Claiming to discern the will of the gods and buddhas behind events

Things I find disturbing:

People who say things under their breath
People who speak in a distant manner
People who speak pedantically
People who don't say what they really mean
People who give stern orders about trivial things
People who want you to lend them things but don't return them
People who say they'll give you things and never do

Things I can't abide:

People who never stop talking

Things I find charmless:

Broaching sensitive points in an insensitive manner

Things I find embarrassing:

Having people praise you to your face

Things you can't trust:

People who try to gauge your reaction as they speak

Things that show a lack of sincerity:

Breaking promises

Things that demonstrate a lack of sensitivity:

People who sing around someone in distress
People who talk constantly about eating around someone who
    is fasting
People who jabber away when someone next to them can't
    sleep
People who wake others violently
People who thoughtlessly issue orders to children
People who lecture drunks
Priests who discuss the amount of the alms they receive
Priests who chatter when attending a religious talk
Priests who chatter during sūtra chanting
People who yawn when they recite the *nenbutsu*
Priests who linger at a patron's house, trying to cadge a meal

Guests who are picky eaters
People who say inappropriate things
People whose actions don't match their words

The things people say when children cry:

Who did it to you?
Just bear it!
If you don't stop, tomorrow there'll be rain!
If you don't stop, we'll put moxa[35] on you!
If you don't stop, we'll send for the doctor!

Pointless things:

People who speak in riddles

Groundless beliefs:

Stories about mountain hermits who fly through the clouds and
    eat only mist[36]

III

Teaching others about things you don't know yourself

. . .

Excessive reasoning

. . .

Speaking thoughtlessly on solemn occasions

. . .

People who always want to be acknowledged
Staring at people one speaks to

. . .

Telling others about one's distinguished lineage

. . .

Treating conjecture as truth

. . .

Mentioning every single thing one sees or hears
Discussing whether a sermon is skillful or not
Discussing whether a government official is good or bad
People who like to lecture about things
Children who grow up too fast

. . .

Speaking with one's hands

Moving one's head up and down while arguing
Mimicking
Misquoting others
People who are always complaining
Pushy behavior
Circulating stale gossip

. . .

Edo-style talk[37] in provincials' mouths
Speaking as if one came from Kyoto

. . .

Uncritically passing on rumors

. . .

Speaking in an overly familiar manner

. . .

Memorizing the words of a sermon so one knows just the right
place to start to cry

. . .

Pretentious talk about enlightenment
Pretentious talk about learning
Pretentious talk about the tea ceremony
Pretentious talk about art

. . .

Feeling grateful only when one enjoys abundant good fortune or
receives lots of things

. . .

Looking down one's nose at others[38]

IV

The following list appears to consist of brief "reminders" that Ryō-
kan noted for his own use.

Offer incense and flowers to the Buddha
Plant trees and shrubs, sweep the garden, carry water, remove
rocks
From time to time, apply moxa to legs
Don't eat fatty fish
Don't eat anything oily
Always eat plain foods
Don't sleep late
Don't overeat

Don't take long naps
Don't do things you know you shouldn't be doing
Don't be lazy
Don't do things halfway
Don't try to hide from your worries
Drink sake hot[39]
Keep your head shaved
Cut fingernails and toenails
Rinse the mouth and clean the teeth
Bathe
Speak out loud[40]

Finder's Lists

Kanshi

Sources for the translations of Ryōkan's kanshi are given below in the order in which the translations appear. Pages in the present work are given at left; the source of the text from which the translation was made appears at right. Unless otherwise indicated, numbers refer to poem numbers in Tōgō Toyoharu, *Ryōkan Zenshū* (Tokyo, 1959), volume 1. Occasionally, the text in the *Zenshū* has been supplemented by texts in two other sources: Iriya Yoshitaka, *Ryōkan shishū*, Zen no koten 12 (Tokyo, 1982), and Iida Rigyō, *Teihon Ryōkan shishū yaku* (Tokyo, 1989). In these instances, the *Zenshū* poem numbers are followed by a second entry, referring to the relevant page numbers in either "Iida" or "Iriya." Poems marked only "Iida" or "Iriya" do not appear in the *Zenshū*.

Page	Source	Page	Source
107	277	114	94
108	192	114	267
108	50	114	210
109	7	115	269
109	311	115	188
110	Iriya 178	115	295
110	393	116	95
111	177	117	100
111	Iriya 149	117	230
112	6	118	83
112	278	118	222
113	212	119	306
113	228	119	321

Page	Source	Page	Source
156	49	179	217
156	226	179	375
157	244	180	8
157	158	180	214
158	159	181	340
158	160	182	334
159	272	183	181
159	119	183	353
160	51	184	82
160	255	184	141
161	34	185	107
161	35	186	180
162	116	186	220
162	143	187	297
163	46	187	348
164-165	69	188	233
166-167	42	189	358
167	263	190	403
168	166	191-192	238
168	314	192	133
169	366	193	261
169	164	193	129
170	285	194	99
170	130	194	165
171	382	195	336
171	273	195	80
172	79	196	185
172-173	70	196	147
174	207	197	106
174	186	197	259
175	87	198	262
175	363	198	75
176	64	199	184
176	391	199	293
177	171	200	309
177	388	200	53
178	329	201	135
178	367	201	195

Waka

Sources for the translations of Ryōkan's waka are given below in the order in which the translations appear. Pages of the present work are given at left; the text from which the translation was made appears at right. Unless otherwise indicated, numbers refer to poem numbers in Tōgō Toyoharu, *Ryōkan zenshū,* volume 2. Waka marked "Yoshino" do not appear in the *Zenshū* and are based on Yoshino Hideo, *Ryōkan: uta to shōgai* (Tokyo, 1975). Waka from *Hachisu no tsuyu* are based on the text in *Zenshū* 2, pages 490–499 and are unnumbered.

Page	Source	Page	Source
203	4	209	513
203	21	210	516
204	25	210	561
204	26	210	566
204	849	211	604
205	850	211	605
205	851	211	638
205	852	212	641
206	855	212	642
206	860	213	657
206	862	213	644
207	865	213	324
207	1239	214	683
207	838	214	Yoshino 83
208	844	214	488
208	835	215	272
208	32	216	402
209	512	216	Yoshino 61

Notes

Introduction

1. Minakami Tsutomu, *Ryōkan* (Tokyo, 1984), p. 3.

2. Miya Eiji, "Ryōkan kenkyū no kaiko to tenbō," in *Ryōkan kenkyū ronshū*, ed. Miya Eiji (Tokyo, 1985), p. 17.

3. Tōgō Toyoharu, ed., *Ryōkan zenshū*, 2 vols. (Tokyo, 1959), vol. 1, no. 192.

4. Hayden White, *Tropics of Discourse* (Baltimore, 1978), p. 2. Also see White, *Metahistory* (Baltimore, 1973), pp. 1–42. For various ways in which contemporary language theories illustrate the primacy of the figurative over the literal in the signifying movements of the text, see Julia Kristeva, *Desire in Language* (New York, 1980), pp. 92–123; Barthes, *Mythologies* (New York, 1972), pp. 109–158; Paul Ricoeur, *Interpretation Theory* (Fort Worth, 1976), pp. 45–69; and J. L. Austin, *How to Do Things with Words* (Oxford, 1962).

Ryōkan of Mount Kugami

1. Quoted from *Kitsuen shiwa* (Stories of Poetry and Poets Told While Smoking), an 1814 anthology edited by Ryōkan's friend and biographer Suzuki Bundai (1796–1870), in Tōgō Toyoharu, ed., *Ryōkan zenshū* (Tokyo, 1959), 2, p. 489 (hereafter abbreviated *Zenshū*).

2. Walt Whitman, "The Biography," manuscript in the Oscar Lion Collection, New York Public Library. Astor, Lenox, and Tilden Foundations.

3. Ryōkan's father's name is also given as Yamamoto Iori and Tachibana Samon Yasuo.

4. *Ryōkan zenji den* (Biography of the Zen Master Ryōkan), in *Zenshū* 1, p. 593. Ōzeki (d. 1834) composed his biography in 1818, during Ryōkan's lifetime.

5. According to Kokusen's biography, in 1779, during a circuit of Sōtō temples in Echigo, Kokusen had been present at Kōshōji for Genjō's ceremonial installation as abbot as well as for an attendant ordination of monks and intensive meditation retreat, and may have met Ryōkan on that occasion. See Okayama Sōtō-shū seinenkai, ed., *Ryōkan no shi, Tainin Kokusen zenji den* (Kurashiki, 1982), 86, 114. Japanese scholars have debated the age at which Ryōkan actually entered the priesthood. Biographies by Ryōkan's contemporaries give his age as either seventeen or twenty-one. It seems likely that both are, in a sense, correct, Ryōkan having left home and entered Kōshōji as a novice at seventeen, formally receiving the ton-

sure and becoming a Zen monk at twenty-one, during Kokusen's 1779 visit to the temple.

6. Published in Okayama Sōtōshū seinenkai, *Kokusen zenji den,* 166-168. The rules were elaborated by Kokusen's successor as abbot, Gentō Sokuchū (1729-1807).

7. The poem is included in the closing section of Kera Yoshishige's *Curious Accounts,* translated below.

8. As a rule, distinguished Japanese Zen monks have two Buddhist names, known respectively as *azana* and *imina.* The names may be received at different times, but are generally read in combination (e.g., Taigu Ryōkan, Dōgen Kigen, and so forth). Ryōkan refers to himself in his letters and poems as "Ryōkan"; the name "Taigu" (or Daigu) is first recorded in autumn 1831, shortly after Ryōkan's death, in the inscription for a proposed mortuary tablet (*Zenshū* 1, p. 596).

9. Teishin's account is translated in "Letters," pp. 391-393.

10. An old province on the island of Shikoku, included in present-day Kōchi prefecture.

11. A *ri* is approximately 2.4 miles.

12. Kōchi, Tosa's capital and site of the daimyo's castle.

13. A *chō* is approximately 119 yards.

14. The incantation *Namu Amidabutsu!* ("Praise to the buddha Amitābha!"). Amitābha, one of the "eternal" buddhas, is said to have vowed that all those who call his name will be reborn in the Pure Land, a kind of Buddhist paradise in the Western Heavens. *Nenbutsu* recitation was practiced widely in Japan, both as a form of prayer and meditation.

15. A Chinese work of the fourth century B.C.E., considered one of the classics of Taoism. It was reportedly a favorite of Ryōkan's.

16. Unidentified.

17. *Zenshū* 2, pp. 508-509.

18. The Shingon, or "mantra," school was the Japanese school of Esoteric Buddhism founded by Kūkai (Kōbō Daishi, 774-835).

19. Dates unknown. Despite the surname Tachibana, he is unrelated to Ryōkan.

20. *Zenshū* 2, p. 507.

21. *Zenshū* 2, p. 197. Quoted from a poem sent by Yamada to Ryōkan. The poem reads in full: "The voices of the children call: / 'Here he comes, Master Ryōkan / Skinny as the season's first sardine!'" In reply, Ryōkan sent the following poem to Yamada: "My punishment from a previous life / For stuffing myself and then falling asleep: / A body like a sardine!" Ibid., p. 197.

22. Suzuki Bundai, a doctor and Confucian scholar who was a close friend of Ryōkan's, was the compiler of the *Sōdōshū* (Grass Hut Anthology), a manuscript collection of Ryōkan's kanshi. The passage is quoted from Suzuki's biographical sketch of Ryōkan, an addendum to his 1849 preface to the *Sōdōshū.*

23. Tōgō Toyoharu, *Shinshū Ryōkan* (Tokyo, 1970), p. 200.

24. Suzuki Tekiken, *Ryōkan zenji mokuhatsu no ki* (Zen Master Ryōkan's Wooden Bowl Record), 1895, in *Zenshū* 1, p. 591. Tekiken's dates are 1836-1896.

25. Ōzeki, *Ryōkan zenji den,* in *Zenshū* 1, p. 594.

26. Quoted in Tōgō, *Shinshū,* 283-284.

27. Ōzeki, *Ryōkan zenji den,* in *Zenshū* 1, p. 594.

28. *Zenshū* 1, p. 588. Bundai's account appears in an inscription he composed in 1867 for a hanging scroll of Ryōkan's work belonging to the Abe family, descendants of Ryōkan's friend Abe Sadayoshi.

29. Selections from this work are translated below in the Waka section.

30. Undated memo from Teishin to the Priest Zōun (1813-1869), an early anthologist of Ryōkan's poetry. *Zenshū* 2, p. 502.

31. N.d. The Tomitori family, traditional headmen of Jizōdō, were among Ryōkan's supporters.

32. Tōgō, *Shinshū Ryōkan,* p. 101.

33. Ibid., p. 102.

34. The bodhisattva Avalokiteshvara.

35. In modern Japan referred to as the Jōdō Shinshū, or "True Pure Land Sect," it was founded by the Japanese Buddhist priest Shinran (1173-1262). The school is based on belief in the saving grace of Amitābha Buddha.

36. The *Heart Sūtra* (Skt. *Mahāprajñāpāramitā hṛdaya sūtra*) is a short sūtra presenting a distillation of essential Mahāyāna teachings. Generally speaking, Buddhist sūtras are records of teachings said to have been given by the Buddha himself. For the Chinese text of the *Heart Sūtra,* see Takakusu Junjirō et al., eds., *Taishō shinshū daizōkyō,* 85 vols. (Tokyo, 1914-1922), vol. 8, no. 250 (abbreviated T.).

A Poetics of Mendicancy: Nondualist Philosophy and Ryōkan's Figurative Strategies

1. Barthes, *The Pleasure of the Text* (New York, 1975), p. 64; italics in original.

2. Tōgō Toyoharu, ed., *Ryōkan zenshū,* 2 vols. (Tokyo, 1959), vol. 2, no. 481 (hereafter abbreviated *Zenshū*).

3. Karaki Junzō, *Ryōkan* (Tokyo, 1971), pp. 10-11.

4. For examples of such episodes, see *Ryōkan zenji kiwa,* in *Zenshū* 2, pp. 524, 530. Also see his letter dated the fourth day of the eleventh month to an anonymous addressee declining a request for his calligraphy. *Zenshū* 2, p. 387. For various anecdotes about Ryōkan's poetry and calligraphy and the villagers' attempts to obtain them, see Tanigawa Toshirō, *Ryōkan no shōgai to itsuwa* (Tokyo, 1984), pp. 354-364.

5. The earliest printed description of Ryōkan can be found in fascicle 6 of Tachibana Konron's *Hokuetsu kidan* (Marvelous Episodes of Echigo) published by Eijudō, one of the major publishing houses in Edo in the late Tokugawa era. Ryōkan was fifty-three years old when Tachibana's work appeared. See *Zenshū* 2, pp. 507-508.

6. In his letter to local chronicler Suzuki Bokushi (1770-1842) dated the seventh day of the twelfth month of Bunsei 13 (1830), Kimura Motouemon of Shimazaki, one of Ryōkan's major patrons, writes: "Even though there are pieces of calligraphy attributed to Master Ryōkan on the market, I would caution you not to purchase them carelessly. Recently, a messenger brought from Mr. Yamada in Yoita two pieces said to be by Master Ryōkan: a verse attached to a painting of Kanzan and Jittoku and a poem with which I was familiar copied on writing paper. Both were for sale, but Mr. Yamada could not tell if they were genuine and wanted to ask

[Ryōkan's] advice. When Master Ryōkan examined them, he kindly wrote me, say-ing: 'Both are fakes.' So, if I may, in light of the above, I would humbly advise you not to purchase such items." This was two years before Ryōkan's death, when he was staying in quarters in the Kimura residence, Motouemon having undertaken to care for Ryōkan in his final years. Kimura's letter is printed in Matsumoto Ichiju's *No no Ryōkan* (Tokyo, 1988), p. 255, n. 6.

7. *Ryōkan zenji kiwa*, in *Zenshū* 2, p. 524.

8. *Zenshū* 1, no. 50.

9. *Sōdōshū jo narabi ni hugen.* See *Zenshū* 1, p. 579.

10. Ryōkan's interest in the ancient poetic tradition is shared by Kamo no Mabuchi (1697–1843), Motoori Norinaga (1730–1801), Kagawa Kageki (1768–1843), and other renowned innovators of poetics in the late Tokugawa period. For the affinity of Ryōkan's waka with the *Man'yōshū,* see Tanigawa, *Ryōkan no shō-gai to itsuwa,* pp. 237–247; Nobuyuki Yuasa, trans., *The Zen Poems of Ryōkan* (Princeton, 1981), pp. 3–15. Also see Asakura Hisashi, "Ryōkan no shiika ni miru kotoba to kokoro," in *Ryōkan kenkyū ronshū,* ed. Miya Eiji (Tokyo, 1985), pp. 189–242.

11. For the stylistic influence of Han-shan and other Chinese poets on Ryō-kan's kanshi, see Nobuyuki Yuasa, *The Zen Poems of Ryōkan,* pp. 14–22. For a gen-eral discussion on the relationship between Zen and poetry, see Burton Watson, "Zen Poetry," in *Zen: Tradition and Transition,* ed. Kenneth Kraft (New York, 1988), pp. 105–124.

12. See, for example, poems 66 and 170 in *Zenshū* 1.

13. Iriya Senkai, ed., *Kanzanshi, Zen no goroku* 13 (Tokyo, 1970), p. 385, no. 281.

14. Two of the "eight diseases" *(pa-ping),* or the eight taboos, of the five-syllable, five-character-line verse identified by Ch'en-yüeh (441–513).

15. For the *p'ing-tse* regulation, see James J. Y. Liu, *The Art of Chinese Poetry* (Chicago, 1962), pp. 20–38.

16. *Zenshū* 1, no. 192.

17. *Zenshū* 1, p. 593.

18. *Zenshū* 1, no. 205. Ancient Style *(ku-feng, ku-t'i)* and Recent Form *(chin-t'i)* are the two major formats of classical Chinese poetry. Ancient Style poetry, exemplified by the poets of the Han (206 B.C.E.–217 C.E.) and Wei (220–265) periods, consists of an undetermined number of four-, five- and seven-syllable lines, characterized by flexible application of *p'ing-tse,* rhyming, and other related rules. Recent Form refers to a highly stylized, strictly regulated poetry composed of five-or seven-syllable lines producing four- or eight-line verse. Besides the *p'ing-tse* and rhyming, which must occur at the end of every even-numbered line, the eight-line verse must observe the parallel contraction on the third and fourth lines, and, again, on the fifth and sixth lines. Recent Form poetry reached its apex during the T'ang period (618–907).

19. Addressed to Yamazaki Ryōhei. See Furukawa Hisashi, ed., *Sōseki no shokan* (Tokyo, 1982), p. 322. Unless otherwise indicated, all the quotations from Japanese and Chinese sources in this introductory essay are my own translation. Excluded from this rule are Ryōkan's works that also appear in the translation sec-tion of this volume, which resulted from the joint work of Peter Haskel and me.

20. Shōō is a literary name of the late Tokugawa Confucian scholar Nukina Kaioku (1778-1863), who was renowned for his painting and calligraphy. Rai San'yō (1746-1816) is another Confucian scholar of the late Tokugawa period who is particularly well known for his kanshi and calligraphy.

21. Furukawa, *Sōseki no shokan,* p. 357.

22. Burton Watson, *Ryōkan, Zen Monk-Poet of Japan* (New York, 1977), p. 1.

23. Originally published by Shun'yōdō, Tokyo. Reproduction in 1974 by Kōkodō Press, Tokyo, with new illustrations by the painter Tomigawa Jun'ichi.

24. Originally published by Ryōkan kai, Niigata.

25. See Miya, *Ryōkan* (Tokyo, 1979), and *Ryōkan bokuseki tanbō* (Tokyo, 1983); Satō, *Izumozaki hennenshi* (Niigata, 1972); Tanigawa, *Ryōkan denki nenpu bunken mokuroku* (Sanjō, 1982).

26. "Ryōkan zenji no shūkyō," in *Ryōkan kenkyū ronshū,* ed. Miya Eiji (Tokyo, 1985), pp. 341-384.

27. Tanigawa, *Ryōkan no shōgai to itsuwa.*

28. *Ryōkan,* 2 vols. (Tokyo, 1978), vol. 2, p. 78.

29. *Ryōkan nyūmon* (Tokyo, 1985), p. 112.

30. *Ryōkan shishū* (Tokyo, 1972).

31. *Zenshū* 1, no. 267.

32. The anthology was *Kitsuen shiwa. Zenshū* 2, p. 489.

33. *Zenshū* 2, p. 489.

34. Ibid.

35. The addendum to the preface to the *Sōdōshū,* dated 1849. *Zenshū* 1, pp. 578-580.

36. *Ryōkan zenji den,* in *Zenshū* 1, pp. 593-594.

37. See my essay "Commemorating Ryōkan" below.

38. *Zenshū* 1, no. 281.

39. *Zenshū* 1, no. 270.

40. *Zenshū* 1, no. 293.

41. See Julia Kristeva, *Semeiotike* (Paris, 1969), pp. 1-26, 246-277. Also see Jonathan Culler, *The Pursuit of Signs* (Ithaca, 1981), pp. 80-118. For the distinction between the literal and figurative levels of text, see Hayden White, *Tropics of Discourse* (Baltimore, 1978), pp. 1-25, 81-100.

42. *Zenshū* 1, no. 69.

43. Paul Ricoeur, *The Rule of Metaphor* (Toronto, 1977), p. 7.

44. "In service to the poetic function, metaphor is that strategy of discourse by which language divests itself of its function of direct description in order to reach the mythic level where its function of discovery is set free" (ibid., p. 247). Ricoeur thus asserts that his expression "metaphorical truth" is not an oxymoron but a characterization of his consistent strategy to demonstrate the inseparability between reality as language construct and metaphoricity. "The 'place' of metaphor, its most intimate and ultimate abode, is neither the name, nor the sentence, nor even discourse, but the copula of the verb *to be.* The metaphorical 'is' at once signifies both 'is not' and 'is like.' If this is really so, we are allowed to speak of metaphorical truth, but in an equally 'tensive' sense of the word 'truth'" (p. 7). "We can presume to speak of metaphorical truth in order to designate the 'realistic' inten-

tion that belongs to the redescriptive power of poetic language. . . . When the poet says that 'nature is a temple where living columns . . .' the verb *to be* does not just connect the predicate *temple* to the subject *nature*. . . . The copula is not only relational. It implies besides, by means of the predicative relationship, that *what is* redescribed; it says *that* things really are this way" (p. 248).

45. *Poetics* 1, trans. Richard Janko (Indianapolis, 1987), p. 12.

46. *Zenshū* 1, p. 593.

47. *Zenshū* 1, no. 119.

48. *Zenshū* 1, no. 139.

49. *Zenshū* 1, no. 181.

50. David Loy, *Nonduality: A Study of Comparative Philosophy* (New Haven, 1988), p. 17. Italics in original.

51. Ibid., p. 1.

52. *Zenshū* 1, no. 334. Compare this poem of Ryōkan's with Nietzsche, who illustrates his nondualist approach to the problem of subject and object as follows:

> That which gives the extraordinary firmness to our belief in causality is . . . our inability to interpret events otherwise than as events caused by intentions. It is belief in the living and thinking as the only effective force—in will, in intention—it is belief that every event is a deed, that every deed presupposes a doer, it is belief in the "subject." Is this belief in the concept of subject and attribute not a great stupidity? . . . We derive the entire concept from the subjective conviction that we are causes, namely, that the arm moves—but that is an error. We separate ourselves, the doers, from the deed, and we make use of this pattern everywhere—we seek the doer for every event. What is it we have done? We have misunderstood the feeling of strength, tension, resistance, a muscular feeling that is already the beginning of the act, as the cause, or we have taken the will to do this or that for a cause because the action follows upon it. . . . when one has grasped that the "subject" is not something that creates effects, but only a fiction.

The Will to Power, trans. Walter Kaufmann and R. J. Hollingdale (New York, 1967), Sect. 550-552.

53. *Zenshū* 1, no. 185.

54. *Zenshū* 1, no. 142.

55. *Daijō kishinron* (Ch. *Ta-ch'eng ch'i-hsin lun*). See Takakusu Junjirō et al., eds., *Taishō shinshū daizōkyō*, 85 vols. (Tokyo, 1914-1922, hereafter abbreviated, T.), 32, no. 1667.

56. Yoshito Hakeda, trans., *The Awakening of Faith* (New York, 1967), p. 83.

57. Ibid., pp. 82-83.

58. *Zenshū* 1, no. 259.

59. Yoshito Hakeda, *Awakening of Faith,* p. 41.

60. *Zenshū* 1, no. 331.

61. Magliola, *Derrida on the Mend* (West Lafayette, 1984), pp. 87-129; Loy, *Nonduality,* pp. 202-260; Coward, *Derrida and Indian Philosophy* (Albany,

1990), pp. 125-146. Magliola, for instance, suggests that the deconstructive movement of Nāgārjuna's Mādhyamika theory exceeds Derrida's in its radicalness, "that Nāgārjuna's Middle Path, the Way of the Between, tracks the Derridean trace, and goes 'beyond Derrida' in that it frequents the 'unheard-of-thought,' and also, 'with one and the same stroke,' allows the reinstatement of the logocentric, too" (p. 87).

62. Jacques Derrida, *Dissemination,* trans. Barbara Johnson (Chicago, 1981).

63. *Zenshū* 1, no. 348.

64. Jacques Derrida, "Différance," in *Margins of Philosophy,* trans. Alan Bass (Chicago, 1982), p. 9.

65. Derrida's neologism from the French verb *différer,* which means both "to differ" and "to defer." "That the difference marked in the 'differ( )nce' between the *e* and the *a* eludes both vision and hearing perhaps happily suggests that here we must be permitted to refer to an order which no longer belongs to sensibility. But neither can it belong to intelligibility. . . . Here, therefore, we must let ourselves refer to an order that resists the opposition, one of the founding oppositions of philosophy, between the sensible and the intelligible." Ibid., p. 5.

66. See Derrida, "Freud and the Scene of Writing," in *Writing and Difference,* trans. Alan Bass (Chicago, 1978), p. 205.

67. *Zenshū* 1, no. 141. The quote "names are the guests of reality" is from the first chapter of the Inner Book of the *Chuang-tzu.*

68. *Ryōkan zenji kiwa,* in *Zenshū* 2, pp. 533-534.

69. *Yamamotoke keifu,* in *Zenshū* 2, p. 513.

70. *Hokuetsu kidan,* fascicle 6. Excerpts of the passages describing Ryōkan in *Zenshū* 2, p. 507.

71. Harada Jakusai's kanshi titled "Ryōkan shōnin o tazunu," dated Kansei 9 (1797), in *Jakusai monjo,* reproduced in Tanigawa Toshirō, *Ryōkan no shōgai to itsuwa,* p. 101.

72. Suzuki Bundai's *Kitsuen shiwa,* composed in the eleventh month of Bunka 11 (1816), reports that Ryōkan's hut was then located at the side of the Otogo shrine. *Zenshū* 2, p. 489. It appears that Ryōkan was using both the upper and lower huts of Mount Kugami for a few years and then finally moved to the lower hut at the Otogo shrine.

73. *Ryōkan zenji hiseki narabi ni jo,* in *Zenshū* 1, pp. 596-597.

74. See *Ryōkan zenji kiwa,* episodes 32, 33, 48, 49, in *Zenshū* 2, pp. 528, 531.

75. See Tamamuro Taijō, *Sōshiki bukkyō* (Tokyo, 1964), pp. 262-274.

76. *Zenshū* 1, pp. 12-16. Translated in this volume, in the section "Reflections on Buddhism."

77. *Zenshū* 1, p. 13.

78. *Zenshū* 1, p. 14.

79. For the rivalry between the two temples, see Heinrich Dumoulin, *Zen Buddhism: A History,* 2 vols., (New York, 1988-1990), 2, pp. 333-334; Takeuchi Michio, *Sōtōshū kyōdanshi* (Tokyo, 1971), pp. 90-110.

80. *Zenshū* 1, no. 116.

81. *Zenshū* 1, pp. 12-16. Translated in this volume, in the section "Reflections on Buddhism."

82. *Butsu suiban neban ryakusetsu kyōkaigyō* (also known as *Yuikyō-gyō*), T. 12, no. 389, pp. 110-112.

83. Ibid, p. 111a.

84. Ibid.

85. *Zenshū* 1, p. 14. The quote from the *Vimalakīrti Sūtra* is found in T. 14, no. 475, p. 540a.

86. *Zenshū* 1, no. 95.

87. *Zenshū* 1, no. 49. The bodhisattva Mañjushrī personifies *prajñā,* the Buddhist wisdom of nonduality. The east, the direction of sunrise, is symbolic of one's awakening to enlightenment.

88. *Nakanoshima sonshi,* quoted in Minakami Tsutomu, *Ryōkan* (Tokyo, 1984), pp. 119-123.

89. *Zenshū* 1, no. 272.

90. *Zenshū* 1, no. 267.

91. *Zenshū* 2, p. 526.

92. *Ryōkan zenji hiseki narabi ni jo,* in *Zenshū* 1, pp. 596-597. Also see Ryōkan's letter thanking Shōgan for his visit and his gifts, in *Zenshū* 2, p. 381.

93. *Zenshū* 1, p. 596.

94. *Zenshū* 1, p. 591.

95. Some scholars believe that the title "Great Fool" was given to Ryōkan only posthumously because there exists no surviving handwritten letter by Ryōkan bearing this name as his signature. True, Ryōkan always signed his letters, simply, with the two characters *ryō-kan.* However, it is highly unlikely that Ryōkan would have used his official Zen name, signing his personal letters with the four imposing Chinese characters *tai-gu-ryō-kan,* which exude a sanctimonious air foreign to Ryōkan's other writings. Moreover, there exist a handful of poems of Ryōkan's in which he describes himself with the character "fool" *(gu).* For a detailed discussion of this name, see Tanigawa, *Ryōkan no shōgai to itsuwa,* pp. 56-60.

96. Peter Haskel, trans., *Bankei Zen* (New York, 1984), p. 80.

97. Ibid., p. 34; Haskel's italics.

98. *Zenshū* 1, no. 160. Maitreya (J. Miroku) is the bodhisattva designated by Shākyamuni Buddha as heir to his throne of Tathāgatahood in the distant future.

99. Georges Bataille, *Inner Experience,* trans. Leslie Boldt (Albany, 1988), p. 95.

100. A fragment of Ryōkan's calligraphy titled "admonition" *(kaigo)* preserved in the collection of the Kimura family, descendants of Ryōkan's patron Kimura Motouemon. *Zenshū* 1, p. 505.

101. T. 14, no. 475, p. 544b.

102. T. 14, no. 475, p. 554c.

103. *Zenshū* 1, no. 118. Samantabhadra is the bodhisattva personifying the original enlightenment shared equally by all beings. Ghoṣa is a renowned master of the Sarvāstivādi school of northern India, a contemporary of King Kaniṣka (r. 132-152) of the Kushāna dynasty.

104. *Zenshū* 1, no. 287.

105. *Zenshū* 2, no. 604.

106. *Zenshū* 2, no. 605.

107. *Zenshū* 1, no. 336.

108. *Zenshū* 2, p. 522.

109. *Zenshū* 1, no. 51.

110. *Zenshū* 1, no. 255.

111. It was only in 1815 (When Ryōkan was fifty-seven) that Dōgen's collected essays first became popularly available though the woodblock edition of the *Shōbōgenzō (honzan ban)*.

112. *Zenshū* 1, pp. 84-86.

113. *Zenshū* 1, no. 69.

114. *Zenshū* 1, no. 195.

115. *Zenshū* 1, no. 133.

116. *Zenshū* 1, no. 106.

117. *Zenshū* 2, no. 539.

118. T. 9, p. 29a.

119. See Ryōkan's letter to Shukumon, in *Zenshū* 2, p. 347. Also see Ryōkan's poem in *Zenshū* 1, no. 212: Begging, I arrive at your house / In the refreshing cool of early autumn / The garden is sparse with spiny chestnut burrs scattered about / In the chilly air, the cicadas' voices are stilled / My nature is to be free of attachment / Whatever I do, my thoughts are at ease / I sit and read the *Lotus Sūtra* / Rolling and unrolling its eight scrolls, which I keep always by my seat.

120. *Zenshū* 1, pp. 457-497.

121. See "Kie buppōsō," in *Shōbōgenzō,* Terada Tooru and Mizuno Yaoko, eds. *Dōgen,* 2 vols. *Nihon shisō taikei* nos. 12-13 (Tokyo, 1970-1972), p. 417. For an elucidation of Dōgen's nondualist perspective, see Carl Bielefeldt, *Dōgen's Manual of Zen Meditation* (Berkeley, 1988), pp. 133-170.

122. T. 8, pp. 25c-26a.

123. *Zenshū* 2, no. 539.

124. *Zenshū* 1, no. 328.

125. In his study of Dōgen's meditation manual, Carl Bielefeldt has illustrated the uniqueness of Dōgen's nondualism of training and enlightenment: "Unlike the famous Ch'an teachings that emphasize the spontaneous, unintentional character of the practice and tend to reduce it—at least in theory—to a sudden return to, or recognition of, the original nature of the mind, Dōgen prefers to stress what might almost be called the intentionality of enlightenment and to interpret Buddhahood as the ongoing commitment to make a Buddha" (Bielefeldt, *Dōgen's Manual,* p. 145). As an inheritor of Dōgen's spirituality, Ryōkan demonstrates his "return" not as a mere recognition of the original enlightenment, but as his ongoing commitment to his practice of mendicant living. "How many times since I came to this place / Have I seen the leaves green and then gold? / Wrapped by vines, the old trees have turned dark / The bamboo has grown tall even in the valley's shade / My staff has rotted from the night rain / My robe frayed from the years of wind and frost / In the vast silence of the universe / For whom do I meditate each morning and night?" (*Zenshū* 1, no. 262).

126. Kristeva, *Revolution in Poetic Language* (New York, 1984), p. 60. Parentheses in original.

127. *Zenshū* 2, no. 852.

128. *Zenshū* 1, no. 80.

129. See his fragmentary notes on phonetics and grammar collected in *Zenshū* 1, pp. 419-437. Also see Kera's remarks in *Curious Accounts,* translated below.

130. See Ryōkan's study of *makurakotoba,* ornamental phrases in waka, in his collection of *Man'yōshū* poems, *Akinono,* in *Zenshū* 2, pp. 441-445.

131. *Zenshū* 2, p. 529.

132. *Zenshū* 2, pp. 395-418. Translated below in the section "Reflections on Buddhism."

133. One was addressed to a young woman named Okano, said to be a daughter of Ryōkan's friend Kimura Motouemon, who provided Ryōkan with a cottage behind his house. Legend has it that Ryōkan gave Okano the Words of Advice when she was preparing for her wedding. See *Zenshū* 2, pp. 411-412.

134. *Zenshū* 2, p. 399.

135. *Zenshū* 2, pp. 402-403.

136. *Zenshū* 1, no. 137.

137. *Zenshū* 2, p. 531.

138. T. 8, pp. 50b-51c.

139. *Zenshū* 2, p. 141, no. 855.

140. *Zenshū* 1, p. 488, nos. 96-98.

141. Yoshino, *Ryōkan: uta to shōgai* (Tokyo, 1975), pp. 24-25. Strictly speaking, it is unknown how accurate this oral tradition is. However, most historians credit this episode because (1) there exist letters from Yoshiyuki that account for Umanosuke's delinquency; (2) there survive letters in which Ryōkan, in response to his friends' requests, provided advice and help to two other delinquent youths. One is Kera Magouemon, the eldest son of Kera Shukumon, Ryōkan's supporter, who ran away from home to Edo in 1818; the other is Kimura Shūzō, the eldest son of Kimura Motouemon, another major supporter of Ryōkan's, who was once disowned by his father and was, through Ryōkan's mediation, finally pardoned. See Ryōkan's letters, in *Zenshū* 2, pp. 354, 358-359.

142. *Zenshū* 2, p. 524.

143. Jacques Derrida, *Of Grammatology* (Baltimore, 1974), p. 158. Italics in original.

144. Ibid., p. 49. Italics in original; notations in brackets added.

145. *Zenshū* 1, no. 141.

146. *Zenshū* 2, no. 516.

Commemorating Ryōkan: The Origin and Growth of Ryōkan's Biographies

1. For the original Japanese characters for the titles of the unpublished primary sources, see Miya Eiji, ed., *Ryōkan* (Tokyo, 1979), pp. 81-82. The primary sources published as woodblock editions can be located in *Kokusho sōmokuroku hoteiban,* 9 vols. (Tokyo, 1989-1991). The characters for the secondary scholarly works can be found in *Ryōkan denki nenpu bunken mokuroku* (Sanjō, 1982). For a detailed annotated bibliography of secondary sources, see Watanabe Shūei, "Ryōkan kenkyūshi," in *Ryōkan kenkyū ronshū* (Tokyo, 1985), ed. Miya Eiji, pp. 31-72.

2. See *Zenshū* 2, p. 507.

3. For Mizue's biography see Ōshima Kasoku, ed., *Ryōkan zenshū fuk-kokuban* (Tokyo, 1989), pp. 712–713.

4. See ibid., p. 713.

5. See Ryōkan's letter to Teichin, in Tōgō Toyoharu, ed., *Ryōkan zenshū,* 2 vols. (Tokyo, 1959), 2, p. 335 (hereafter cited as *Zenshū*). Teichin made available to Ryōkan many books from his family library. In his letter, Ryōkan thanks Teichin for locating a particular manuscript of the *Man'yōshū* in the library of Miwa Gonbei, a mutual friend.

6. Tōgō Toyoharu suggests its date of compilation as ca. 1867 (see *Zenshū* 2, p. 27). The printed edition of *Shamon Ryōkan shi kashū* is available in Watanabe Shūei, ed., *Mikan Ryōkan kashū goshu* (Tokyo, 1979).

7. Among several sources that record Bōsai's praise for Ryōkan are Kera Yoshishige's *Ryōkan zenji kiwa* (*Zenshū* 2, p. 532) and Suzuki Bundai's *Sōdōshū ji narabi ni fugen* (*Zenshū* 1, p. 581).

8. Quoted in Kojima Masayoshi, "Ryōkan sōsho no genryū o tazunete," in Miya Eiji, ed., *Ryōkan kenkyū ronshū* (Tokyo, 1985), pp. 267–295.

9. Ibid., p. 275.

10. See Tanigawa Toshirō, *Ryōkan no shōgai to itsuwa* (Tokyo, 1984), p. 171.

11. *Zenshū* 2, p. 517.

12. See *Zenshū* 2, p. 489.

13. Ōshima Kasoku, *Ryōkan zenshū fukkokuban,* p. 702.

14. All of Bundai's prefaces and commentarial writings on *Sōdōshū* and on other poems of Ryōkan are collected in *Zenshū* 1, pp. 571–589.

15. *Zenshū* 2, p. 594.

16. See also Ryōkan's letter to Genjō, in *Zenshū* 2, p. 372. The letter shows that Genjō treated Ryōkan, providing him with some medicinal herbs and tea leaves. For Genjō's biography, see Ōshima Kasoku, *Ryōkan zenshū fukkokuban,* p. 720.

17. *Zenshū* 2, pp. 371–372.

18. *Zenshū* 2, p. 595.

19. *Zenshū* 1, p. 95.

20. *Zenshū* 2, p. 516. For the complete text of *Koshi no shiori,* see Uchida Takeshi and Miyamoto Jōichi eds., *Sugae Masumi yūranki* (Tokyo, 1965). For the dating of the *Shiori,* see Tanigawa, *Ryōkan no shōgai to itsuwa,* p. 220.

21. Tōgō's *Zenshū* contains twenty-five letters Ryōkan sent to Kera Shukumon and his relatives. See *Zenshū* 2, pp. 347–357.

22. See Harada Kanpei, *Ryōkan zenji kiwa kaisetsu* (Sanjō, 1989), p. 34. For a detailed study of this manuscript, see Matsumoto Ichiju, *No no Ryōkan* (Tokyo, 1988).

23. Watanabe Shūei gives its date of composition as ca. 1857. See Watanabe, "Ryōkan kenkyūshi," in *Ryōkan kenkyū ronshū,* ed. Miya Eiji, p. 43. For a printed edition available under the same title, see Yoshino Hideo, Asada Sōtarō, Hayashi Takeshi, et al., eds., *Ryōkan zenji kashū* (Tokyo, 1977).

24. See Ryōkan's letter to Shukumon, in *Zenshū* 2, p. 347.

25. Printed edition in *Zenshū* 2, pp. 517–534. The reproduction of the

original handwritten manuscript was edited by Harada Kanpei in *Ryōkan zenji kiwa ikōbon* (Sanjō, 1989).

26. Yoshishige was born on the eighth day of the first month of Bunka 7 (1810). Because both the first month *(shōgatsu)* and the number eight *(hachi)* are considered auspicious, he was given the childhood name "Shōhachi."

27. *Zenshū* 2, p. 356.

28. Shukumon's first son, Magouemon, died at age thirty in 1828; his second son, Kumanosuke, died of illness at age fifty-three in 1858. See Harada Kanpei, *Ryōkan zenji kiwa kaisetsu,* p. 33.

29. Matsumoto Ichiju, *No no Ryōkan,* p. 24.

30. Suzuki Bundai, "Ryōkan shōnin no ōkan ni daisu," in Zenshū 1, pp. 577-578.

31. For the dating of the *Kiwa,* see Matsumoto Ichiju, *No no Ryōkan,* pp. 23-33.

32. *Zenshū* 2, p. 532.

33. Banjō's description of his encounter with Ryōkan in Shikoku is translated in Peter Haskel's introductory essay. For a detailed biographical study of Banjō and for the bibliographical background of his work, see Inoue Keiryū, "*Nezame no tomo* no Ryōkan to kinsei Echigo no bunkateki fūdo," in *Ryōkan kenkyū ronshū* ed. Miya Eiji, pp. 533-560.

34. The entire section on Ryōkan in this manuscript is printed in Inoue Keiryū's article "*Nezame no tomo* no Ryōkan." The section on Ryōkan in Kera's manuscript has its date of composition inscribed by Banjō as "Kōka 2" (1845). The other two surviving manuscripts, preserved, respectively, in the National Diet Library and the Seikadō Library in Tokyo, carry the date of composition "Kōka 4" (1847).

35. Yoshishige's colophon is printed in its entirety in Harada Kanpei, *Ryōkan zenji kiwa kaisetsu,* pp. 35-36.

36. Zōun's preface to *Ryōkan dōjin ryakuden,* in *Zenshū* 1, p. 599. See also, Ōshima Kasoku, *Ryōkan zenshū fukkokuban,* pp. 735-736. For Zōun's biography, see Okamoto Katsumi, *Ryōkan sōkō* (Tokyo, 1984), pp. 209-225.

37. For a detailed study of Teishin's poems and her relationship with Ryōkan, see Hori Chōha, *Ryōkan to Teishinni no ikō* (Tokyo, 1962).

38. A reproduction of the original manuscript was published by Nijima shuppan, Sanjō, Niigata, in 1970. Most parts of *Hachisu no tsuyu* are printed in Zenshū 2: *kaigo,* pp. 413-418; the preface and exchange poems, pp. 490-500; Teishin's letter, p. 500.

39. Printed in *Zenshū* 2, pp. 502-503. Originally, all the letters Teishin addressed to Zōun were collected in her manuscript *Jōgyō yoji,* preserved in the collection of the city library of Hakozaki, Niigata prefecture.

40. Printed in Ōshima Kasoku, *Ryōkan zenshū fukkokuban,* pp. 733-734.

41. For Henchō's biography see Kuwahara Jinrai, "Ryōkan to hōtei Henchō," in *Ryōkan no bannen,* ed. Kuzumi Kumasaburō et al. (Wajima, Niigata, 1980), pp. 157-176.

42. For the development of the collections of Ryōkan's kanshi, see Tōgō Toyoharu's introduction in *Zenshū* 2, pp. 1-36.

43. For photographic copies of the original letters, see Zenkoku Ryōkan kai, eds., *Teihon Ryōkan shoseki taikei*, 10 vols. (Tokyo, 1990). Tōgō's *Zenshū* collects 173 of Ryōkan's letters. See *Zenshū* 2, pp. 323-392.

44. Printed in *Zenshū* 1, pp. 596-597.

45. *Zenshū* 2, p. 381.

46. See Ryōkan's letters in *Zenshū* 2, pp. 323-392.

47. The edition of Teichin's *Man'yōshū* studied by Ryōkan was the 1643 standard edition by the Kyoto publisher Yasuda Jūbei. The dating of these Man'yō-related letters to Teichin was determined from Ryōkan's condolences to Teichin in a letter after the death of one of Teichin's daughters in 1819.

48. See Ryōkan's letter to Miwa Gonbei, in *Zenshū* 2, p. 360. It appears that it was the nun Ikyō, one of Gonbei's daughters, who first informed Ryōkan that Chikage's commentary was in her father's possession. See Kitagawa Shōichi, *Esshū shamon Ryōkan* (Tokyo, 1984), pp. 244-262.

49. *Zenshū* 2, pp. 439-445.

50. *Zenshū* 2, p. 528.

51. See Ryōkan's letter to Rihei, in *Zenshū* 2, p. 377. The date of the letter is determined from Ryōkan's condolences in the letter for Rihei's father's death in 1827.

52. See Ryōkan's *kaigo*, in *Zenshū* 2, pp. 395-418.

53. *Zenshū* 2, p. 529.

Curious Accounts of the Zen Master Ryōkan

1. A quotation from the sixth chapter of the *Great Learning,* one of the Confucian classics. See *Shinshaku kanbun taikei*, 100 vols. (Tokyo, 1950–1990), vol. 2 (1967), p. 53.

2. Actually, a box containing a pipe, a small *hibachi* or charcoal brazier, tobacco, and so forth, which smokers in Japan would traditionally carry. This was a highly personal item, shared only by lovers and the like, so that people probably resented having to lend it to Ryōkan. According to local tradition, Ryōkan lost his tobacco box so often that someone attached it to a six-foot cord, which was then tied to the belt of Ryōkan's robe. A contemporary portrait by the doctor and painter Sugimoto Shunryō shows the aged Ryōkan with his pipe hanging by a cord from his monk's staff, lending credence to the story.

3. Tōgō Toyoharu, ed., *Ryōkan zenshū*, 2 vols. (Tokyo, 1959), 1, p. 516.

4. That is, the Buddhist scriptures. They are commonly recited by Buddhist monks, in whole or in part.

5. A town just southeast of Ryōkan's home on Mount Kugami.

6. A unit of money in premodern Japan. In 1825, one *kan* could purchase slightly under forty grams of silver. Though hardly a vast sum, to the chronically destitute Ryōkan it may well have seemed a small fortune.

7. "I," here and throughout, refers to the author of the *Kiwa*, Kera Yoshishige.

8. Unidentified. The Tomitori were hereditary headmen of Jizōdō.

9. Control of the breath is a fundamental aspect of Zen meditation and of Buddhist meditation practice generally.

10. A village just south of Ryōkan's hut at Otogo shrine on Mount Kugami.

11. A Shingon-school temple located in the city of Sanjō, southeast of Mount Kugami.

12. A traditional Japanese weighted doll that, when struck, always springs back to an upright position.

13. Sugawara Michizane (845-903), a celebrated court official of the Heian period (794-1191), revered as the patron deity of learning and calligraphy.

14. A cursive, often highly abstract style of calligraphy.

15. Huai-su (725-785) was a calligraphy master of the mid-Tang dynasty.

16. Fujiwara Sukemasa (944-988) was a famous calligrapher of the Heian period. The *Akihagichō* (also read *Sazanamichō* or *Shūshūchō*) is actually the work of another celebrated Heian calligrapher, Ono no Tōfū (896-966).

17. In 1826, at the invitation of his longtime patron Kimura Motouemon, Ryōkan left his hut on Mount Kugami and moved to the nearby village of Shimazaki, where he occupied a cottage behind the Kimura family home.

18. A fan is considered an auspicious object at ceremonies such as weddings, and Ryōkan may have used it as a prop in delivering the formal address.

19. N.d. She was a member of a branch of the Tomitori family living near the town of Jizōdō. Hokusen was a doctor and a close friend of Ryōkan's.

20. D. 1843. An abbot of the Jōdo Shinshū school, who was also a calligrapher and poet.

21. "Dream Play." An inspirational Buddhist work, portraying the frailty of worldly ambition and the importance of the spiritual life. It appears to have been a favorite of Ryōkan's. Ryōkan's copy still survives with his distinctive inscription, "This is mine." The *Muyūshū* has been attributed by the Japanese scholar Matsumoto Ichiju to the celebrated medieval writer Kamo no Chōmei (1153-1216).

22. N.d. A local village headman and literatus.

23. Moxa cautery is a homeopathic cure still popular in East Asia. Small cones of moxa—a combustible substance derived from the leaves of the mugwort plant *(yomogi)*—are burned at particular points on the body. The procedure is traditionally believed to stimulate the flow of vital energy, whose unobstructed circulation is regarded as the key to physical health.

24. Yamada Nagayoshi (n.d.), headman of Na'nokaichi (Na'nukaichi according to local dialect), a town southeast of Izumozaki.

25. Maki Ryōkō (1777-1843), a famous professional Edo calligrapher, also known as Kōsai. Large folding screens, sometimes used to protect sick people from drafts, might be decorated with calligraphy.

26. Contests in which poets would compete at composing poems on a particular theme—the autumn moon, cherry blossoms, and so on.

27. *Tanzaku,* referring to small vertical "poem cards" traditionally used by Japanese poets.

28. A type of tea ceremony in which the guests sit in a row in a special tea hut. The host prepares a bowl of very strong green tea *(koicha)* from which each guest in turn takes a sip.

29. In premodern Japan, impoverished families were at times driven to sell their daughters to brothels, often at a very young age.

30. Referring to Ryōkan's friend Yamada Tokō (1775–1844), a haiku poet and painter and member of a wealthy sake-brewing family. The town of Yoita lies southeast of Mount Kugami and was the birthplace of Ryōkan's father, I'nan.

31. The *Man'yōshū,* or "Ten-Thousand Leaves Collection," is the earliest anthology of Japanese poetry. It was compiled in the mid–eighth century but includes verses from earlier periods.

32. "Old and New [Poems] Collection," the first of the Imperial Court anthologies of poetry. It was completed in 905.

33. Motoori Norinaga (1730–1801) and Kamo no Mabuchi (1697–1769), early scholars of Japanese language and literature. It was during their lifetimes that the principles of classical Japanese were first critically studied and explained.

34. Traditionally in rural Japan, people carry firewood by tying it to their backs with a rope, which is then fastened under the arms in such a way as to leave the hands free. Ryōkan's fastening the rope under his crotch must have considerably impeded his movement and given him a comical appearance as he stumbled down the mountainside with his load.

35. A means of storing the unhulled rice as seed for the next year's planting.

36. The bodhisattva Ksitigarbha ("Earth Store"). He is said to intervene to rescue the souls of the dead from torment, particularly those of dead children. In rural Japan, roadside statues of Jizō are often treated like living beings, given rain-hats, straw coats in cold weather, and so on. Ryōkan here seems to be making use of the bodhisattva's straw rainhat by standing under it himself to keep from being drenched.

37. *Iroha uta.* A Buddhist-inspired poem that used to be given to children to teach them the Japanese syllabary. The crafty peasant here seems to have taken advantage of Ryōkan's predicament to wheedle some calligraphy out of him.

38. An important port city in Ryōkan's day, Niigata lies some 120 miles north of Ryōkan's native Izumozaki and is now the capital of Niigata prefecture.

39. A school of Japanese Buddhism founded by the medieval monk Nichiren (1222–1282). Known for its militancy and its intolerance of other Buddhist teachings, the school stresses the unique efficacy of the recitation of the title of the *Lotus Sūtra* and forbids its adherents to recite any other sūtra.

40. A well-known Edo Confucian who visited Ryōkan on Mount Kugami. His dates are 1752–1826.

41. A ninth-century Japanese poet-recluse.

42. A Shingon-school temple that was the Kera family's *bodaiji,* or family funerary temple.

43. A priest of the Jōdo Shinshū school.

44. Notoya was the "shop" or commercial name of the Kimura family, Ryōkan's longtime patrons, referred to above. Commercial families in premodern Japan frequently had separate family and "shop" names, the latter indicated by the suffix *ya,* meaning "store" or "house."

45. Present-day Kōchi prefecture on the island of Shikoku.

46. Kondō Banjō (1776–1848), author of *Nezame no tomo* (A Bedside Companion), which includes the record of his encouter with Ryōkan in Tosa. For

Banjō's description of Ryōkan, see Haskel's essay; for Yoshishige's relationship with Banjō, see Abé's essay "Commemorating Ryōkan."

47. Henchō (1801-1876) was among those closest to Ryōkan during the Master's later years. A native of Shimazaki, Henchō first visited Ryōkan in 1815 and asked to stay and assist him at his hut. The young monk remained with Ryōkan till 1826, when he became abbot of a temple in the nearby town of Jizōdō.

48. It is unclear what these titles refer to. Possibly they served as reminders to Kera Yoshishige to include these items in the *Kiwa* at some point.

49. Tainin Kokusen (1722-1791). Kokusen's poem together with the wooden staff were apparently testimony to Ryōkan's enlightenment. Inscribed by Kokusen and dated 1779, the poem remained with Ryōkan throughout his life and is still preserved at the Kimura family residence, where Ryōkan spent his final years.

Kanshi (Poems in Chinese)

1. The Saitō in the title of this poem is sometimes said to refer to a friend of Ryōkan's who was headman of the village of Komegura, a hamlet to the northeast of Mount Kugami.

2. Traditionally, Chinese and Japanese poets have often borrowed lines or phrases from famous poems of the past and used these in constructing their own poems, a tribute to and comment on the works of their predecessors.

3. Gold-colored rings are suspended from the staffs of Buddhist monks and pilgrims in order to warn insects and other small creatures of their approach.

4. This poem appears on a scroll in the collection of the Abe family. It was probably written by Ryōkan during a visit with his poet friend Abe Sadayoshi (1779-1838), perhaps as a note to alert his host that he had gone off begging in the fine spring weather. A Japanese verse in Ryōkan's hand precedes the Chinese poem:

> Birds are singing
> And everywhere in the surrounding hills
> Cherry trees are in bloom
> What is one to do with this mind of spring?
> (*Zenshū* 2, no. 593)

5. Takakusu Junjirō et al., eds., *Taishō shinshū daizōkyō,* 85 vols. (Tokyo, 1914-1922, hereafter abbreviated T.), 9, no. 262. Among the most popular of Buddhist scriptures, the *Lotus Sūtra* is revered by most Japanese schools of Buddhism. The sūtra was a favorite of Ryōkan's, and he composed a series of religious poems based on its text.

6. This poem is said to have been composed in 1827, when Ryōkan was staying temporarily at Mitsuzō-in. This was a cloister on the grounds of Shōmyōji, a Shingon-school temple in the seaside town of Teradomari, located about midway between Ryōkan's native Izumozaki to the south and Mount Kugami to the northeast.

7. Ryōkan compares his pitifully threadbare robes to mist or fog, parting at the slightest breeze to the point of transparency.

8. A mountain covered with swords in one of the Buddhist hells.

9. Referring to a Buddhist hell in which sinners are boiled in cauldrons.

10. Zen traditionally traces its "wordless transmission" to an incident in which the Buddha, during a sermon on the Vulture Peak, held up a golden lotus flower. Of all those present, only the Buddha's senior disciple Mahākāshyapa grasped the Buddha's intention and smiled, becoming the first Indian patriarch of Zen.

11. "Jewel of the Shākyas," a title of the Buddha, Siddhārtha Gautama (approximate dates: midsixth to early fifth centuries B.C.E.). The Shākyas were the North Indian tribe into which the Buddha was born.

12. Ryōkan paraphrases a famous passage in the *Vimalakīrti Sūtra.* T. 14, no. 475, p. 540a.

13. A poet friend of Ryōkan's, Chikukyū was a native of Takebana, a village just southeast of Mount Kugami. His dates are not known.

14. Ryōkan's hermitage on Mount Kugami.

15. Verses in Buddhist scriptures recapitulating the contents of sections and chapters.

16. Ryōkan would have used the bamboo steamer primarily to prepare left-over cooked rice or barley that had become hard and dry and could be "reconstituted" by steaming. But with his rations meager at times and the rice pot itself standing empty for days, the steamer must often have seemed superfluous.

17. Possibly a reference to one of Ryōkan's literary friends and patrons from the towns near Mount Kugami.

18. At the end of the year in Japan, it is customary to bring gifts to people to whom one owes an obligation of some sort, such as one's teachers, bosses, clients, and so forth.

19. From about 1813 to 1816 Ryōkan seems to have alternated between his retreat Gogō-an and a new hut in the precincts of the Otogo Shintō shrine, farther down Mount Kugami, which eventually became his regular hermitage.

20. The opening lines of this poem paint a deliberately morbid picture of Ryōkan's mountain home, a scene of unrelieved loneliness, desolation, and decay. But this, Ryōkan finally confesses, only reflects the conventional view of his surroundings. For one who knows how to appreciate it, such a place is nothing short of perfection. For a poet or a calligrapher, for a lover of nature and serenity, this life has everything one could wish.

21. Literally, the "sound of the insects." Ryōkan, however, is probably referring to the *suzu-mushi,* a cricketlike nocturnal insect whose wings rub together to produce a high-pitched musical sound resembling glass bells, greatly appreciated in China and Japan.

22. In 1836, weakened by age, Ryōkan was persuaded by his old friend Kimura Motouemon to move from Mount Kugami to a small cottage behind the Kimura family mansion, located a few miles from his native Izumozaki. Still preserved, the Kimura residence is an impressive compound of multistoried wooden buildings in traditional Japanese style. Ryōkan, however, seems to have missed the peace and remoteness of his hut on Mount Kugami. The poem appears to refer to this difficult period in Ryōkan's life and may have been addressed to Motouemon as a kind of jocular expression of thanks for his hospitality.

23. A narrow wooden board known as *zenpan,* used to support the back

during zazen, or sitting meditation. It may also serve as a chin rest. Presumably, the cushion, too, was used by Ryōkan when meditating.

24. The *Han-shan shih-chi,* the collected poems of Han-shan, Shih-te, and Feng-kang, the legendary T'ang dynasty recluses of Mount T'ien-t'ai.

25. A container for water, one of the Zen monk's basic appurtenances.

26. The traditional Japanese child's ball, or *mari,* consists of tightly wound colored threads. Usually, the object of the game of ball is to see how many times the *mari* can be bounced on the ground, and special children's songs often accompany the count. One reaches the second song, the third song, and so on, depending on one's skill, so that the songs and bouncing go together—similar to skipping rope in the West. In Japan, this game was one of the ways in which children learned to count. Ryōkan recorded what are apparently the lyrics to one of these "ball-playing songs" in a document published by Professor Suzuki Hōken, grandson of Ryōkan's friend and anthologist Suzuki Bundai:

> On the mountain over yonder
> What's that something shining bright?
> The moon? A star? A firefly?
> Not the moon
> Not a star
> But the pine torch of my lord
> Down it comes, after the girl
> Burning up her silken robe
> Tell us, how much did it burn?
> Just three inches burned away
> Too short for a belt, too long for a sleeve
> Let's use it for the cord on the gong
> Of the temple over there!

Tōgō Toyoharu, *Shinshū Ryōkan* (Tokyo, 1970), p. 200.

27. Hachiman is an important Shintō god, or *kami,* associated with war and the military arts. He is also worshiped in Japan as a bodhisattva. Shrines, like churches in medieval Europe, were often popular spots for begging, and their large, open spaces are still used by Japanese children to play games.

28. "Dueling grasses" refers to a Japanese children's game in which players loop two blades of grass and pull to see which will snap the other.

29. *Hi-i! fu-u! mi-i! yo-o! i-i! mu-u! na-a!* The numbers song the children chant as they bounce the ball. Unlike a tennis ball or a volleyball, the traditional ball played with by Japanese children is difficult to bounce, and the game demands concentration as well as skill. One must not only bounce the ball at a steady speed but keep track of the count as well—a kind of impromptu meditation practice. A phrase similar to the last line of this poem appears in case 47 of the celebrated Sung dynasty koan collection *Pi-yen lu* (Blue Cliff Record): "One, two, three, four, five, six—even the blue-eyed barbarian monk isn't able to count it" (T. 48, no. 2003, p. 183b). But it is hardly necessary to know this to appreciate Ryōkan's meaning.

30. "Wolves and tigers" is a common Buddhist metaphor for destructive human passions. Wolves actually roamed areas of Echigo in Ryōkan's day, as attested to in *Hokuetsu seppu,* a popular account of Echigo life and customs by Ryōkan's

contemporary the merchant-literatus Suzuki Bokushi (1770–1842), with comments by Bokushi's editor Iwase Momoki (or Kyōzan, 1767–1858). The book's chapter on wolves contains a discussion of people's "wolfish" minds reminiscent of the concluding line of Ryōkan's poem:

> Consider for a moment: at least a wolf is a wolf and acts like a wolf. When men act like wolves, they hide their wolfishness and do not dare to show it openly. . . .
>
> The wolfishness of man is far more terrible and hateful than that of real wolves. Men who give themselves the appearance of honest persons but inside are full of insatiable greed we call wolf men, and a mother-in-law who treats her daughter-in-law badly is an old wolf woman. Well they might be able to hide the wolfishness in their hearts; yet the wise man's eye still sees the truth's reflection.
>
> Wolves! Wolves! How terrible, how disgraceful! Be on guard against wolves!

Translated by Jeffrey Hunter with Rose Lesser in *Snow Country Tales* (New York, 1986), pp. 244-245.

31. A famous river-crossing in Ryōkan's native Echigo. The poem apparently refers to Ryōkan's return to Echigo following his period of training at the Tamashima Entsūji and may be a description by Ryōkan of an enlightenment experience at this critical juncture in his life. The original text for the last line, here rendered in the general sense of "long," reads literally "ten" or "twenty" years, depending on the manuscript.

32. According to certain accounts, Ryōkan undertook another *angya,* or Zen pilgrimage, during his years at Otogo shrine, and the poem may refer to his return from such travels.

33. An important pilgrimage site and headquarters of the Shingon school of Japanese Buddhism, established in the early ninth century by the school's founder, Kūkai (774–835). By Ryōkan's period, the approach to Mount Kōya was lined with stalls selling robes and other Buddhist clerical appurtenances.

34. Though employed to some extent by most Japanese Buddhist schools, *nenbutsu* practice was frequently favored by less-educated and less-sophisticated believers and was often emblematic of a simple Buddhist piety.

35. Eizō was Ryōkan's secular name before he became a monk and took the religious name Ryōkan.

36. The temple in Tamashima where Ryōkan received his monk's training under the Zen Master Kokusen.

37. Such signboards, generally banning liquor, meat, and the "forbidden" vegetables—leeks, onions, scallions, ginger, and garlic—were common outside Buddhist monasteries during the Tokugawa period. These foods were thought to have an adverse effect on practitioners.

38. Unidentified.

39. A lotus-shaped device filled with water, which runs out through tiny holes. The amount of water remaining indicates the time. The clock would have been important in maintaining the monastery's rigorous training schedule.

40. There are several places called Yonezawa in Japan, including a famous

scenic spot in present-day Yamagata prefecture, but it is uncertain which of these the poem refers to.

41. Following the alternate version in Tōgō Toyoharu, ed., *Ryōkan zenshū*, 2 vols. (Tokyo, 1959), 1, no. 251 (hereafter cited as *Zenshū*).

42. The location of the Tamagawa Station referred to here is uncertain.

43. As a rule, a monk granted lodging in a layman's home would not remain more than a single evening. A stay of two nights would be considered an unusual courtesy, and the layman's invitation here indicates the respect and affection for Ryōkan among the laypeople he encountered on his travels.

44. Matsuno-o is a scenic spot in Ryōkan's native Echigo.

45. Referring to a story that appears in *The Five Vermin of the State (Wu tu)*, a work by the early Chinese philosopher Han Fei-tzu (d. 233 B.C.E.): "A man of Sung was tilling a field in which there was a stump. A rabbit accidentally collided with the stump, broke its neck and died. The delighted farmer then threw away his plow and just sat watching by the stump, waiting for the next rabbit to fall into his lap. But there would never be another rabbit, and the farmer became the laughing-stock of the entire province. Likewise, those who would use the laws of ancient rulers to govern the men of the present are all 'guarding the stump.'"

46. Referring to Otogo shrine, site of Ryōkan's mountain hermitage. Ryōkan is apparently describing his return from a pilgrimage that had taken him away from Mount Kugami for several years.

47. The proper posture for zazen, or sitting meditation. Ryōkan quotes these instructions from *Fukan zazengi*, a celebrated meditation manual composed by Dōgen. T. 82, no. 2580, p. 1a.

48. Ryōkan uses the metaphor of a hired laborer to describe his life of begging. Like the hired worker, Ryōkan suggests, he sustains himself by going from place to place and accepting whatever people offer him. With a mischievous wink, he contrasts his present seemingly passive and shabby, yet actually enlightened, mode of life with the ardent striving of his youth, when he charged from teacher to teacher in search of Zen wisdom—failing to realize that, all the time, it was his own original, "everyday" mind.

49. A common metaphor in Buddhism. The moon is symbolic of enlightenment, of ineffable original mind, which can only be revealed by "pointing" with the finger of the Buddha's teaching.

50. A famous phrase appearing in the *Mahāvairocana Sūtra*, T. 18, no. 848, p. 1c.

51. Following Iida Rigyō, *Teihon Ryōkan shishūyaku* (Tokyo, 1989), p. 501.

52. Referring to a parable in the *Lotus Sūtra*. A traveler visiting a friend becomes drunk and falls asleep. His host must leave but first places a precious gem in the man's robe. Unaware of this, the traveler awakens and continues his journey, arriving in another land, where he must labor hard to sustain himself. One day, he meets his friend, who is surprised to find him in such poor circumstances and reveals to him the existence of the jewel, which all the time had remained in his robe. The jewel is, of course, a metaphor for enlightened wisdom, or *prajñā*, the intrinsic wisdom that, according to Buddhism, we have always had but fail to realize.

53. Buddhist texts often liken enlightenment to a castle, impenetrable to ignorance and delusion. Mañjushrī, the bodhisattva who personifies intuitive wisdom, frequently appears in the eastern portion of Buddhist mandalas. The east, where the sun rises, symbolizes the origin, or beginning, and Ryōkan suggests that instead of wasting their time in discursive thinking, Zen students should come directly to enlightenment through intuitive wisdom, the source of realization and the true point of departure for religious practice.

54. In Japan and much of East Asia, rice is the mainstay of the diet, and the word "rice" is often interchangeable with notions of sustenance and existence. The question Ryōkan poses thus contains a meaning that transcends its somewhat whimsical expression.

55. Maitreya (J. Miroku) is the buddha foretold to appear in the future.

56. India, where Buddhism originated with the teachings of Shākyamuni Buddha. The expression derives from the fact that the Indian subcontinent lies to the west of China and Japan.

57. An old state in what are now Fukien and Chekiang provinces in south China. Hence, the "south."

58. Kokusen's temple in Tamashima, where the young Ryōkan studied from 1779 to 1795. Although this poem has usually been interpreted as a paean to life at Entsūji, composed during Ryōkan's years in training, it reads more naturally as a wry reflection on how the course of Ryōkan's life has changed in the years since leaving the temple. As one of Kokusen's prominent disciples, Ryōkan would have been expected to occupy an important position at Entsūji, perhaps eventually receiving abbacy of the temple and rising through the Sōtō Zen hierarchy. Ryōkan, however, abandoned Entsūji, Tamashima, and the entire Zen temple establishment to live as a mendicant in his native Echigo.

59. The *Kao-seng chuan,* a celebrated collection of biographies of eminent Buddhist priests, compiled during the Liang dynasty (502-556). Further similarly titled collections appeared during the T'ang (618-906) and Sung (960-1279) dynasties.

60. Referring to the thirty-four legendary patriarchs said to have transmitted the Zen teaching "from mind to mind" in an unbroken line from the Buddha Shākyamuni. These include the twenty-eight Indian patriarchs, from the Buddha's disciple Mahākāshyapa, who received the Master's "wordless teaching," to Bodhidharma (d. 532), who carried the teaching from India to the east; and the six patriarchs of Zen in China, from Bodhidharma to Hui-neng (638-713), the "Sixth Patriarch" celebrated in the *Platform Sūtra,* one of the school's seminal works.

61. Kannon is Avalokiteshvara, an important Mahāyāna bodhisattva celebrated as the embodiment of compassionate wisdom.

62. Reference is to the *Laṅkāvatāra Sūtra,* T. 16, nos. 670-672.

63. Literally, the three temples. Ryōkan may be referring to the three great Sōtō-school temples in the Kansai district of Japan—Ryūonji, Daichūji, and Sō'neiji —or to those of Kaga in Ryōkan's native district of Chūbu—Daijōji, Tentokuin, and Hōenji.

64. The twelve categories of Buddhist scriptural texts, i.e., (1) scriptural discourse *(sūtra),* (2) summary verses *(geya),* (3) hymns *(gāthā),* (4) stories of the past *(nidhāna),* (5) stories of the disciples' former lives *(itivṛttaka),* (6) stories of

the Buddha's former lives *(jātaka),* (7) miraculous stories *(adbhutadharma),* (8) parables *(avadhāna),* (9) logical discussions *(upadesha),* (10) the Buddha's personal utterances *(udāna),* (11) extensive discourses *(vaipulya),* and (12) the Buddha's proclamation of disciples' future lives *(vyākarana).*

65. Desire, form, and formlessness, the three realms in which sentient beings transmigrate.

66. Tung-shan Liang-chieh (807–869), member of the Ch'ing-yüan line of Ch'an and a founder of the Ts'ao-tung (J. Sōtō) school. The phrase is actually the response of another Ch'ing-yüan master, Shih-shuang Ch'ing-chu (807–888), to Tung-shan's statement "Go to where for ten thousand miles not an inch of grass is to be found." *Ching-te Ch'uan-teng lu,* in T. 51, no. 2076, p. 321a.

67. There is some confusion over the precise identity of the "Eihei Record" (J. *Eihei roku*). The Japanese scholar Ishida Yoshisada has argued that it is the *Eihei koroku,* a collection of works by the Sōtō school's founder, Dōgen Kigen. In the course of his research on the poem, Ishida found a copy of the *Eihei koroku* at Kōshōji—the Echigo Sōtō temple where Ryōkan first studied Zen—bearing notes in a hand similar to Ryōkan's.

68. The Zen master Tainin Kokusen, under whom Ryōkan studied at Entsūji in Tamashima.

69. *Shōbōgen,* a phrase describing the living essence of the Zen transmission, the enlightened mind passed directly from master to disciple through the generations of Zen patriarchs and teachers. Ryōkan may also be referring to Dōgen's seminal work by this name, the *Shōbōgenzō,* "Treasury of the Eye of True Enlightenment," or he may simply be using the expression to indicate the essence of Dōgen's Zen.

70. The Vulture Peak (Skt. Gṛdhrakūṭa), referred to previously, was said to be the site of many of the Buddha's sermons. The reference here is probably to the legend of the origins of Zen's "mind-to-mind" transmission, according to which the Buddha Shākyamuni held up a lotus flower at an assembly on the Vulture Peak, whereupon of all his disciples, only Mahākāshyapa understood and smiled. The Buddha, acknowledging Mahākāshyapa's attainment of the Eye of True Enlightenment, transmitted his teaching to him, making Mahākāshyapa the first patriarch of Zen. The Sixth Patriarch is the seventh-century Chinese master Hui-neng. Precisely why Ryōkan connects the Vulture Peak and the Sixth Patriarch with the autumn moon is unclear, though the full moon—in Japanese, *gachirinkan*—is a common Buddhist metaphor for enlightened mind. As such it was a favorite of Ryōkan, who even inscribed the characters for *gachirinkan* on the wooden lid of a storage jar. Another possible connection may be a reference to the moon by the celebrated Zen master Hsüan-sha Shih-pei (835–908), appearing in the eleventh-century collection of Zen monks' biographies *Ching-te ch'uan-teng lu.* In the course of a talk, Hsüan-sha remarks: "It is just as when on the Vulture Peak, of the Buddha's one million followers in the assembly, Mahākāshyapa alone understood. . . . [The Buddha said]: 'I entrust to Mahākāshyapa the true eye of my teaching. This is just like the moon of which I spoke.' And when the Sixth Patriarch raised his whisk, this, too, was just like pointing to the moon."

71. Referring to a story concerning the masters Ma-tsu Tao-i (709–788) and Nan-ch'üan P'u-yüan (748–835). When Ma-tsu was observing the moon with his

disciples Nan-ch'üan P'u-yüan, Hsi-t'ang Ching-ts'ang (735–814), and Po-chang Huai-hai (d. 850?), he asked them: "What about this moment?" Hsi-t'ang said: "Perfect for an offering." Po-chang said: "Perfect for practice." Nan-ch'üan simply went off flapping his sleeves. Ma-tsu declared: "Nan-ch'üan alone has transcended the phenomenal world." The story appears in the *Ching-te ch'uan-teng lu.*

72. Yüeh-shan Wei-yen (751–834). "One evening, the Master [Yüeh-shan] climbed the mountain. Suddenly the clouds parted, revealing the moon, and he gave a great laugh, whose sound was heard as far off as Ling-yang, ninety *li* to the east." This episode appears in the *Ching-te ch'uan-teng lu.* T. 51 p. 312b.

73. Ryōkan, his meager possessions, and the landscape of his mountain retreat all grow old together, a reminder that everything in this world is merely temporary, subject to change. Ryōkan then poses a rhetorical question: If, as Buddhism maintains, existence is truly "empty"—void of any enduring substance or identity—for whom does one practice meditation? The answer lies in the nature of the bodhisattva, the Buddhist ideal of the fully realized being, dedicated to the enlightenment of others. Because he embodies absolute emptiness, the bodhisattva transcends selfish aims or desires and is one with the world around him, both human and natural. The bodhisattva's compassion flows directly from this transcendence of subject and object, self and other that forms the core of Buddhist meditation, a practice that impartially benefits all sentient beings.

74. The farmer offers Ryōkan a form of "home brew," a locally produced raw sake with a thick, often porridgelike consistency. Straining of the muddy, unrefined liquid is an expression of the couple's rustic hospitality.

75. Bodhidharma (d. 532), said to be the first transmitter of the torch of Zen from India to China.

76. This day, known as "Little New Year's" *(koshōgatsu),* was the first full-moon day after the New Year, traditionally a time for family gatherings and remembering friends, relatives, and ancestors. The day is still observed in some rural areas of Japan. This poem was addressed to the nun Ikyō (d. 1821), a member of the Miwa merchant family of Yoita, a town about ten miles southeast of Ryōkan's hermitage at Mount Kugami. The daughter of Ryōkan's friend Miwa Gonbei, she had become a nun after her husband's death and resided in Edo. Ikyō may have been visiting with her family when she received Ryōkan's letter, which is addressed to her at Yoita and consists of the present poem followed by a waka. *Zenshū* 2, p. 362.

77. Kera Shukumon (1765–1819) was a member of a wealthy Echigo farming family and an important patron of Ryōkan's. Shukumon's son Yoshishige was the compiler of the *Curious Accounts of the Zen Master Ryōkan.*

78. In Zen temples in Japan, the first week of December is devoted to intensive meditation, culminating on 8 December, when the Buddha is said to have attained enlightenment on seeing the morning star. At this time, a ceremony is held at which customary offerings are the vegetable stew *(atsumono)* and assorted sweets or fruits *(saka)* mentioned below.

79. That is, the Buddha.

80. Two of the basic foodstuffs for temple offerings in Japan, following Chinese tradition. The cakes and fruits, which may accompany tea, are piled in neat mounds. The hot stew, which is served in a porcelain pot with a lid, consists of various vegetables—radish, mushrooms, burdock root, and so on—cooked in a spe-

cial stock. As the poem indicates, Ryōkan first helped himself to the food he had prepared with Kera's gift and reserved the leftovers as offerings, probably placing them on the altar in his hut.

81. A popular Japanese game, played with white and black stones on a square wooden block. The object is to surround one's opponent's stones and take possession of the board.

82. Kankan-sha means "Quiet Retreat" and was the name of the country home of Ryōkan's patron and literary friend the doctor and poet Harada Jakusai (1763-1827). This poem may describe Ryōkan's return to Echigo after his years of traveling on pilgrimage. Although Harada is no doubt delighted to find him alive and well, Ryōkan sympathizes with his old friend, inconvenienced by a lodger who brings with him nothing but his poverty and the inclement weather.

83. Ryōkan's younger brother Yoshiyuki became the Tachibana family heir when Ryōkan, the designated successor, left home to become a monk. The brothers remained close and shared an active interest in calligraphy and Japanese poetry.

84. Both unidentified. The term *shōnin* ("exalted one") was generally used in Japan for Buddhist priests; *rōjin* ("elder," "venerable," or simply "old boy") was the way Ryōkan commonly referred to his literary friends.

85. Ugan (d. 1808) was a close friend of Ryōkan's noted for his calligraphy. Ugan had become a monk as a young man but apparently had returned to lay life at this time. Ugan's retreat, Tanomo-an, is said to have been situated beside a tributary of the Shinano River, an important local river and possibly the stream referred to in the poem's last line.

86. In China and Japan, "red dust" is a common metaphor for the transient world of the senses.

87. A phrase from the opening fascicle of the *Chuang-tzu.*

88. Ryōkan is referring to a celebrated story in the second fascicle of the *Chuang-tzu:* "Once Chuang Chou dreamt he was a butterfly, a butterfly fluttering around, happy with himself and doing as he pleased. He didn't know he was Chuang Chou. Suddenly he woke up and there he was, solid and unmistakable Chuang Chou. But he didn't know if he was Chuang Chou who had dreamt he was a butterfly, or a butterfly dreaming he was Chuang Chou." Translated by Burton Watson in *The Complete Works of Chuang Tzu* (New York, 1968), p. 49. The bustling port scene of the poem's opening lines may reflect the fact that Ryōkan's native area, facing the sea of Japan, was an important center for shipping and commerce.

89. This curious poem suggests a sort of dream journey, through which Ryōkan presents a forthright description of the difficulties of meditation practice. It begins with Ryōkan seated in his hut trying to concentrate his mind in meditation. But, gloomy and ill-at-ease, he soon finds his thoughts wandering riotously in every direction. Ryōkan's original intention of a period spent in quiet practice is left behind, dissolved amid a welter of distractions, anxieties, and sobering reflections on the passage of time. Given this interpretation, the poem testifies to the disarming candor with which Ryōkan presents himself in his writings.

90. Literally, "Eternal Peace." Located in what is now Shensi province, Ch'ang-an was the capital of China during the T'ang dynasty.

91. Composed in reply to a poem by Ryōkan's literary friend Harada Jakusai. Harada's original poem may have been a message urging Ryōkan to visit and gently taxing him with hiding from the world—an accusation that Ryōkan deftly refutes, while declining his friend's invitation.

92. The mountain in present-day Hunan province in China, where, according to tradition, Bodhidharma, the Zen school's semilegendary founder, practiced austerities.

93. Ryōkan's literary colleague Ōzeki Bunchū (d. 1834). Bunchū, a doctor in the village of Magari, became blind in his later years.

94. "Crimson gates and golden pavilions" may be Ryōkan's sarcastic reference to the palatial appointments of wealthy Zen temples, which he compares unfavorably with his tumbledown mountain retreat.

95. Presumably referring to Zen's Indian progenitors, such as Shākyamuni, the Buddha, and Bodhidharma.

96. Suzuki Ryūzo (n.d.) was a doctor and poet friend of Ryōkan's, living in the Echigo town of Aozu. His brother Bundai compiled the *Sōdōshū,* the earliest collection of Ryōkan's Chinese poems.

Waka (Poems in Japanese)

1. Here again, Ryōkan may be alluding to the story of Mahākāshyapa's transmission, when the Buddha held up a flower at his sermon on the Vulture Peak.

2. Reportedly Ryōkan's favorite bodhisattva, the Bodhisattva Jōfukyō ("Never-Despising-Anyone") appears in the twentieth chapter of the *Lotus Sūtra.* He would bow down to and praise each person he met, declaring that all human beings possess the potential to become buddhas. At times, he would be chased off, or even stoned, but he would always return and resume bowing and praising everyone he encountered. According to the sūtra, he was later reborn as Shākyamuni, the historical Buddha. Ryōkan dedicated several poems to the bodhisattva, including the following, from his collection of poems on the *Lotus Sūtra:*

> Some throw stones, some beat him with sticks
> He retreats, then stops and calls to them aloud
> Since this fellow has left the world
> No one has heard from him
> But the wind and moonlight that fill the night
> For whom do they reveal their purity?

Tōgō Toyoharu, ed., *Ryōkan zenshū,* 2 vols. (Tokyo, 1959), 1, no. 97 (hereafter cited as *Zenshū*).

3. The three worlds are the past, present, and future.

4. Susuki *(Miscanthus sinensis).* A tall, arching plant that turns a golden color in fall.

5. Saigyō (1118–1190) was a former courtier who became a priest of the Shingon school and a wandering poet. He is among the most highly regarded of Japanese poets and was greatly admired by Ryōkan.

6. The notation attached to this poem appears in the *Yaegiku,* a waka collection compiled by Ryōkan's brother Yoshiyuki. Yoshiko was a member of the Yamada family of Yoita.

7. That is, the buddha Amitābha's (J. Amida) vow to save all those who call his name. Although Amitābha is associated particularly with the Pure Land schools, reverence for Amitābha and the practice of the *nenbutsu* (*Namu Amida butsu!* the recitation of Amitābha's name) were integral features of popular Buddhist belief generally. By invoking them in his poems, Ryōkan demonstrates his sympathy with the ordinary faith of the common people.

8. The full moon hidden among floating grasses such as duckweed is a common metaphor in Japanese Buddhism, symbolizing the manner in which the original mind of enlightenment is temporarily concealed by the "floating world" of illusion.

9. In contrast to the rigid, hereditary class system of his day—with samurai lording it over farmers, artisans, and merchants—Ryōkan reminds us that everyone is equal when it comes to Buddha Nature. When carefully planted and tended, he insists, the seed of enlightenment will blossom in anyone's mind, regardless of birth or social station.

10. The notation attached to this poem appears in the *Ryōkan zenshū* edited by Tamaki Reikichi in 1918.

11. Ryōkan paraphrases here a celebrated line in the *Diamond Sūtra.* See Takakusu Junjirō et al., *Taishō shinshū daizōkyō,* 85 vols. (Tokyo, 1914-1922), 8, no. 239, p. 775b.

12. A district of the coastal town of Teradomari.

13. *Fujibakama (Eupatorium fortunei).* A variety of chrysanthemum with lavender-colored petals.

14. Vulture Peak is said to have been the site of many of the Buddha's sermons and of the Buddha's transmission of mind to Mahākāshyapa that, according to legend, is the origin of Zen's "mind-to-mind transmission."

Letters

1. The village chief of Makigahana, Shukumon (1755-1819), was one of Ryōkan's closest friends and supporters. Kera Yoshishige, the author of the *Ryōkan zenji kiwa* (Curious Accounts of the Zen Master Ryōkan), was Shukumon's third son.

2. In Japan it is customary to send gifts at the end of the year to people with whom one has a special relationship, such as teachers, relatives, or business associates.

3. In the lunar calendar in use in premodern Japan, the sixth month was equivalent to our late summer. The actual season for bamboo shoots is early spring, when Ryōkan may have composed the poem included in this letter. In rural Japan, gathering the new bamboo shoots is a favorite pastime in early spring, popular with children and adults alike. Considered a great delicacy, the fresh young shoots may be eaten raw as they are plucked from the ground or cooked over hot coals. Ryōkan apparently delighted in this seasonal treat, which must have provided a welcome addition to his larder.

4. Unidentified. Apparently a local Buddhist priest. Mosquito netting was a valuable and indispensable fixture in traditional Japanese homes and in a poor household like Ryōkan's would have been one of the few objects to attract a thief's attention. The well-to-do Kera apparently lent the netting to Ryōkan, who then returned it at the end of the season.

5. Eating warm yams was a folk remedy believed to cure the lower abdominal pain associated with lumbago.

6. During slack seasons and in times of crop failure, Japanese farmers frequently migrated to other areas to perform nonagricultural labor. The practice continues today, with some farmers drifting to Tokyo and other cities to do temporary work in the construction trades.

7. This note was apparently given to the woman in question by Ryōkan to present to one of his regular patrons. New Year's is a particularly important day in Japan, and one's actions at this time are thought to determine, for better or for worse, one's fortunes during the ensuing year. Though he would no doubt be annoyed to find the lady begging on his doorstep during the holiday, even the most hard-nosed householder would find such a charitable request, particularly from a prominent priest, difficult to refuse.

8. Kera Magouemon (1798-1828) was the son and heir of Ryōkan's friend Kera Shukumon. The tone of the letter suggests that Magouemon had broken with his father, who seems to have accused him of dissipation. Ryōkan may have Magouemon in mind when he refers to Shukumon's concern over his son's departure for Edo in the letter above.

9. A printed copy book for calligraphy practice consisting of models attributed to the famous Heian period calligrapher Ono no Tōfū.

10. During the first three days of the New Year in Japan, one is not supposed to transact any business. The fourth day of the year is the first day when normal business may be resumed, indicating that Abe dispatched his messenger to Ryōkan at the earliest possible opportunity.

11. Teichin (1779-1838), also known as Sadayoshi, was a literary friend and supporter of Ryōkan. The Abe family mansion was located just below the western slope of Mount Kugami in the village of Watabe, where the Abes were the traditional *shōya,* or village heads. During Ryōkan's years on Mount Kugami, Sadayoshi was his closest friend and leading patron. The Abe family still preserves many letters and poems in Ryōkan's hand, including corrected drafts of poems that Sadayoshi presumably collected around Ryōkan's hut.

12. The shop name of the Miwa family of Yoita.

13. Notoya was the shop name of the Kimura family. In 1826, at the urging of Ryōkan's old friend and patron Kimura Motouemon, the family head, the aging Ryōkan left his spartan hermitage on Mount Kugami and moved into a cottage on the Kimura property.

14. It is customary in Japan for parishioners to invite Buddhist priests to breakfast or luncheon. The occasion serves as an opportunity for the patron to acquire merit and for the priest to lecture on Buddhism.

15. Another close friend of Ryōkan's, Yamada Tokō (1775-1844) was a haiku poet and painter and member of a wealthy sake-brewing family. The town of Yoita lies southeast of Mount Kugami and was the birthplace of Ryōkan's father, I'nan.

16. *Odori tenugui,* a kind of towel-kerchief tied under the chin and worn by participants in the folk dances that accompany many Japanese festivals and celebrations.

17. A severe earthquake struck Ryōkan's area of Echigo on the twelfth day of the eleventh month of 1828. Some fourteen hundred people were killed and

nearly eleven thousand homes destroyed. Ryōkan's letter is dated the eighth day of the twelfth month, only several weeks after the quake.

18. Referring to the *kamachi,* a raised bench on which one stands to reach the tatami-covered formal area in which guests are received or on which one sits to talk familiarly with the people inside.

19. Gon'uemon was an adopted son of and heir to Nakamura Kuzaemon, a prosperous sake brewer in the village of Jizōdō. As children, Kuzaemon and Ryōkan were fellow students and friends at the school run by the Confucian teacher Ōmori Shiyō.

20. The earliest historical text on Japanese antiquity, edited and compiled in 712 by Hieda no Are. The *Kojikiden,* a voluminous commentarial text completed in 1798 by Motoori Norinaga, made this ancient text readily accessible to the late Tokugawa literati and laid the foundation for the rise of the Kokugaku movement. It is possible that Ryōkan, who was familiar with Motoori's other works, studied the *Kojiki* as a result of his interest in ancient Japanese phonetics.

21. The informal name of Ryōkan's literary friend Yamada Gon'uemon. Gon'uemon was a resident of the village of Na'nokaichi, located a short distance east of Ryōkan's native Izumozaki. One of Gon'uemon's daughters was the wife of Ryōkan's nephew Umanosuke.

22. Hakuyū (1646–1709) was a hermit of the mid–Tokugawa period, whose real name was Ishikawa Jishun. He lived in the hills of Kyoto's Shirakawa district and practiced reciting both the *Lao-tzu* and the *Diamond Sūtra.* In his works *Yasen kanna* and *Orategama,* the famous Rinzai Zen master Hakuin Ekaku (1686–1769) claims to have received training from Hakuyū in a variety of yoga techniques that cured him of a nervous disorder apparently brought on by his Zen training. See Philip Yampolsky's translation of *Orategama* in *The Zen Master Hakuin: Selected Writings* (New York, 1971), pp. 41–43.

23. Apparently referring to a Taoist meditation practice.

24. Probably indicating Taoist-style longevity practices advocated by Hakuyū.

25. Lily bulbs *(yurine)* remain a Japanese delicacy. They are often boiled in a sweet syrup and eaten cold as a side dish.

26. Ryūzen is unidentified. It is possible he was abbot of Kokujōji, a large Shingon-sect temple situated on Mount Kugami. The letter suggests that he had invited Ryōkan to attend a temple festival.

27. Apparently Ryōkan had been ill during the previous period, suffering from some sort of delirium.

28. Unidentified; apparently a local Buddhist priest.

29. Presumably the head of the Chikiriya, a merchant family of Izumozaki.

30. Referring to the traditional Japanese children's game of keeping count while bouncing a ball.

31. Identified elsewhere as Miuraya Kōsuke. Like Chikiriya, above, he was apparently head of a local merchant family.

32. A coastal town facing the Sea of Japan, about two and one-half miles southwest of Ryōkan's retreat on Mount Kugami. The Toyamas, Ryōkan's sister and brother-in-law, lived in Teradomari, and Ryōkan stopped there at times in the course of his begging expeditions.

33. Unidentified. The anonymous recipient's address.

34. Addressee unidentified. Ryōkan's friends in Niigata included the physician Nakahara Genjō, the confectionery shop owner Shibagaki (Ameya) Manzō, and the waka poet Tamaki Shōryō.

35. Presumably, because he was ill, Ryōkan had been unable to shave his head.

36. Ryōkan's contemporary the merchant-literatus Suzuki Bokushi (1770–1842) was the author of *Hokuetsu seppu,* a popular account of Echigo life and customs.

37. The legendary Zen practitioners of Mount T'ien-t'ai, Han-shan (J. Kanzan) and Shih-te (J. Jittoku), popular subjects of Zen ink painting.

38. Komatsu Shigemi, "Ryōkan nisemaneshi," *Geijutsu shinchō* 40, no. 2 (February 1989): p. 58; and Yoshino Hideo, *Ryōkan: uta to shōgai* (Tokyo, 1975), p. 33.

39. As a guest at the temple, Ryōkan would have been obligated to join the resident monks at the regular early morning service.

40. This chapter, referred to in Japanese as *Fumonbon,* is dedicated to the bodhisattva Kannon (Avalokiteshvara) and is commonly recited in many Japanese Zen temples.

Reflections on Buddhism

1. The site of many of the Buddha's sermons as depicted in the *Prajñā-pāramitā,* the *Lotus,* and other scriptures.

2. A celebrated exponent of Mahāyāna Buddhism, said to have lived in India during the second and third centuries. He is regarded as the founder of the Mādhyamika school.

3. The first Buddhist temple in China, erected in Lo-yang in A.D. 67.

4. The T'ang dynasty lasted from 618 to 906.

5. Referring to the divisions between the followers of the Sixth Patriarch Hui-neng (638–713) and his Dharma brother, the Ch'an master Shen-hsiu (605?–706). According to the account in the *Platform Sūtra,* Hui-neng's followers, known as the Southern school, are said to have maintained that enlightenment was sudden; those of Shen-hsiu, known as the Northern school, maintained it was gradual.

6. The Sung dynasty lasted from 960 to 1126.

7. The five branches of the Southern school of Zen: Lin-chi, Kuei-yang, Ts'ao-tung, Yün-men, and Fa-yen.

8. The eight schools of Buddhism in China apart from the Ch'an (J. Zen) school: Hua-yen, Lu, Fa-hsiang, San-lun, Ch'eng-shin, Chu-she, T'ien-t'ai, and Chen-yen.

9. I.e., Dōgen, founder of the Sōtō school of Zen.

10. Dōgen's Chinese teacher, T'ien-t'ung Ju-ching (1163–1228).

11. The celebrated compendium of Dōgen's writings.

12. Tōgō Toyoharu, *Ryōkan zenshū,* 2 vols. (Tokyo, 1959), 1, no. 1 (hereafter cited as *Zenshū*).

13. The entirety of the world, the threefold universe (Skt. *triloka*) consisting of the realms of desire, form, and formlessness.

14. A scene from the opening of the tenth chapter of the *Vimalakīrti Sūtra,* in which the Buddha's disciple Shariputra is considering how he will feed the assembled bodhisattvas. Vimalakīrti, the enlightened layman, dispatches an illusory bodhisattva to the "Fragrant Land" to beg offerings of food from the Buddha of Fragrance. The Buddha gives the messenger a bowl of fragrant rice that, though seemingly meager, proves inexhaustible. See Takakusu Junjirō et al., *Taishō shinshū daizōkyō,* 85 vols. (Tokyo, 1914-1922, hereafter T.), 14, no. 475, p. 552.

15. Cunda was a lay follower of the Buddha Shākyamuni. Various sūtras relate how, overjoyed at receiving the Buddha's teaching, he invited the sage to his house the following morning and offered him a meal. The Buddha died at midnight the same day.

16. The princely name of the Buddha.

17. A heretical practitioner. He was among the teachers the Buddha is said to have visited when he first left his palace in search of enlightenment. The name Ārāda Kālāma is often taken to indicate two different teachers but actually refers to a single person.

18. *Butsu suihan nehan ryakusetsu kyōkaigyō* (popular name, *Yuikyōgyō*), T. 12, no. 389, pp. 110-112.

19. Ibid., p. 111a.

20. Ibid.

21. T. 14, no. 475, p. 540a.

22. *Fukan zazengi,* in *Dōgen 7, Nihon shisō taikei,* vol. 12 (Tokyo, 1970), pp. 125-126.

23. A verse recited in Zen temples at mealtimes.

24. See *Eihei fushuku nanpō,* in *Dōgen zenji zenshū,* 7 vols. (Tokyo, 1989-1991), vol. 6 (1990), p. 61.

25. One of the Buddha's ten titles. Like the charioteer who guides and controls his horses, the Buddha keeps mind and body in order.

26. A passage in the *Book of Documents,* in the chapter "Pronouncements of the Great Yü." See *Shōkyō, Shinshaku kanbun taikei,* vol. 26 (1983), p. 371.

27. The six leading religious teachers of the Buddha's day in India.

28. Arhats are beings who through solitary practice have freed themselves from the cycle of birth and death. The six supernatural powers are the powers to travel anywhere at will, to see all things, to hear all things, however distant, to read others' minds, to know one's own and others' past lives, and to rid oneself of defilements.

29. Gods and dragons who serve as protectors of Buddhism.

30. T. 12, no. 389, pp. 110-112.

31. Indra and various other Hindu gods were amalgamated by Buddhism as protective deities, defending the religion and its adherents.

32. The truth, or teaching, of Buddhism. *Buddha Dharma .*

33. *Zenshū* 1, no. 137.

34. *Zenshū* 2, pp. 395-399.

35. A homeopathic cure used in Chinese medicine popularly practiced in Japan. Small cones of moxa—a combustible substance derived from the leaves of the mugwort plant *(yomogi)*—are burned at particular points on the body.

36. *Zenshū* 2, pp. 406-410.

37. Edo (present-day Tokyo) and Kyoto were, respectively, the new and old capitals of Japan and thus connoted "big-city" sophistication and prestige.

38. *Zenshū* 2, pp. 412–417.

39. Warm sake is appreciated in Japan, particularly in cold weather. Heating also diminishes the liquor's alcohol content, apparently the point of Ryōkan's advice.

40. *Zenshū* 2, pp. 410–411. Ryōkan spent much of his time alone and here seems to be reminding himself for health reasons to exercise his voice occasionally, even if no one is available to speak with.

Select Bibliography

Works in English and Other Western Languages

Aristotle. *Poetics 1*. Trans. Richard Janko. Indianapolis, 1987.

Austin, J. L. *How To Do Things with Words*. Oxford, 1962.

Barthes, Roland. *Mythologies*. Trans. Annette Lavers. New York, 1972.

———. *The Pleasure of the Text*. Trans. Richard Miller. New York, 1975.

Bielefeldt, Carl. *Dōgen's Manual of Zen Meditation*. Berkeley, 1988.

Bownas, Geoffrey, et al. *The Penguin Book of Japanese Verse*. New York, 1964.

Coward, Harold. *Derrida and Indian Philosophy*. Albany, 1990.

Culler, Jonathan. *The Pursuit of Signs*. Ithaca, 1981.

Derrida, Jacques. *Dissemination*. Trans. Barbara Johnson. Chicago, 1981.

———. *Of Grammatology*. Trans. Gayatri Spivak. Baltimore, 1974.

Dumoulin, Heinrich. *Zen Buddhism: A history*. 2 vols. New York, 1988–1990. Vol. 2., *Japan*.

Haskel, Peter, trans. *Bankei Zen*. New York, 1984.

Hunter, Jeffrey, et al. *Snow Country Tales*. New York, 1986.

Keene, Donald. *Anthology of Japanese Literature*. New York, 1955.

Kodama, Misuo, et al. *Ryōkan the Great Fool*. Kyoto, 1969.

Kraft, Kenneth, ed. *Zen: Tradition and Transition*. New York, 1988.

Kristeva, Julia. *Desire in Language: A Semiotic Approach to Literature and Art*. Ed. and trans. Leon Roudiez et al. New York, 1980.

———. *Revolution in Poetic Language*. Trans. Leon Roudiez. New York, 1984.

———. *Semeiotike*. Paris, 1969.

LaFleur, William. "Too Easy a Simplicity: Watson's Ryōkan." *Eastern Buddhist* 13, no. 1 (Spring 1980): pp. 116–127.

Loy, David. *Nonduality: A Study of Comparative Philosophy*. New Haven, 1988.

Magliola, Robert. *Derrida on the Mend*. West Lafayette, 1984.

Maloney, Dennis, et al., trans. and eds. *Between the Floating Mist: Poems of Ryōkan*. Buffalo, 1992.

Ricoeur, Paul. *Interpretation Theory*. Fort Worth, 1976.

———. *The Rule of Metaphor*. Toronto, 1977.

Stevens, John, trans. *One Robe, One Bowl: The Zen Poetry of Ryōkan*. New York, 1977.

Watson, Burton. "Zen Poetry." In *Zen: Tradition and Transition*, ed. Kenneth Kraft, pp. 105–124. New York, 1988.

Watson, Burton, trans. *Cold Mountain, 100 Poems by the T'ang Poet Han-shan.*
New York, 1962.
———, trans. *Ryōkan, Zen Monk-Poet of Japan.* New York, 1977.
White, Hayden. *Tropics of Discourse.* Baltimore, 1978.
Yoshimoto Takaaki. "Asian Thought and Ryōkan." *Iichiko Intellectual,* no. 5
(1993), pp. 102–128.
Yuasa, Nobuyuki, trans. *The Zen Poems of Ryōkan.* Princeton, 1981.

Works in Japanese

Asakura Hisashi. "Ryōkan no shiika ni miru kotoba to kokoro." In *Ryōkan kenkyū
ronshū,* ed. Miya Eiji, 189–242. Tokyo, 1985.
Furukawa Hisashi, ed. *Sōseki no shokan.* Tokyo, 1982.
Harada Kanpei, ed. *Ryōkan zenji kiwa.* Sanjō, 1979.
———. *Ryōkan zenji kiwa ikōbon.* Sanjō, 1989.
———. *Ryōkan zenji kiwa kaisetsu.* Sanjō, 1989.
Hasegawa Yōzō. *Ryōkan no shisō to seishin fūdo.* Tokyo, 1974.
———. "Ryōkan zenji no shūkyō." In *Ryōkan kenkyū ronshū,* ed. Miya Eiji, pp.
341–384.
Hori Chōha. *Ryōkan to Teishinni no ikō.* Tokyo, 1962.
Horie Tomohiko. "Kokō no sho." In *Ryōkan no sekai,* ed. Miya Fuyuji, pp. 17–28.
Iida Rigyō. *Ryōkan goshaku Taichi geju yaku.* Tokyo, 1988.
———. "Shūgaku shisō no naka no Ryōkan." In Miya, *Ryōkan no sekai,* pp. 49–68.
———. *Taigu Ryōkan no fūkō.* Tokyo, 1986.
———. *Teihon Ryōkan shishū yaku.* Tokyo, 1989.
Iijima Tachio et al. *Ryōkan bokuseki taikei.* 6 vols. Tokyo, 1992–1993.
Imoto Nōichi. *Ryōkan.* 2 vols. Tokyo, 1978.
Inoue Keiryū. "*Nezame no tomo* no Ryōkan to kinsei Echigo no bunkateki fūdo."
In Miya, *Ryōkan kenkyū ronshū,* pp. 533–560.
Iriya Senkai. *Kanzanshi. Zen no goroku* 13. Tokyo, 1970.
Iriya Yoshitaka. *Ryōkan shishū.* Tokyo, 1982.
Iwanami shoten kokusho kenkyūshitsu, eds. *Kokusho sōmokuroku hoteiban.* 6
vols. 1989–1991.
Kanaya Osamu et al., eds. *Shinshaku kanbun taikei.* 100 vols. Tokyo, 1950–
1990.
Karaki Junzō. *Ryōkan.* Tokyo, 1971.
Katō Kiichi. *Ryōkan no sho.* 5 vols. Sanjō, 1974–1975.
Kikkawa Shōjun. "Tainin Kokusen oshō to Ryōkan." In Miya, *Ryōkan kenkyū ron-
shū,* pp. 411–446.
———. "Tamashima no shugyōsō." In Miya, *Ryōkan no sekai,* pp. 159–176.
Kitagawa Shōichi. *Esshū shamon Ryōkan.* Tokyo, 1984.
———. *Teihon Ryōkan yuge.* Tokyo, 1983.
Kojima Masayoshi. "Ryōkan sōsho no genryū o tazunete." In Miya, *Ryōkan kenkyū
ronshū,* pp. 267–296.
Kuno Hisashi. "Dōgen to Ryōkan." In Miya, *Ryōkan no sekai,* pp. 121–138.
Kurita Isamu. *Ryōkan nyūmon.* Tokyo, 1985.
———. "Ryōkan michi: Tōtō tenshin ni makasu." *Geijutsu shinchō* 40, no. 2 (Feb-
ruary 1989): pp. 19–39.

Komatsu Shigemi. "Ryōkan nisemaneshi." *Geijutsu shinchō* 40, no. 2 (February 1989): pp. 57-63.

Kojima Masayoshi. "Ryōkan sōsho no genryū o tazunete." In *Ryōkan kenkyū ronshū,* ed. Miya Eiji, pp. 267-295. Tokyo, 1985.

Kuwahara Jinrai. "Ryōkan to hōtei Henchō." In *Bannen no Ryōkan,* ed. Kuzumi Kumasaburō, pp. 157-178. Wajima, 1980.

Matsumoto Ichiju. *No no Ryōkan.* Tokyo, 1988.

Matsuzawa Sagoe. "Ōmori Shiyō to sono shūhen." In Miya, *Ryōkan kenkyū ronshū,* pp. 483-532.

Minakami Tsutomu. *Ryōkan.* Tokyo, 1984.

Miwa Kenji. *Ryōkan e no apurōchi.* Sanjō, 1975.

Miya Eiji. *Ryōkan.* Tokyo, 1979.

———. *Ryōkan bokuseki tanbō.* Tokyo, 1983.

———. "Ryōkan kenkyū no kaiko to tenbō." In Miya, *Ryōkan kenkyū ronshū,* pp. 15-30.

———, ed. *Ryōkan kenkyū ronshū.* Tokyo, 1985.

Miya Fuyuji, ed. Ryōkan no sekai. Tokyo, 1969.

———. "Ryōkan no hito to uta." In Miya, *Ryōkan no sekai,* pp. 1-16.

Nakamura Shūichi. *Ryōkan no ge to Shōbōgenzō.* Tokyo, 1984.

———. *Ryōkan no hokketen hokkesan no ge.* Tokyo, 1987.

Nomura Takuji. "Bannen no Ryōkan." In *Bannen no Ryōkan,* ed. Kuzumi Kumasaburō, pp. 49-136. Wajima, 1980.

Okamoto Katsumi. *Ryōkan sōkō.* Tokyo, 1984.

Okayama Sōtōshū seinenkai, eds. *Ryōkan no shi, Tainin Kokusen zenji den.* Kurashiki, 1982.

Ōshima Kasoku. *Ryōkan zenshū.* Tokyo, 1929.

———, ed. *Ryōkan Zenshū Fukkokuban.* Tokyo, 1989.

Ryōkan kai, eds. *Ryōkan no ayumi.* Tokyo, 1983.

Satō Kichitarō. *Izumozaki hennen shi.* Niigata, 1972.

———. *Ryōkan no chichi Tachibana I'nan.* Niigata, 1935.

Sōma Gyofū. *Taigu Ryōkan.* Tokyo, 1918.

Susa Shinchō. *Ryōkan shi chūkai.* Tokyo, 1961.

Takakusu Junjirō et al., eds. *Taishō shinshū daizōkyō.* 100 vols. Tokyo 1914-1922.

Takemura Makio. *Ryōkan no shisō to Dōgen zen.* Tokyo, 1978.

Takeuchi Michio. *Sōtōshū kyōdanshi.* Tokyo, 1971.

Tamaki Reikichi, ed. *Ryōkan Zenshū.* Niigata. 1918.

Tamamuro Taijō. *Sōshiki bukkyō.* Tokyo, 1964.

Tamashima Ryōkan kenkyūkai, eds. *Ryōkan: shugyō to tamashima.* Niigata, 1975.

Tanaka Keiichi. Ryōkan no jitsuzō. Tokyo. 1994.

Tanigawa Toshirō. "Ryōkan denki ni okeru shomondai." In Miya, *Ryōkan kenkyū ronshū,* pp. 73-116.

———. *Ryōkan no shōgai to itsuwa.* Tokyo, 1984.

———, ed. *Ryōkan denki nenpu bunken mokuroku.* Sanjō, 1982.

Terada Tooru and Mizuno Yaoko, eds. *Dōgen.* 2 vols. *Nohon shisō taikei.* Nos. 12-13. Tokyo, 1970-1972.

Tōgō Toyoharu. *Shinshū Ryōkan.* Tokyo, 1970.

———, ed. *Ryōkan zenshū.* 2 vols. Tokyo, 1959.

Uchida Takeshi, and Miyamoto Jōichi, eds. *Sugae Masumi Yūranki.* Tokyo, 1965.

Uchida Tomoya. "Ryōkan shi no seiritsu ni tsuite." In Miya, *Ryōkan kenkyū ronshū,* pp. 141–188.

Watanabe Hideei. "Ryōkan kenkyūshi." In Miya, *Ryōkan kenkyū ronshū,* pp. 31–72.

———. *Ryōkan shukke kō.* Niigata, 1974.

———, ed. *Mikan Ryōkan kashū goshu.* Tokyo, 1979.

Yokoyama Hide. *Mikan Ryōkan kashū goshu.* Niigata, 1980.

———. "Ryōkan kashū no shohon ni tsuite." In Miya, *Ryōkan kenkyū ronshū,* pp. 117–141.

Yoshino Hideo. *Ryōkan: uta to shōgai.* Tokyo, 1975.

Yoshino Hideo, Asada Sōtarō, Hayashi Takeshi et al., eds. *Ryōkan zenji kashū.* Tokyo, 1977.

Index

Abe family: collection of, 233, 261 n. 28, 274 n. 4, 285 n. 11

Abe Teichin (Sadayoshi): descendants of, 261 n. 28; letters to, 227–229, 269 n. 5; mentioned, 16; patron of Ryōkan, 77, 80, 285 n. 11; poem for, 274 n. 4; text of *Man'yō wakashū*, 85

Abhidharmakosha, 39–40

"admonitions," 245, 266 n. 100. See also kaigo; "Words of Advice"

Advaita Vedanta, 41

affiliated family system, 49

Aizu Yaichi, 24

Akatsuka, 78. *See also* Niigata

Akihagichō, 97, 272 n. 16

Akinono (Autumn Field), 85, 268 n. 130

Akita province, 79, 80

All-Japan Ryōkan Study Society (Zen-koku Ryōkan kai), xii

Amaze, 5, 30

Amitābha Buddha, 260 n. 14, 261 n. 35, 284 n. 7. *See also* Buddha Amida

Analects, 30

Ancient Style poetry, 262 n. 18

ango (meditation retreats), 8

angya (pilgrimage), 8. *See also* pilgrimage

Aozu, 81

Ārāda Kālāma, 242, 288 n. 27

Araki family, 5

arhats, 244, 288 n. 28

autobiographical poems, 39, 67–69

Avalokiteshvara. *See* Kannon

Awakening of Faith, 43–44, 46, 56

Baisaō (Maisaō), 7

ball-playing songs, 132, 276 n. 26, 276 n. 29. *See also* children's games

balls, 233, 234

bamboo shoots, 103, 106, 224, 284 n. 3

bandits, 128. *See also* thieves

Bankei Yōtaku, 56, 58

Barthes, Roland, 23

Bataille, Georges, 57

beggars, 225, 285 n. 7; and beggar-monks, 7. *See also* begging; mendicancy

begging: and the bureaucratization of Buddhism, 49, 53–54; compared to life of hired laborer, 278 n. 48; forms of, 242; heretical practices in, 244; and nonduality, 39, 47; poems on, 54, 111–117, 186, 274 n. 4; by Ryōkan, xiii, 13–14, 34, 101; and transmission of the Buddha Dharma, 21, 63, 116, 243. *See also* mendicancy; "On Begging One's Food"

Bielefeldt, Carl, 267 n. 125

biographical sources, xv–xvi, 4, 9, 33–34, 39, 86–87, 261 n. 5; figurative strategies in, 74; Japanese characters for, 268 n. 1. *See also* Kera Yoshishige; Kondō Banjō; letters; Ōzeki Bunchū; Suzuki Bundai; Suzuki Tekiken

Bitchū, 6. *See also* Entsūji; Tamashima

Bodhidharma, 29, 32, 34, 241, 279 n. 60, 281 n. 75; and Mount Sung, 197, 283 n. 92

bodhisattva path, 43–44, 59

Itoi River, 140, 277 n. 31
Iwase Momoki (Kyōzan), 277 n. 30
Izumozaki: headman of, 5, 8, 11; mentioned, 30; merchant families of, 286 n. 29, 286 n. 31; return to, 12, 47, 62, 275 n. 22; Ryōkan Museum in, 122; Ryōkan's native place, xiii, 4-5, 47

Jakusui, 105
Jittoku. *See* Shih-te
Jizen Shōnin, 178
Jizō, 81, 103, 122, 273 n. 36
Jizōdō: Henchō settled at, 18, 274 n. 47; identified, 271 n. 5; mentioned, 95, 104, 286 n. 19; Ryōkan's education in, 5; Tomitori family of, 19, 98, 261 n. 31, 271 n. 8, 272 n. 19
Jōdo Shinshū school, 261 n. 35, 272 n. 20, 273 n. 43. *See also* True Pure Land Sect
Jofukyō (Never-Despising-Anyone), 71-72, 206, 283 n. 2
Johnson, Barbara, 45-46

Kagawa Kageki, 262 n. 10
kaigo (words of advice), xiv, 247. *See also* "admonitions"; "Words of Advice"
Kairyū-in, 83
Kameda Bōsai, 77, 78, 80, 86, 105, 106; calligraphy of, 77
Kamo no Chōmei, 272 n. 21
Kamo no Mabuchi, 86, 102, 262 n. 10, 273 n. 33
Kaniṣka, King, 266 n. 103
Kankan-sha, 175, 282 n. 82
Kankoku, 99, 272 n. 20
Kannon, 21, 113, 161, 279 n. 61, 287 n. 40
Kansai district, 279 n. 63
kanshi, 25-26, 92; manuscripts, 83-84; sources of, 93; titles of, 92
Kanshōji, 105, 273 n. 42
Kanzan. *See* Han-shan

Kao-seng chuan (Record of Eminent Priests), 160, 279 n. 59
Karaki Junzō, 24
Kashiwasaki, 235
Katsura River, 5
Keizan Jōkin, 50
Kera family, 91; funerary temple, 273 n. 42; library, 81, 82
Kera Kumanosuke, 270 n. 28
Kera Magouemon, 226, 268 n. 141, 270 n. 28, 285 n. 8
Kera Shukumon, 281 n. 77; buried copy of *Lotus Sūtra*, 80-81; letters to, 65, 80-81, 223-225; poem expressing gratitude to, 172-173, 282 n. 80; as Ryōkan's friend and supporter, 91, 94, 281 n. 77; sons of, 81, 268 n. 141, 270 n. 28, 285 n. 8; as village chief, 78
Kera Yoshishige, 81, 94, 270 n. 26, 284 n. 1; account of Ryōkan, 34, 55; colophon for *Shiki zatsueisō*, 82-83; on Ryōkan and the *Man'yōshū*, 85, 102; on Ryōkan's calligraphy, 24; on Ryōkan's interest in phonetics, 86; on Ryōkan's silence, 61; on Ryōkan's visits, 70-71, 104; *Ryōkan zenji kiwa* (Curious Accounts) by, xiii-xiv, 81, 82, 83, 91-92, 94-106, 260 n. 7, 269-270 n. 25, 281 n. 77
kigo, 92
Kimura family, 22, 30; collection of, 245, 266 n. 100; preserved poem by Kokusen, 274 n. 49; residence of, 275 n. 22. *See also* Kimura Motouemon
Kimura Motouemon: daughter Okano of, 268 n. 133; hospitality of, in Ryōkan's final years, 18, 217, 262 n. 6, 272 n. 17, 275 n. 22, 285 n. 13; on Ryōkan's calligraphy, 237, 261-262 n. 6; son of, 230, 268 n. 141. *See also* Shimazaki
Kimura Shūzō, 230-231, 268 n. 141
Kisen, 105, 273 n. 41
Kodama Rihei, 85, 271 n. 51

About the Translators

RYŪICHI ABÉ is currently an associate professor in the Department of Religion at Columbia University. His research interests include Japanese Buddhism, Japanese Buddhist literature, and contemporary theories on sign, text, and ritual. He has published several articles in both English and Japanese, including studies of the poetic writings of Kūkai and Kakuban.

PETER HASKEL holds a doctorate from Columbia University's Department of East Asian Languages and Cultures, where he specialized in the history of Japanese Zen Buddhism during the Tokugawa period. He is the author of *Bankei Zen* (Grove Press), translations from the record of the seventeenth-century Zen master Bankei Yōtaku, and coeditor of a collection of lectures on the *Platform Sūtra* by the Zen master Sōkei-an Sasaki (Tuttle).

 Production Notes

Composition and paging were done in
FrameMaker software on an AGFA AccuSet
Postscript Imagesetter by the design
and production staff of University of
Hawai'i Press.

The text typeface is Garamond Book
and the display typeface is Hiroshige.

Offset presswork and binding were done by
The Maple-Vail Book Manufacturing Group.
Text paper is Glatfelter Offset Smooth Antique,
basis 50.